MW00780532

Totally Unofficial

Totally Unofficial

The Autobiography of

RAPHAEL LEMKIN

Edited by Donna-Lee Frieze

Yale

UNIVERSITY PRESS

New Haven & London

Yale University Press books may be purchased in quantity for educational, business, or promotional use. For information, please e-mail sales.press@yale.edu (U.S. office) or sales@yaleup.co.uk (U.K. office).

Designed by Sonia Shannon.
Set in Electra type by Keystone Typesetting, Inc.
Printed in the United States of America.

Library of Congress Cataloging-in-Publication Data
Lemkin, Raphael, 1900–1959.
Totally unofficial : the autobiography of Raphael Lemkin / Raphael Lemkin, Donna-Lee Frieze.
pages cm
Includes bibliographical references and index.
ISBN 978-0-300-18696-3 (hardback)
1. Lemkin, Raphael, 1900–1959. 2. Lawyers—Poland—Biography.
3. Lawyers—United States—Biography. 4. Human rights workers—Poland—Biography. 5. Human rights workers—United States—Biography.
6. Genocide—Prevention. 7. Convention on the Prevention and Punishment of the Crime of Genocide (1948) 8. World War, 1939–1945—Atrocities. I. Frieze, Donna-Lee. II. Title.
KKP110.L46A3 2013
345′.0251092—dc23
[B] 2012051175

A catalogue record for this book is available from the British Library.

This paper meets the requirements of ANSI/NISO Z39.48–1992 (Permanence of Paper).

10 9 8 7 6 5 4 3 2 1

Contents

Acknowledgments   vii

INTRODUCTION. *The "Insistent Prophet,"*
by Donna-Lee Frieze   ix

Preface   1
ONE. Early Years   3
TWO. The Flight, 1939   25
THREE. The Flight, 1939–1940   41
FOUR. A Refugee in Lithuania, Latvia, and Sweden   60
FIVE. From Sweden to the United States   79
SIX. First Impressions of America: April–June 1941   98
SEVEN. Alerting the World to Genocide   112
EIGHT. The Birth of the Convention   118
NINE. Geneva, 1948   133
TEN. Paris, 1948   150
ELEVEN. Climbing a Mountain Again   180
TWELVE. Nearing the End   219

Appendixes   223
Notes   241
Bibliography   267
Index   277

Acknowledgments

I would like to thank the Jewish Holocaust Centre in Melbourne, New York Public Library and Thomas Lannon, Center for Jewish History, Alfred Deakin Research Institute, American Jewish Archives and Kevin Proffitt, American Jewish Historical Society, Yeshiva University Museum and YIVO Institute for Jewish Research. Thanks also to everyone at Yale University Press, in particular Jaya Chatterjee and Heidi Downey. Thanks to Cynthia Crippen for meticulous indexing. Much gratitude to my patient and erudite editor, William Frucht.

I am also very grateful to Saul Lemkin and Nancy Steinson Ehrlich for their time, hospitality, and generosity.

The following people have been instrumental with their guidance and support: Joyce Apsel, Steven Cooke, Rita Frieze, Ron Frieze, Heidi Groen, Alex Hinton, Tony Joel, Simone Judowski, Leah Kaminsky, Robert Jay Lifton, Yohanan Loeffler, Pam Maclean, Viki Markoff, Denis Meehan, A. Dirk Moses, Judith Siegel, Ileene Smith, Andrew St. John, Jay Winter, and Andrea Witcomb. And of course thanks to my son, Gene, for being you, all the time. I am deeply appreciative of Peter Balakian's support and encouragement, which has been steadfast since the beginning.

The "Insistent Prophet"

Donna-Lee Frieze

WHEN RAPHAEL LEMKIN collapsed at a bus stop on 42nd Street in New York City on August 29, 1959, he either had just visited the Curtis Brown Agency on Madison Avenue or was on his way there to discuss his autobiography, *Totally Unofficial*. The manuscript was nearly complete. According to those who knew him, Lemkin was taken by the NYPD to the nearest police station, where he died. Abe Bolgatz, the son of friends of Lemkin's, had the sad job of identifying the body at the Bellevue Hospital morgue. Bolgatz says that Lemkin might have been conscious after his collapse, "as something was said about a publisher's office, and [the NYPD] might have taken him there."

Only weeks before, his dear friend Nancy Ackerly (now Nancy Steinson Ehrlich), a public law and government student in a graduate program at Columbia University, had accompanied him to Spring Valley to the home of family friends—where, as she recalls, Lemkin would go to relax and "tell jokes"—to help with the manuscript and "smooth out the language." English was far from his native language: it was one of at least twelve he had acquired in his wanderings.

Lemkin was eager to see his autobiography published. The last two years of his life were absorbed in writing, editing, and sending chapters to his agent, Naomi Burton at Curtis Brown. Possibly the last letters written to Lemkin were from Burton. On August 6, 1958, before a certain Arthur Roth suggested that he approach Curtis Brown, Lemkin had submitted two chapters of his manuscript ("Geneva" and "Paris") to the Lower East Side publishers Duell, Sloan and Pearce. He received a rejection letter less than two weeks later. The publishers concluded: "It would not be possible . . . to find a large enough audience of buyers for a book of this nature," even though they found the chapters "fascinating" and an "important record" of the Genocide Convention and the United Nations. Lemkin then sent an outline to Curtis Brown, and he corresponded with Burton from September 1958 until shortly before his death. Burton was pleased with the outline and sent a copy to Simon and Schuster along with Chapter Two of *Totally Unofficial*. Between November 7, 1958, and July 20, 1959, Burton wrote several letters to Lemkin inquiring about the manuscript and his health. His life was a worthy subject for an autobiography: Lemkin did not just invent the word "genocide," he labored for years to ensure the act became an influential component within international law.

Rafał Lemkin was born on June 24, 1900, the second child of Joseph and Bella Lemkin (née Pomerantz), and was raised in eastern Poland (now Belarus) on a farm with his parents, two brothers, uncles, aunts, and cousins. He lived on the outskirts of Wolkowysk for the first ten years of his life among a community of Poles, White Russians, and Jews who shared the region with a "feeling of common destiny." Fittingly for a child who would become a man of law, Wolkowysk was named after two villains whose felonious activities, including robbing and killing travelers who entered the village, cemented their names in Polish history.

Lemkin was an impressionable child who played freely with his brothers and cousins, who pretended to be pirates and conquistadors. He could also be mischievous and unkind, violating his parents' rules by stealing fruit from a neighbor's orchard and showing off his new shoes to the barefoot children of farmhands. These childish acts, however, helped shape Lemkin's moral conscience, as did singing proverbs from the prophets in the Bible and learning the "brevity of the Hebrew language." His early life was immersed in poetry, music, and literature, which fueled his love of world cultures.

Around eleven years of age, Lemkin read Henryk Sienkiewicz's novel *Quo Vadis*, which detailed Nero's persecution of Christians in 64 A.D. The book made an impression on this intellectual child, who was home-schooled by his highly educated mother. Pogroms against the Jews, and the Russian and German invasions of eastern Poland, also left an impact. When he was fourteen, during World War I, the Germans occupied Wolkowysk, and the Ottoman Empire embarked on what Lemkin characterized as the "sinister panorama of destruction of the Armenians," a deft synopsis of what he later became the first to label the Armenian genocide. According to Steinson Ehrlich, it was the intended destruction of the Armenians that triggered Lemkin's moral interest in the protection of groups.

Lemkin later attended school in Vilnius and studied philology at the University of Heidelberg and Lwow, where he eventually completed his doctorate in law in 1926. The medley of law and languages mobilized his quest for the ratification of the Genocide Convention. Two events in the 1920s had considerable bearing on his thinking: the assassinations of Talaat Pasha in 1921 and Symon Petliura in 1926 by Soghomon Tehlirian and Shalom Schwarzbard, respectively. Talaat, as minister of the interior of the Turkish government in 1915, was unarguably the primary planner of the Armenian genocide, and, contentiously, Petliura oversaw the pogroms of thousands of Jews in Ukraine. Their murders did not repel Lemkin as much as did the trials of Tehlirian, whose family was killed in the Armenian genocide, and Schwarzbard, whose parents were murdered in the pogroms. As a young law student, Lemkin was deeply disturbed that a government could attempt to destroy a national group with impunity while a person could be tried for the murder of an individual. The trials highlighted the details of the genocide and the pogroms "like an open wound before the world." Both Tehlirian and Schwarzbard were deemed insane, based on the trauma they had gone through, and therefore were acquitted. After the Tehlirian trial in 1921, Lemkin notes that his "worries about the murder of the innocent became more meaningful." In 1927, after the Schwarzbard trial, he wrote an article in which he condemned "the absence of any law for the unification of moral standards in relation to the destruction of national, racial, and religious groups."

The next ten years of Lemkin's life, spent in Warsaw, were prosperous and successful. He was appointed deputy public prosecutor of the city and secretary of the Committee of Codification of the Laws of the Polish Republic, and he managed to publish almost a book a year. But these achievements seemed ephemeral to Lemkin. The one task that he prized was his work, at the 1933 League of Nations conference in Madrid, to outlaw genocide. Although the word "genocide" was not yet invented, it was described in its incipient forms: "barbarism" and "vandalism." The time was ripe. Hitler had just become chancellor of Germany, and in Iraq, acts of "barbarity" and "vandalism" were being committed against the Assyrians. To prevent a military alliance between France and Poland, Hitler began to negotiate a nonaggression pact with Poland. This, along with pressure from an anti-Semitic Polish newspaper that viewed Lemkin as "acting solely for the protection" of his own "race," forced the Polish minister of justice to oppose Lemkin's presence at the Madrid conference, but his paper was presented (although tabled) and published and circulated around Europe. Shortly after, under pressure from the Polish foreign minister, Lemkin resigned from his public prosecuting duties and became a private solicitor.

On September 6, 1939, Lemkin's house on Kredytowa Street in Warsaw was bombed by the Nazis, who had invaded Poland six days earlier. The prosperous international lawyer suddenly became an internally displaced refugee. After weeks of dodging German bombs while wandering the Polish countryside, Lemkin faced Russian interrogation. To avoid incarceration, he shed his intellectual sensibility, cast off his city clothes, exchanged his expensive glass rims, and assumed the demeanor of a White-Ruthenian peasant with enough conviction to secure his release.

In November he reached his family home in eastern Poland and saw his parents for the last time.

Arriving in Lithuania in early 1940, while it was still neutral, Lemkin noted the chaos and fragility of its capital, Vilnius: the Russians were voraciously buying consumer goods, others were profiting by smuggling people from Warsaw, and black marketers were profiteering. It is here that Lemkin articulates his desire to dispense with material pleasure and devote his life to outlawing intended group destruction. The money and material benefits he earned, he writes, never made him happy. "As a public prosecutor and a lawyer I served power and enjoyed false prestige. I really lived only when I was fighting for an ideal. I will devote the rest of my life to my work—outlawing the destruction of peoples." He began organizing his escape to Sweden through his publishing and legal contacts there. A week later he reached Riga, Latvia, fighting the refugee's "loss of self-esteem." There, during a conversation with the Jewish historian Simon Dubnow, he further crystallized his ideas about intended group destruction. Sitting at Dubnow's hearth, weeks before the Sovietization of Latvia and a year and a half before Dubnow's execution by the Nazis, Lemkin emphasized the imperative of outlawing the destruction of peoples on an international stage. Dubnow agreed: "I have always felt that history must sit in judgment." Within a short time, Lemkin transformed himself from a powerless refugee in Latvia and Lithuania to a self-possessed intellectual in Sweden. He spent much of his time in the Stockholm library, studying the "crime without a name" that was sweeping Europe.

But Lemkin's goal was always to reach the United States, and with help from his American colleague Malcolm McDermott at Duke University, he traveled to North Carolina via Russia and Japan to teach at Duke Law School. When he first arrived in the United States, in April 1941, his impressions were of a large, friendly, welcoming country, flush with industrialization and modernity. The fatherly and optimistic McDermott guided him through his first year. On arriving in bustling Durham, Lemkin was informed that he was to give the keynote speech at a university dinner that evening, and in the presence of the president of the university. Lemkin's spoken English was poor, but his speech, a meditation on past and current genocides, was nevertheless inspirational: "If women, children, and old people would be murdered a hundred miles from here, wouldn't you run to help? Then why do you stop this decision of your heart when the distance is five thousand miles instead of a hundred?"

New York became Lemkin's home for the remainder of his life. He took contract positions at prestigious universities, became a consultant for the U.S. Board of Economic Warfare and Foreign Economic Administration, advised the U.S. Supreme Court Justice and Nuremberg trial chief counsel Robert Jackson, and did work for the U.S. War Department. While working for the Board of Economic Warfare in Washington in 1942, Lemkin was staggered by the "complete unawareness that the Axis planned destruction of the people under their control"—in other words, genocide. He uncovered the unimaginable: that mass annihilation was occurring in Europe. And he uncovered the unconscionable: that the Allies were aware of the atrocities and were ignoring the messages. Lemkin wrote to President Franklin D. Roosevelt, warning him of Hitler's intention to commit atrocities that were well beyond warfare. Roosevelt's passive response, urging "patience," was, to Lemkin, a green light for Hitler to commit genocide. As Lemkin notes, " 'Patience' is a good word for when one expects an appointment, a budgetary allocation, or the building of a road."

Lemkin's pioneering work was yet to come. When the newly formed United Nations opened the first regular session of its General Assembly in 1946, Lemkin was there, armed with his new magnum opus, *Axis Rule in Occupied Europe*, in which the word "genocide" first appeared in print. After many years of intense lobbying, and with the help and support of diplomats and organizations around the world, the Convention on the Prevention and Punishment of the Crime of Genocide was ratified in 1951 by the United Nations. Lemkin was nominated for the Nobel Peace Prize twice in the 1950s.

When told with such brevity, Lemkin's story could give the impression that the fight for the Genocide Convention was uncomplicated and that he strode confidently, even effortlessly through his chaotic times. This, of course, is not true.

After the Holocaust, many nations and nongovernmental organizations finally listened to Lemkin. These influential players on the international stage in the newly formed United Nations—delegates from the United States, France, Egypt, Chile, India, Cuba, Panama, Czechoslovakia, the United Kingdom, and eventually the Soviet Union—understood that Hitler's crimes must never be repeated. Diplomats and many women's and religious organizations rallied around the cause, prompting Lemkin to write that he may "have been doing an injustice to others, and to myself, by thinking that I am a lonely fighter for this cause." However, if the aftermath of the Holocaust woke the moral and ethical consciousness of the international community, it did not obliterate or even shake the realist notion of state sovereignty. Self-interested nation-states that opposed the Genocide Convention feared that international law would trump the sanctity of their domestic laws. Lemkin viewed the leaders of these states and their spokespeople as adversaries. He perceived sabotage in their politics, which weighed on him personally. In a few delegates he confronted acrimony; in documents such as the Universal Declaration of Human Rights he found the convention's bête noire. Plagued by ill health most of his life (high blood pressure was a familial condition), he often found it physically impossible to sustain the demands of his intensive work. After the U.N. adopted the Genocide Convention in France, in 1948, he had to convalesce in a Paris hospital. The doctors could not define his illness, so Lemkin made a self-diagnosis: "genociditis: exhaustion from the work on the Genocide Convention."

The energy and time required to concentrate on lobbying often forced Lemkin to abandon his contract positions at universities. He often had no income and was reduced to eating unpalatable and unhealthy food. He also suffered from isolation, as his only surviving immediate relative, his brother Elias (Eliyahu), lived in Canada. Apart from some cousins, aunts, and uncles scattered in the United States, his family had been murdered in the Holocaust. There is evidence that his parents were gassed in Treblinka not long before Lemkin coined the word "genocide." He had no wife (not for a lack of suitors) or children. As he told Steinson Ehrlich, "I have no time for married life, or the funds to support it."

Mendacious diplomats often underestimated Lemkin's political ingenuity and psychological strength. While he faced stubborn opposition to the convention, the diplomats who opposed Lemkin and his ideas faced someone who, in his own words, was "sentenced to constant struggle, until the end" of his days. During the drafting of the Genocide Convention he often "felt like a pilot of an airliner who had managed to restart a couple of dead motors." His description of his feelings regarding the U.N. Assembly of 1950, "a mixture of innocent joy, great success, distress, deceit, and danger to my life and health," can serve as a vignette for Lemkin's life beyond 1946. It is no wonder he could empathize with the "futile struggle of the waves" on a transoceanic trip.

Today we might call Lemkin a Holocaust survivor, yet despite his personal experiences and tragic losses, he never allowed genocide to be defined by one case study. The world may have been motivated to outlaw genocide because of the Holocaust, but Lemkin insisted that we not "describe a crime by one example. . . . It is necessary to describe the division of the roles and to foresee all modalities, all possible techniques. The formulation must be made valid for all times, situations, and cultures." For Lemkin, genocide was not only the gas chambers in the Holocaust, it was intended group destruction. And as he demonstrated throughout his comparative genocide research, there are many ways to destroy a group. His driving passions were fueled by his ability to interpret legal intricacies and to articulate this "intended group destruction" in international law.

Lemkin's intellectual and legal skills did not prevent him from being labeled naive and a fanatic. In fact, these traits are palpable in *Totally Unofficial*. Some characterizations were used to marginalize him; others, such as Genêt's description of him as a "sad, witty, middle-aged man," were used for caricature. But to label Lemkin with these qualities alone overlooks his diplomacy and wisdom, his astute intelligence and brilliant accomplishments. As *Totally Unofficial* demonstrates, the people he encountered captivated him. Indeed, he is also informed by a less self-conscious persona. When an Indian/Chilean casino dancer in Montreux tells him that he will be famous after his death, Lemkin interprets this as a reflection of her depth and the power of the convention rather than an endorsement of his achievements: "The little dancer in Montreux with the innate vision of a great extinguished race saw, in her own way, the immortality of the law in which I so firmly believed."

Despite his need for solitude, Lemkin was rejuvenated when delegates to the U.N. displayed genuine enthusiasm for the ratification of the Genocide Convention. He was reignited with passion and determination when, for instance, he was welcomed in the Australian delegate's lounge "not as a poor relative and petitioner but as a full-fledged partner in the most beautiful adventure that a man could imagine." At times, his loneliness was accentuated by his inability or lack of desire to engage in small talk, or by the perception that he could be encountered only "on an exceedingly high plane." For a short period in 1948, Lemkin decided to abandon conversations regarding the Genocide Convention during social events. When approached, he would laugh with the delegates, playfully feigning ignorance: "'Genocide, what's that?'" He was not trying to socialize but rather to strategize, to use social functions to advance pertinent legal and moral issues. Still, there is no doubt that the solitude he craved often ricocheted into loneliness, and the long years of researching historical cases of intended group destruction were not all intellectualized. As he notes, he suffered deeply when one diplomat threatened him: "For more than violence, I detest threats. Violence is directed against the body, but threats are meant to paralyze the will of a man who might remain by force. When I met this man I looked at him as if there was an empty space before me."

Despite his strong will and resilience, Lemkin describes himself as a "habitual pessimist." Considering his loss of family and home, his itinerant lifestyle, and his consequent poverty and hunger, we may plausibly suspect he suffered from depression. He saw advantages in loneliness: "Only lonely persons can reach the borders of the unconscious and achieve the state of intuition which were so necessary for appraising situations at once and for acting quickly." Nevertheless, he would need remedies to counter these states.

There is little evidence that Lemkin was religious, but there can be no doubt that he was immersed in spirituality, high culture, poetry, philosophy, and aesthetics, all of which gave him relief from his research into the destruction of nations. It is possible that, like a citizen of post-revolutionary France, he viewed progress as a "new religion for modern man" and woman. He lamented that "western man has relegated beauty" into a "single compartment." But during his quest for the Genocide Convention he encountered many who inspired in him a spiritual illumination, especially diplomats from distant lands and cultures. One was Judge Riad of Egypt, who helped Lemkin understand the "scope of spirituality of the Arab mind" and believed that the Genocide Convention, like "real spiritual values of any period," would live on in history. Another was Pakistan's Zafarullah Khan, who was Lemkin's guide: "There are meetings with people," Lemkin writes, "that make you feel something of value has entered into you." It was Sir Zafarullah who suggested that the Genocide Convention be known as the Lemkin Convention.

A key to Lemkin's inner life lies in a book he gave to Nancy Steinson Ehrlich, *Rainer Maria Rilke: His Last Friendship*, edited by Marcel Ravel. The volume is a series of edited letters from Rilke to Nimet Eloui Bey, a young Egyptian woman with whom Rilke maintained a spiritual and loving friendship during the last years of his life. Lemkin's relationship with Steinson Ehrlich bears a strong resemblance to that between Rilke and Bey, and the book Lemkin gave Steinson Ehrlich had been well read, many of its passages underlined in Lemkin's thick red pencil. He found in Rilke's poetry and prose a sensibility that echoed his own and embodied an era of mid-twentieth-century European intellectual modernity, Romanticism, and spirituality. But how Lemkin felt about the cosmos is clear in Ravel's description of Rilke, which Lemkin bracketed (the passage in italics was underlined by Lemkin):

> He received no thrill from supernatural terrors, nor did he seek to delude himself, but it was not his nature to believe either in life or in death, in an absolute way; for him, *life and death were the reverse and the obverse of the same phenomenon; past, present, and future were one for him, and all the proofs that our appearance as living creatures is inseparable from the presence of the departed were precious to him.* It was to some extent an experimental view, and it was as peculiar to him as the greenish color of his eyes, or the musical softness of his voice. The *Duino Elegies* and the *Sonnets of Orpheus* are dazzling evidence of this conception of existence.

"Our appearance as living creatures is inseparable from the presence of the departed": the ghosts of his parents and the genocide victims Lemkin could not save lived deep within him and spurred him to fight for the Genocide Convention. Most revealingly, Lemkin underlined Ravel's observation that Rilke "lived all his life as if he had neither country nor family, nor issue, nor even a religion." Was Lemkin envious of Rilke for having the luxury of choosing a life he himself could not help but live, or did he simply understand that Rilke too embraced these disjunctions of life?

Lemkin's metaphysical life is not explicitly illuminated in *Totally Unofficial*, and even the early chapters of the book conceal intricate personal details. Because Lemkin died before he completed the manuscript, some chapters were unedited and others unwritten. Had he lived longer, perhaps he would have contemplated adding more detail. Regardless, some aspects of Lemkin's life are behind an iron curtain, begging the reader who knows the outlines to speculate on why he fails to write about the death of his younger brother Samuel, who, according to Lemkin's nephew, died from the Spanish flu around 1918. What about his years as an undergraduate, graduate, and doctoral student? Was daily life in Warsaw in the 1930s perilous for a Jewish public prosecutor? Why no mention of love interests and a mere allusion to his surviving brother, Elias? What were the "disasters of my mature age"? Why the large gap between Chapter Seven (the middle of the war) and Chapter Eight (which begins at the end of the Nuremberg Tribunal)? To answer these and other inscrutabilities, I offer some theories, arguing that *Totally Unofficial* is part autobiography, part biography, part memoir, and part report.

First, this volume is not solely an autobiography. Lemkin also saw it as his biography of a living, breathing entity, the Genocide Convention, which had the capacity to forever change international law and the world's societies. At times he refers to the convention as a child, and it is felicitous that the father of this law should write the story of how it was conceived, and how some of its adversaries desired "aborticide." It is an enriching and insightful account of how the components of the Genocide Convention were determined, including Lemkin's argument that specific techniques of genocide "cannot be mentioned . . . by name, because another important means of genocide might be left out." Most revealing is Lemkin's methodological approach to obtaining ratifications: he targets Latin America because of its size and its "new humanitarianism." Lemkin also knew he could engage with Latin Americans through their conceptual and philosophical intellectualism. And "more working than talking" was his new method of activism in the late 1940s. If personal or social events are related to his endeavor to outlaw genocide, Lemkin usually includes them: one such instance is his conversation with the casino dancer. Another is his last letter from his parents, which coincides with the German invasion of his hometown in Eastern Europe. He also mentions the ill health that delays his work on the convention. The book is an autobiography (or, as its author calls it, a "narrative report") inasmuch as it is a parable of Lemkin's inclination toward idealism, wisdom, commitment, and passion, told through conversations and stories about old friends, colleagues, delegates, and diplomats.

Lemkin's account is enriched with major historical moments of the mid-twentieth century: he describes the postwar world as "trembling under convulsions of change, impatience, fear, and anxiety." Some may find it remarkable that Lemkin concedes that as far as human rights are concerned, the golden age of the U.N. is over—by 1948. *Totally Unofficial* sheds light on major figures in this golden age, characters who, as Lemkin generously notes, were foundational if not integral to ratification of the convention. It is their historic contributions that Lemkin gracefully memorializes. He is able to express in almost elegiac terms the tortured history of people in Haiti embodied in the Haitian ambassador to the United States; he thought deeply about "their wounds, their sweat, their fears and longings" in an effort to comprehend a past scarred by human rights abuses. These are the book's memoirist moments.

If *Totally Unofficial* conceals many details of Lemkin's life (apart from its autobiographical passages, such as moving reminiscences of childhood), it does reveal salient components of his personality. At times the book is what Jaume Aurell defines as a constructivist autobiography, one in which authors establish a "critical distance from their own lives to present it objectively." Constructivists "view their autobiographies as stories that contribute to a larger history." In the beginning of *Totally Unofficial*, Lemkin's life is the dominant theme, but as the Genocide Convention is brought to life, the two become entwined. Everything that is in Lemkin is in the Genocide Convention, and vice versa. Part memoir, part autobiography, and part biography, *Totally Unofficial* becomes larger than Lemkin's life. Or, as Sigrid Arne put it in 1947, "There is not a bomb, a bullet, or a torpedo in Raphael Lemkin's story. Yet this is one of the more fantastic stories of World War II. It is the story of an idea and a word." The silences must be forgiven.

As Hazel Rowley writes, "A biography is not a life; lives cannot be recovered. . . . We are continually revising our memories and hopes, rationalizing disappointments. Modifying the way we present ourselves to ourselves and others. Everything we do has a hidden aspect; every incident has several versions; each moment of our lives is invisibly shaped by our unpruned, tangled past." No memoir is complete and no autobiographical narrative is the bona fide version of one's life: memories are variegated and people are convoluted. Lemkin may avoid details of his personal life, and it seems clear that he selected a narrative of his life that would complement the birth of his "child." Yet his feelings of pleasure or pain are flagrant and overt; his observations, adroit.

A student of philology, Lemkin embraced languages for their ability to express cultural nuances. He learned new languages with lightning speed. Even though English was possibly his tenth or eleventh language, it is evident that Lemkin is a fine chronicler of detail. This is epitomized in Chapters Two and Three, perhaps his most contemplative chapters, in which he describes his flight from Warsaw. In this vivid snapshot of Poland in the early weeks of the war, Lemkin stalls the chaos of the Nazi blitz to provide us with sapient insights and observations about the people around him. In one passage he pauses from the commotion of war to contemplate the ants crawling on the ground around him, superstitiously believing that their behavior may "predict" his fate. Noted are the mundane realities: the inability to shave, perform ablutions, and wash clothes. He witnesses intimacy among strangers, which he treats perceptively and solicitously, without resentment or prudishness. Lemkin animates the disaster of the war: the sun is ignorant or indifferent to pleasure or pain, and the overcrowded train, full of internally displaced people ("nomads") with nowhere to go, moves "like a tired old man." One train, bombed during a blitzkrieg, "stretched on the slope like a dead black horse"; elsewhere, "wounded trees" groan. Nature is attentively contemplated—its artistry, its indifference, and its cruelty.

The defeat of the Polish army (*before* battle) signifies for Lemkin the moral and spiritual decline of the Polish state in 1939 and the fragmentation of the state "as the outward symbol of social order." Despite their desperation, fear, and hunger, the "nomads" are nevertheless moved to leave a final potato for a hungry child and buy a cow for a woman who displays great generosity despite her destitution. At this stage of the war the nomads in Lemkin's group express anger at their nation's disgrace and blind reliance on dictatorship. Others proudly declare their fierce patriotism. With the concentration of an erudite professor, Lemkin revels in the intellectual discussions. But once he leaves the group his journey becomes more perilous, in particular during his brief incarceration by the Russians. Yet he is saved by his intellect, his knowledge of many languages, cultures, and customs, his experience as a prosecutor, and his ability to perform. He will again employ these traits in persuading diplomats to outlaw genocide.

In Chapters Five and Six, as Lemkin leaves Sweden for the States, traveling through Russia (remembering the thirteenth-century Mongol invasion of Russia, Poland, Silesia, and Hungary) to Japan, Canada, and finally America, he again displays his acute observational skills and thirst for knowledge of different cultures. He notes the "impassive" Russian authorities and people in Moscow whose "movements were slow, their faces [showing] concern, preoccupation, heavy responsibility, as of men and women who had long carried a sad burden." In Kyoto, people walking the streets in kimonos "would stop before each other, bow slowly and gravely, and continue their leisurely pace." His impressions of American social life and of academic and political culture in Washington, D.C., are perceptive and eloquently articulated views of America by the newly arrived émigré. Lemkin compares American and European students, as well as the methods and means of the different legal systems. He accustoms himself to American cultural habits and practices, sometimes with ease but at other times with difficulty and impatience, from societal rituals to topics of conversation. For instance, as a European mid-twentieth-century intellectual, Lemkin could not fathom why American dinner conversations centered on "what kind of refrigerator or vacuum cleaner was the best."

But genocide is never far from his mind. Because he had studied genocide for years—even before he invented the word—he feared its occurrence and spent the war years pleading in vain. But he did not believe that the birth of the Genocide Convention was an antidote to genocidal destruction; it is, he explains, a "framework . . . a rallying point for thinking and acting." In short, he hoped that because of the convention, "moral condemnation [of the crime] will become easier." For Lemkin, the convention's moral weight is as important as its legal status.

This continued exigency propelled Robert Merrill Bartlett to describe Lemkin as an "insistent prophet," underscoring Lemkin's assiduous and tenacious desire for the unanimous ratification of the Genocide Convention and his profound metaphysical perspective. Even as he saw the convention's legal possibilities he predicted that the world would again lapse into complacency, forgetting past genocides or ignoring ongoing atrocities. We are struck by his lifelong insistence that genocide will occur repeatedly but that fighting for the convention on the international stage, no matter how feeble a force it is for the prevention of genocide, is wiser than living as a halfhearted idealist.

In Chapter Two of *Totally Unofficial* we witness the devotee at work in the Polish province of Wolynia, where he attempts to warn a religious Jewish baker of the intended destruction of Jews. Lemkin tells the baker that this "war" will have cataclysmic effects on the cultures of specific national, racial, ethnic, or religious groups. Lemkin's detailed description of the baker, the world of the *shtetl*, and the religious life of impoverished Jews reveals not simply his mourning for a vanished world. It also provides insight into the loss of religion and, especially, culture in genocide. These are the "wealth of all humanity" and "essential foundations"—expressions he used to describe the destruction that occurs in the process of genocide.[1] Here, he elegantly demonstrates his deep Jewish identity, displayed in culture, rituals, literature, and observations of the religion. His struggle to convince the baker that genocide is distinct from war foreshadows his later struggles to convince people that genocide is a recurring theme throughout human history.

On his escape from Poland, Lemkin offers similar warnings in discussions with the president of the district court of Kaunas, with the famous Jewish historian Simon Dubnow, and with his parents, during his last face-to-face conversation with them. He attempts to convince his listeners that this evil is not war; it is another incubus. But by vividly depicting the cultural, religious, and ethnic life of Poles and Jews on the precipice of genocide, he reenergizes the lives of those he encounters. Lemkin expresses guilt at failing to prevent the genocide even as he acknowledges that this feeling is specious: "I was ashamed of my helplessness in dealing with the murderers of humanity, a shame that has not left me to this day. Guilt without guilt is more destructive to us than justified guilt, because in the first case catharsis is impossible." What Bartlett described as his "insistence" was his benediction; the "prophecy," a burden.

Lemkin chose the title for his autobiography from a *New York Times* editorial in 1957 that questioned why the United States had not ratified the Genocide Convention (it did not do so until November 1988).[2] The editorial advised that something "might be learned from that exceedingly patient and totally unofficial man, Prof. Raphael Lemkin." As *Totally Unofficial* is the title that is typed on his agent's copy of the manuscript, I have retained it, even though there is evidence that Lemkin was considering "Totally Unofficial Man" or "The Unofficial Man."

As the outlines for the chapters suggest, Lemkin eventually decided to combine the original Chapters One and Two (see appendixes). His childhood and life in Warsaw as a young public prosecutor would be revealed through reminiscences during his flight from Poland. Methodologically and philosophically I understand Lemkin's reasoning: his last months as an internally displaced person serve as a marker between a relatively secure and established life and an uncertain and nomadic future. But I separated the chapters for two reasons. First, the two chapters together were simply too bulky. Second, the writings on his early years are different from his other writings because he remembers his childhood as a time of innocence. We know that after the age of fourteen or fifteen Lemkin set himself a mission to outlaw group destruction, thus his time before this awakening is perceived as untainted. I felt it was also important to emphasize Lemkin's love of nature and his rural upbringing. This chapter, with its revelation of his traumatic losses, helps us understand another side to Lemkin, and the description of the Jewish

Polish childhood prior to the Holocaust is important for history. The memory of wholeness is perhaps the genocide survivor's key to living.

Because most chapters exist in several drafts, I tried to transcribe and edit the last versions Lemkin wrote. Yet this was not always practical or realistic. Some of the typewritten manuscript pages are long faded, some have wide gaps between or within sentences, and some are illegibly scribbled in ink. Sometimes it was easier to use the first typed draft of a page or even a chapter than to decipher Lemkin's handwriting over the crossed-out lines. In the end, to create a cohesive narrative I was forced to choose from various drafts of each chapter and even some phrases and paragraphs that had been crossed out by Lemkin or an editor. I have also added notes, where possible, on the many characters and world decision makers mentioned by Lemkin. Some of the chapters had titles, which I have used; others did not, and for these I have created titles. Throughout the manuscript are blank spaces between words. Like most writers, Lemkin continued to write even when he could not fill in the blanks. Given that he was retelling a convoluted history, Lemkin can be forgiven for misspelling some names or misremembering some dates. We must remember that Lemkin wrote most of his text while suffering from poor health, poverty, and loneliness.

While "smoothing out" Lemkin's English, I tried to retain the "retrospective charm" of his language to reflect the period of the 1950s in which he wrote the majority of *Totally Unofficial*.

It was twenty-three years after Lemkin's death, in August 1982, that Alexander Gabriel from the Transradio News Agency, U.N. Bureau, donated some of Lemkin's papers, including *Totally Unofficial*, to the New York Public Library. A Meyer Burston Scholarship from the Jewish Holocaust Centre in Melbourne transported me to the New York Public Library on 42nd Street—the street where Lemkin collapsed in 1959—to read through the drafts of *Totally Unofficial*. It was here that I first encountered Lemkin's voice and his remarkable journey. This was the beginning of four years of editing, researching, and transcribing the autobiography, and many hours of peering at faded manuscripts, deciphering indistinct typewritten words and hastily handwritten edits. Reading the manuscript brought Lemkin to life. He had been seen as one-dimensional, as either a fanatic or a dreamer, terms used to underestimate him as early as 1933. I hope that this autobiography offers readers a truer picture of who Lemkin was.

Rumors, anecdotes, and repetitions abound in discussions regarding genocide and Lemkin's life. Several works and events have redressed these issues, including John Cooper's detailed biography *Raphael Lemkin and the Struggle for the Genocide Convention* and a one-day conference titled "Genocide and Human Experience: Raphael Lemkin's Thought and Vision," organized by Judith Siegel and hosted by the Center for Jewish History in New York in 2009. In addition, Yeshiva University Museum in November 2009 opened a six-month exhibition on Lemkin, and his archives have been digitized at the American Jewish Historical Society. It was Siegel's visionary decision to initiate these activities. These and other events have resulted, as Alex Hinton has remarked, in a resurgence of Lemkin scholarship. The scholarly community also owes a great debt to Jim Fussell for his PreventGenocide.org website, which displays many primary documents by Lemkin, some of which Fussell has meticulously translated into English. Steven Jacobs has been publishing Lemkin's academic and personal works for years, including a small portion of *Totally Unofficial*. But the shroud surrounding Lemkin's persona remains. His major archival papers are spread across three institutions in the United States. Many research papers and letters are clearly written by Lemkin, but many are not. And many more are unsigned and ambiguous, possibly written by one of the research assistants Lemkin relied upon in compiling his exhaustive studies of genocide throughout history. But even though he had the help of several friends in editing his autobiography (including, in the end, an enthusiastic young Nancy Steinson Ehrlich), one thing is clear: *Totally Unofficial* is Lemkin's life the way he wanted it heard.

Totally Unofficial

Preface

AS SOON AS I COULD read, I started to devour books on the persecution of religious, racial, or other minority groups. I was startled by the description of the destruction of the Christians by Nero. They were thrown to the lions while the emperor sat laughing on the Roman arena. The Polish writer Henryk Sienkiewicz's book on this subject, *Quo Vadis,* made a strong impression on me, and I read it several times and talked about it often.[1] I realized, vividly, that if a Christian could have called a policeman to help he would not have received any protection. Here was a group of people collectively sentenced to death for no reason except that they believed in Christ. And nobody could help them.

I became so fascinated with this story that I looked up all the similar instances in history, like the destruction of Carthage, of the Huguenots, of the Catholics in Japan, of so many Europeans by Genghis Khan. I was indignant at the French king who watched the hanging of the Huguenots from his balcony. The king ordered his servants to throw more light on the scene so that he might see better the tormented faces of the dying. My conscience protested when I read that the Huguenots in Lyon were roasted alive by being compelled to sit with naked bodies on heated irons. The Moors were deported on boats. While on deck they were stripped of their clothes and exposed for hours to the sun, which finally killed them. Why should the sun, which brought life to our farm and reddened the cherries on our trees, be turned into a murderer? I was fascinated by the frequency of such cases, by the great suffering inflicted on the victims and the hopelessness of their fate, and by the impossibility of repairing the damage to life and culture.

As I grew older I realized that such persecution cannot go on endlessly. Those who destroy others also destroy themselves—if not bodily, then in their souls. I was an impressionable youngster, my sentiments nourished by the tremendous number of books I was reading, but on the other hand I had the strange and profound conviction that feelings of sympathy for one's fellow man require actual implementation. To do something about the thing that is close to your heart became natural to me from early childhood. I always wanted to shorten the distance between the heart and the deed. To live an idea, not just to talk about it or to feel it, was my slogan. Thus my basic mission in life was formulated: to create a law among nations to protect national, racial, and religious groups from destruction. The need for the innocent to be protected set off a chain reaction in my mind. It followed me all my life.

Once I conceived of the destruction of groups as a crime, I could not rest quietly. Neither could I stop thinking about it. When I later coined the word "genocide," I found too an expression for my own use, but at the same time I was prepared to work more for the actual transformation of this word into the subject of an international treaty.

Now that the parliaments of forty-one nations have accepted this law, I feel grateful to Providence for having chosen me as a messenger boy for this lifesaving idea.[2] My task was difficult. I had to inspire people to accept this idea, which sometimes required a great deal of moral persuasion. When I felt that I was failing to inspire people, I would withdraw into myself, where I could face my conscience and draw moral force from meditation. To be successful with one's fellow man one must learn to be fully alone in the sublime world of feelings and faith. I learned to love the obstacles by making them tests of my own moral strength. In this moral strength I believe fervently. It is stronger than any temporal power. It is stronger than technology and government. It is life itself.

CHAPTER ONE

Early Years

I WAS BORN IN A PART of the world historically known as Lithuania or White Russia, where Poles, Russians (or, rather, White Russians), and Jews had lived together for many centuries. They disliked each other and even fought, but in spite of this turmoil they shared a deep love for their towns, hills, and rivers. It was a feeling of common destiny that prevented them from destroying one another completely. This area was between ethnographic Poland to the west, East Prussia to the north, Ukraine to the south, and Great Russia to the east.

The Russians and Poles had fought for centuries for political supremacy in this area, while the Jews struggled for bare survival. A common proverb among the Jews went, "When three persons are in one bed under a common blanket, and when the man to the right pulls the blanket to himself, while the man to the left does likewise, the man in the middle is sure of being covered by the blanket."

I lived my first ten years on a farm called Ozerisko, fourteen miles from the city of Wolkowysk.[1] The city was named after two brigands, Wolk and Wysk. In the seventeenth century these two men controlled a village built within a huge forest. From this village they led the people to rob and kill travelers and tradesmen. Wolk and Wysk were ultimately caught and hanged.[2] But this ignominy did not prevent them from perpetuating themselves, if modestly, on the map of the world.

The city built on the site of their murderous exploits was later connected with many historic events. The Swedish and Napoleonic armies marched through it, and innumerable skirmishes took place there between the Russians and the Poles, Lithuanians and Ukrainians, and, earlier, between the Mongols and the Tartars.

Ozerisko lay in a large clearing between huge forests. It was a joint tenancy of two families, my father's and my uncle's. We children, who were mostly of the same age, spent our days together in one happy gang. When our parents were busy on the farm, especially in the summer months, the children escaped the control of eight parental eyes and had full freedom to explore and play in every corner of the farm.

Summer days on the farm started at sunrise. The alarm was given with amazing regularity by the roosters. They led the farm in its daily resurrection from oblivious sleep to the rhythm of toil. The earth was fresh from the chill of the night and silvery with dew. The animals breakfasted fast. The cows were prevented from kicking during the early milking by directing their personal attention to food. The fields again received their guests for the day: the farmhands and shepherds, sheep, horses, and cows. We were not permitted to get up so early, but from the windows we regularly watched the exodus of our friends. We were so much part of them that we could not miss this great moment.

When the timidity of the early sun changed to a bright flush of living gold, we ran to join the workers in the fields. Ahead of us was our friend and faithful companion, a dog called Riabczyk. He was all white except for a black button nose. He kept us company from early morning to night. Dogs usually absorb the moods of children more easily than those of adults. They integrate themselves forcefully into the lives of children because of the latter's spontaneity. Our dog always seemed to adjust his movements to the rhythm of our life. Sometimes it seemed to us that we were jumping with his feet or barking with his friendly voice. The dog and we were one.

This harmonious flow of busy happiness was sometimes interrupted by disasters. One day Riabczyk followed a rider on a horse who was passing on the road behind our farm. For some reason he started to bark at him. Then we suddenly heard a shot from the side of the road. The dog came running to us with a bleeding mouth. After several days of groaning, Riabczyk died. We cried bitterly, carried him to the top of a hill, and buried him at a spot we could see from our windows.

Although the farmhands treated us like nuisances, they missed us when we were not around. Occasionally they got help from us. We loved to listen to the metallic whisper of the swinging scythes and to the sighs of the clover and rye falling like wounded heroes. The workers used to laugh at our screams when we hurt our bare feet on the sharp stubs of the cut rye.

At noon, when the sun was in the middle of the sky, work stopped for luncheon and rest. The food was meager: black bread, raw onions, potato pudding, and sometimes cold tea or water. Then, within a minute, the farmhands' tired heads would fall on bundles of rye in heavy sleep. We watched how the sun would play on their noses and how they struggled through their sleep with fleas trying to enter their open mouths. While they were sleeping we jumped to the horses having their luncheon of grass. What fun we had stroking their thighs and plunging our fingers into their manes. If we were lucky we could gently caress one horse's silky nose. The horse would answer with a look of tender detachment, by sneezing or raising his ears. We were then sure he had returned our friendship.

Another outlet for our energies was riding horses. We were not permitted to disturb the farmhands during their day work. But at sunset we joined the workers in the fields, when they were ready to return to the farms. I remember with pride that I was three years old when I first rode a horse. My playmates argued that I was too small for this heroic sport. I felt humiliated and resented this inequality. I could not wait endlessly to grow up. I bribed myself into my first horse ride by offering a croissant to our farmhand. He ate the croissant with one hand and used the other hand to put me on the back of the white horse. I grabbed its mane and the world around me started to move as fast as a whirlpool. The sun was shining in my eyes. I saw nothing but the neck of the horse. When I approached the farm and the stables, my frightened mother and our barking dogs greeted me. Then I descended the horse, having achieved much cherished equality with my playmates. As I continued to ride the white horse every day, the feeling of joy deepened. I looked with pride from the horse downward at the earth, and my perception of the world unconsciously gained a new dimension.

The climax of farm life was the return of the entire animal world at sunset. The farm received each of us like a loving mother. First came the sheep and the cows, in a serious procession, some still chewing a last mouthful of grass. When the impatient shepherd put the sheep to run, the whole herd would descend upon the farm in a cloud of dust.

The first duty of the evening was to care for the thirsty. We, the happy gang of children, busily helped water the animals. The water was poured from buckets lifted by hand from the well. I can never forget how intensely they drank. It was as if new life was entering every part of their bodies. Their nostrils were enlarged and their eyes fixed as they sucked the water into their necks. There is a difference in the quenching of thirst between men and animals. Usually a man drinks when he wants, but an animal drinks when man wants it to drink. Desperate thirst exists always with animals, and fulfillment is overwhelming.

Several years later, in Paris, I was reminded of this difference when I saw the sketch by Daumier called "They Are Thirsty."[3] It consists of two parts. In the upper part, men are drinking coffee in a Parisian cafe. They hold their cups nonchalantly and their faces express a blasé indifference. In the lower part, a worker and a horse are drinking directly from a stream with absorbing intensity.

The reception for our four-legged friends was like a huge cocktail party, crowded and noisy, all the animals clamoring for attention under the caresses of a sinking sun. Its rays set afire the windows of our house or tossed playful reflections on the horn of a cow or the shining steel of scythes put to rest. The doors of the stables were wide open, sending smells of manure and sweat into the evening air. The cows and horses were then driven into the stable for food and rest.

Image of Entirety

The adult population of the farm, lost in their daily chores, didn't realize how beautiful it all was. They saw only the part they touched with their hands and senses. But we were hungry to see all the marvels of our world at once. We climbed to the tops of trees and hay carts. When the hay and the clover was brought from the fields to be put into the hay barns, we rode on top of the mountainous carts. From there we could see the distant outskirts of the fields, the neighboring villages, and the roads. The joy of conquering space from the vantage point of a hay top was equaled only by the enchantment of the smell of hay and fresh clover.

Another way to look at the world from above was to climb trees. When the cherry season arrived we almost lived in the trees, like birds. We hid from our parents between the leaves. Who could resist the darkening fullness of a ripe cherry smiling alluringly from the green leaves? From the top we could see the dark green potato fields or the challenging yellow greeting of a carpet of flowers in the grass fields. The roads looked to us like wrinkles on a dear face and the forest like hair on the head of a giant.

The Forest

The forest was the heart of the farm. A great part of our food, like mushrooms, blackberries and raspberries, nuts and game, came from it. It sustained life on the farm by providing wood for fuel. In the winter, it replaced the warmth of the sun.

Many roads and paths led from the farm to the forest. We used each of them. To us little children, and especially to me, it was a place of a thousand miracles to be discovered every day, with more left over for tomorrow.

The trees were ancient and so broad in their trunks that sometimes it took the joined hands of five or six children to encircle them. When we thus felt our hearts pressed against the trunk of an oak, it was like listening to his secret and giving him our own. I especially liked the small clearings in the forest where shadows struggled with the jumping rays of the sun. This constant fight made green carpets on the green underbrush. Here we would find discreet mushrooms and timidly hidden raspberries, between the oaks and nuts growing on winding underbrush. What a joy it was to spy a bundle of nuts growing closely together high up, and then plan the strategy of bending the branches close to our grasping hands.

The ground of the forest was covered with dried leaves and pine needles, a ready-made bed for tired heads of child explorers, hungry for dreams. This was the world that gave me my first lessons in solitude. From an early age I took a special delight in being alone, so that I could think and feel without disturbance. At that time I did not understand the meaning and purpose of this feeling, but I fully enjoyed the delight of contemplation. Away from my companions, I spent hours in the forest listening through my third ear to how the story of life was sung by the sparrows, robins, crows, and blackbirds, the innumerable mosquitoes and insects. Though they played discordant instruments, they still produced harmonious melodies.

The Lake

On one end of the farm was a lake that slept peacefully in the summer in the shade of a row of white birches. To us children this lake exercised the special attraction of a tale begun and never ended. When we looked at the water and couldn't see the bottom, we felt that this lake held a mystery that it wouldn't reveal to us. On this lake we used to build barges with my brothers and playmates.

The barges were small, but when we were on top of them they appeared huge to us. We moved them by leaning on long sticks placed into the mud beneath the water. We played pirates, modern Vikings conquering foreign lands and castles that we built lavishly in our imagination.

On top of the rafts we felt like grown-ups. This desire to prove that we were doing things like adults was with us most of the day.

Once I put on my new trousers for our seafaring and fell into the water. It was my first spanking, by my mother, who in principle did not believe in violence. Apparently she wanted to save her son from future gallows, as Dr. Samuel Johnson's teacher said when he spanked his pupil.[4]

Birch Tree

Somewhere between our house and the lake stood a lonely birch, leaning in the summer against a rye field. The birches on our farm, especially this one, had a special quality of containing and giving a white, aromatic juice. Sometimes it ran down the trunk into the soil. We would make a little hole in the trunk and soon see it fill with juice. We used straws to drink its lemonade. I was especially enamored of this birch. I used to lie for hours on the grass under its shadows after having quenched my thirst. To me the birch was more than a tree. I loved her dearly and was sorry when she got into trouble with the elements of nature. I watched from our house as she bravely defied the onslaughts of storms and lightning and stood half naked during the winter. Many years later, when I was searching for strength in the recollections of my youth, I wrote the following poem: [Poem not included.][5]

Stealing

In a larger sense, the world of nature is one. Nature does not care why man has divided the rye field or the loam between two owners, or why he put down stones to mark a line of ownership. The same flowers grow on both sides of the property line, and the same sky, sun, and rain cover them. Children follow nature. While renting out the farm to our parents, the farm's owner retained for himself two fruit gardens and left to us only some fruit trees scattered over the farm. When summer came, the full ripeness of the black cherries, the juicy yellow pears and apples in both gardens exercised a powerful attraction upon us. Merely noticing that the gardens were empty was enough to send us jumping on the trees and plucking the fruit. Our parents pleaded with us to stop this mischief. We were caught several times by the aggrieved owner, sometimes at the very moment when our hands were stretching out for an alluring cherry or plum. This prohibition, we felt, was against nature. We simply could not look indifferently through the fence at the fruit, and we succumbed to our temptation.

In one of the gardens we removed a plank in the fence behind a bush. Through this hole we slipped inside. My heart was beating fast, and my head was almost dizzy with a feeling of danger. But my eye was already caressing the voluptuous fullness of a pear or an apple. One instant—the apples were already plucked and put quickly into our hats, which we wore especially for this. Then we ran to the hole in the fence. Our faces shone with excitement. I distinctly remember that this danger of stealing touched off waves of pleasure, quickening my pulse and firing my imagination.

I was, I think, three or four years old when I joined my playmates in the raids on the gardens. Despite my inclination for loneliness, I joined the raids because I wanted this excitement and equality. I was the youngest and had to fight my way up for the right to play on an equal footing. Participation in the fruit raids was the price I paid for acceptance.

One day my parents broached the subject. My father told me and my elder brother that stealing is forbidden by God, and God would punish us. I wondered how God could see what we were doing, but then it was explained that he sees everything. It was not, however, until we started to read and were shown the words in the Bible, "Do not steal," that we believed the prohibition was true. Originally we thought our parents were inventing another prohibition, like the one against driving barges. Our raids stopped: there was no way of preventing God from seeing us. There must have been symbolic power in the written words of the prohibition.

The Harvest

The labors of the summer culminated in the ceremony celebrating the harvest. On this memorable occasion the workers were served vodka and sausages in abundance. They drank and sang. The women put garlands of blue field flowers in their hair. A belt was made of rye, and each year a different person was chosen as the king of the harvest, around whom the belt was tied. Later, everyone danced around the "king." I remember that once I was given this honor. It was so abrupt that I stood blushing and almost burst into tears from happiness. The entire community was one song, one joy, and one big pride.

Children of Farmhands

We not only played on our farm but performed useful tasks. One of our activities, performed with great solemnity, was the selection of chickens for egg-laying. Every chicken had to be examined by introducing a finger into a discreet part of her body to ascertain whether she was expected to lay an egg during the night. This was usually done by our mother or one of the female workers. After the examination, we carried the expectant chick-ens to a separate barn and put them in the straw. Next morning we collected the delicate rosy eggs from the barn and brought them into the house.

Another task and great joy was planting potatoes. These first had to be cut in such a way that every part would have a bud on its skin. When the planting started, we followed behind the plow with baskets in our hands and put pieces of potatoes at equal intervals in the freshly dug furrow. On the next turn the plow produced another furrow while the newly turned earth fell and covered the potato seeds we had just planted. It was simple but it bore witness to an iron logic in nature that made the earth the chief nutritionist of mankind, from time immemorial.

Not far from our houses stood the dwellings of the farmhands. We had cordial relations with them, because riding horses and participating in all chores depended very much on their permission. We played sometimes with their boys and girls, but we always were aware of the difference between us. Whereas we were compelled to wash our heads with soap every day, they, being without soap, were compelled to have their heads cleaned of lice. This was done at noon on Sundays, when the boys and girls would lay their heads on their mothers' knees in front of the whole farm. On weekdays, when playing with the children, we shared our sandwiches, because their parents, who worked for us, often left them for the entire day without food.

Still, we displayed our pride to them in a rather crude way. We boasted about our new clothes, especially new shoes, delighting in making them squeak. I was so enraptured with the importance of these new shoes that I even wanted to sleep in them. We went barefoot for pleasure, but the farmhands' children did so by necessity. In the summer their bare feet were brown with permanent dirt, and in the winter they wrapped their feet in rags and wore sandals made of bark.

Although in later years I suffered from other people's vanity and pride, I was guilty of the same injustice toward the poor children of the farmhands.

Buying the Right to Live

Our lives on the farm moved in accordance with the rhythm of nature. We were part of her indeed. The farm supplied the basic ingredients of my personality and made me a combined product of the life energies of my parents and the elements of nature in whose command I was released into this world.

And yet my personal life and the life of the two families around this farm was illegal. For many years the Russian czars had enforced a decree that forbade the Jewish population from dwelling upon or owning farms. Jews could live only in cities and villages of a certain size. This decree, however, was circumvented by bribing the authorities, especially the local police. My parents were compelled to pay not only tenure for the farm but an additional sum to a police official. At regular intervals he would come riding on a horse, which he would dismount and tie to a fence near the house. We saw him often, waiting for our parents to return from the fields. We were impressed by his beautiful horse and greatly admired his uniform, especially his shining high boots. He had a long moustache and an arrogant face, and he was waiting. There was something ominous and oppressive in his waiting, for we learned later why he was coming and we were aware that most of the time our parents had no money. When they would greet him with profuse politeness and guilty faces, we instinctively felt sorry for them. We learned very early in our childhood to dislike this man and to fear him as a symbol of our bondage.[6]

First Love and Early Education

I remember my face and body from the age of perhaps five years, when I first saw myself in a large cracked mirror hanging on the wall of our living room. The little boy with short trousers, white shirt, blond locks, and vivacious eyes looked at me with a questioning face. But something disturbed me deeply. I discovered that large areas on both sides of my nose were covered with freckles. I was told there was no cure for them, and I felt distressed about being thus crippled for life. My playmates soon took advantage of this disability and named me "the freckled one." My brother, who had a darker complexion, got the title in our gang of "the gypsy." Every one of us had a nickname, which was supposed to destroy him. Thus, the two young men and all the others were marked for life, but this did not diminish my worries about the freckles.

One afternoon, visitors came from the next village. The parents brought with them a boy the age of my brother and a girl of my age. The adults discussed plans for hiring a teacher for Hebrew education. In the meantime, the younger generation of visitors joined us.

I was impressed by the girl's beauty. She had hair of reddish gold, large blue eyes, and, by the grace of God, a face full of freckles. Bella's freckles cured me from despair about my own, for I then understood that one can be beautiful having freckles. When we started to play, I felt that I was losing the lightness and freedom of my movements. I didn't know exactly what I was doing because I kept looking at her. This was the beginning of my first love. Timidly, I introduced her to my dog and told her the miracles of the farm.

Bella didn't have miracles to offer in exchange. Her parents ran a combined boarding house and restaurant in the next village. She didn't have horses, cows, or sheep with bells on their necks to cheer her up, and she was frightened of the villagers who were always getting drunk in their house. When children meet, they tell each other more about the things with which they live than about themselves. My world was richer than Bella's and she was obviously impressed. This was exactly what I wanted. After she left, I kept thinking about her. How nice it would be, I thought, to run with her again tomorrow, over the fields, to drive barges with her on the lake, and maybe even put my hand on her golden hair.

Blushingly, I found out that we would see Bella and her parents next week. With a beating heart I rode in a cart to the house of Bella. On second sight she appeared even more beautiful to me, and I knew definitely that I was in love. At dinner, we were seated at different corners of the table, looking in separate directions, and still trying to have our eyes meet.

As I was returning to the farm, the sky of the summer night lying low over our heads, I thought how God had been good to me by giving me her brother as a study partner, which meant many, many times seeing Bella.

Somehow my feelings became known to my playmates and family. Everybody teased me with a serious face. I was told that since the name of the young lady was the same as my mother's, I would be unable to marry her. This despair made me only love her more. Thoughts of Bella made it easier for me to bear my personal troubles, even the worries about my freckles.

When winter came, we moved to Bella's house, where the teacher lived. More boys from the village joined us in common classes. Because our parents had taught us to read Hebrew well, we were able to join more advanced classes.

The teacher was stern and earnest. The Bible was his entire world and he sincerely desired that it become ours as well. Some of the chapters he sang to us, and songs children seldom forget.

On winter mornings he started classes at six o'clock. The room was cold, the only warmth coming from the kerosene lamp. Our teacher's chanting voice would set the tone. The brevity of the Hebrew language, the words loaded with meaning, made a lasting impression on my style of writing and speaking in other languages. The imagery was vivid, and on every page we discovered scenes pulsating with life. I came to the image world of the Bible through the images of my farm.

I used to see Bella at meals. She grew more beautiful and I was only unhappy that she was not taking classes with us. Since the teacher praised my progress before the other pupils, I wished that Bella could know. Soon I found out to my delight that her brother had been telling her. Bella's love gave alertness to my feelings and to my mind. It helped me to grow into an understanding pupil, loving not only the girl but also the yellow pages of the ancient book.

The evenings were a delight. Our mother gathered us near the warm stove. She taught us to sing songs and taught us poetry through the songs. These were sonnets of poets, to which we invented our own music. Sometimes we used known melodies to accompany them. The melodies were simple, the words soared, plain and moving. Because they were naïve, they could fertilize my mind and plant seeds which bore fruit later.

As I try to reconstruct the content of those sonnets-songs, the following picture of the world appears from them. There is much evil on earth and there is much injustice. The innocent and the poor suffer. They are often murdered in cold blood. People bow to false gods, the gods of greed and power. The poor and the innocent must be helped. Those who suffer should be loved and raised from their destitution. The songs offered hope for a better world, for the cessation of evil, for the protection of the weak.

This was told by millions of parents to their children. However, a spoken word is not as strong as a word sung. For this reason the ancient

Greeks used to promulgate their laws by singing them. A song by a mother to a child is bound to exercise the greatest influence, especially when it is repeated often. It invades all the senses and stays forever because the child's consciousness is being formed as it listens. It opens up like a flower to receive the rays of the sun.

My dear brother, beloved and suffering
Whoever you are, don't lose heart,
Although falsehood and evil are ruling the world,
And the earth is soaked with distress;
Though the sacred ideals are reviled,
And the blood of the innocent flows,
Trust the Bal will be destroyed,
And love will return on earth.

This song by the young Russian poet Nadson, who died at twenty-four of tuberculosis, became our second Bible.[7] But it was stronger than the Bible to us, because the Bible contained murders that our teachers had difficulty explaining. There was a pure repudiation of violence, without exception, in Nadson. A child likes a clear picture that does not require elaborate explanations.

The following winter we started on the prophets. I felt strongly drawn to them. Their words were like hot iron to me. They had lived thousands of years and were resounding on the hills of Judea and heard as far as our village. These words lived long because they were deeds dressed as words. When Isaiah ran naked through the streets of Jerusalem or wore a rotten girdle, he did so to show how God would strip Israel and let her decay for her sins.

"Cease to do evil; learn to do well; relieve the oppressed; judge the fatherless; plead for the widow." This call of Isaiah sounded to me so urgent, as if the oppressed stood now outside our door. The appeal to create peace by converting swords into plowshares seemed to re-create his presence. I thought of the power of our own plows, which brought life and not destruction.

I felt deep compassion for the prophets who had to suffer for what they believed. My thoughts were with the prophet Urijah, who fled Egypt to escape King Jehoiakim but was returned by his persecutors and killed. I saw Zachariah stoned to death in the courts of the temple, and Jeremiah as he was led like a sheep to his slaughter, before being saved. The lives and deeds of poor men who challenged kings and priests to obey the religion of the heart, kindled fire in the heart of a small village boy studying the Bible.

News of a pogrom in the city of Bialystok, several miles away in southern Russia, came to our farm. The mobs had opened the stomachs of their victims and stuffed them with the feathers from the pillows and feather comforters. Poems appeared by the Hebrew poet Bialik about the pogroms.[8]

A line, red from blood, led from the Roman arena through the gallows of France to the pogrom of Bialystok. I could not define history with my childish mind, but I saw it with my eyes vividly and strongly as a huge torture place of the innocent, about which my mother sang to us the poems of Nadson.

Another name comes to mind: Krylov, the Russian writer who wrote beautiful fables based on those by the French writer Jean de La Fontaine and the Greek fable writer Aesop.[9] These fables dealt mostly with the lives of animals who personified the virtues or vices of men. There was a half-hidden lesson in many of these fables: hidden enough not to kill the fascination of the story and not so hidden as to prevent children from seeing it. These basic lessons could be reduced to what one could call a human sense of justice. It amounted factually to maintaining equilibrium between two scales—on one was put vice or virtue, on the second retribution or reward. A fox invited a stork for luncheon and made him eat from a flat plate. The stork reciprocated by making the fox eat from a narrow neck of a bottle. Unfairness or injustice never pays in the long run. Nemesis catches up with the guilty.

Our mother read these fables to us. We recited them later, almost by heart. They provided the much-needed complement to Nadson's naïve idealism. Equity, justice, and fairness are basic elements of reason. The unjust person is made a fool because he destroys the reasonable basis of life. To us, the lesson of these fables was plain: the unjust are basically fools.

The power of these lessons was increased by the fact that the main actors were animals or birds, which are close to the imagery of all children. I grew up with a strong feeling that persecution must cease and that justice and love will finally prevail. I could put this idea into practice in my own little world of dogs, birds, horses, and playmates. When I started to read Tolstoy I realized that believing in an idea means to live it. I decided to become a vegetarian. I could not eat the meat of chickens and other animals because I loved them so much. But I could carry out my convictions for only three months. It became increasingly difficult to prepare special vegetarian food for me. I am forever grateful for the seriousness with which my family treated the short-lived vegetarianism of a seven-year-old child.

One day I found an owl in the grass. Her wing was broken, leaving her helpless. I carried her to the roof and made her a nest. For an entire year, I fed her every morning. She was so accustomed to me, and waited so eagerly to be fed, that it gave me a strong feeling of fulfilling a duty. I did not differentiate at that time among human beings, animals, and birds. The feeling of being needed gave me satisfaction. The conviction that I was saving a life made me happy. I did not have the feeling that my care for the owl came from something outside, but rather that it was connected with my inner self.

In 1913 a Jew with the name Beĭlis was accused of having killed a Christian child to use his blood for Jewish Easter.[10] The entire world trembled with interest and indignation. Our family discussed it every day. It was a test case for justice. By that time we had moved from the farm to the city of Wolkowysk. Our parents had reached the decision that their children needed formal education. We were enrolled in a city school that offered the equivalent of the first four years of high school.

The pressure of political bias on the life of the school was unbearable. All Jewish pupils were called by the collective name Beĭlis. The same thing happened in the city, where tensions were increasing. The Jewish population faced the possibility of a pogrom. It seemed as if the whole Jewish population of Russia were on trial. When Beĭlis was freed it temporarily relieved the tensions, but it did not remove the clouds from my mind. I saw clearly that the lives of millions of people depended on the vote of the jury. The axes, hammers, and guns were already prepared while the jury deliberated. I could not see how a situation of this kind could be bearable for long.

As the years went by, I kept thinking of these problems. I thought so hard that sometimes I felt physically the tension of blood in my veins.

In 1915 the Germans occupied the city of Wolkowysk and the surrounding area. I began to read more history to study whether national, religious, or racial groups, as such, were being destroyed. The truth came out only after the war. In Turkey, more than 1.2 million Armenians were put to death for no reason other than that they were Christians. They were driven from their homes along the Euphrates River and then, suddenly, the escorting gendarmes started shooting at both ends of the long line of deportees. Only a handful survived, hidden by the bodies of their comrades. The Turks later accused the unarmed Armenians of having started the shooting.

Early Adult Years

After the war, some 150 Turkish war criminals were arrested and interned by the British government on the island of Malta. The Armenians sent a delegation to the peace conference at Versailles to demand justice. Then one day I read in the newspapers that all Turkish war criminals were to be released. I was shocked. A nation was killed and the guilty persons were set free. Why is a man punished when he kills another man, yet the killing of a million is a lesser crime than the killing of an individual? The Turkish criminals released from Malta dispersed all over the world. The most frightful among them was Talaat Pasha, the minister of the interior of

Turkey, who was identified with the destruction of the Armenian people. Talaat Pasha took refuge in Berlin. One day he was stopped in the street by a young Armenian with the name Tehlirian. After identifying Talaat Pasha, Tehlirian shot him, saying, "This is for my mother." Tehlirian, one of the few survivors of the Armenian massacre, had been saved because the body of his dead mother had fallen over him. His trial became, in actuality, a trial of the Turkish perpetrators. The sinister panorama of destruction of the Armenians was painted by the many witnesses the Armenians brought to the court. Through this trial the world finally obtained a real picture of the tragic events in Turkey. The same world that was conveniently silent when the Armenians were murdered and had intended to hide the fact by releasing the Turkish war criminals was now compelled to listen to the awful truth.

The court in Berlin acquitted Tehlirian. It decided that he had acted under "psychological compulsion." Tehlirian, who upheld the moral order of mankind, was classified as insane, incapable of discerning the moral nature of his act. He had acted as the self-appointed legal officer for the conscience of mankind. But can a man appoint himself to mete out justice? Will not passion sway such a form of justice and make a travesty of it? At that moment, my worries about the murder of the innocent became more meaningful to me. I didn't know all the answers but I felt that a law against this type of racial or religious murder must be adopted by the world.

At Lwow University, where I enrolled for the study of law, I discussed this matter with my professors.[11] They evoked the argument about sovereignty of states. "But sovereignty of states," I answered, "implies conducting an independent foreign and internal policy, building of schools, construction of roads, in brief, all types of activity directed toward the welfare of people." Sovereignty, I argued, "cannot be conceived as the right to kill millions of innocent people."

In 1926, just after obtaining my doctorate of law, another bomb exploded. In a rare moment of clarity that seething indignation instills, I further understood the concept of the crime I was trying to establish.

In Paris, Shalom Schwarzbard,[12] a Jewish tailor whose parents had perished in a pogrom in Ukraine in 1918, shot the Ukrainian minister of war, Symon Petliura,[13] a man generally blamed for the massacres. Like Tehlirian before him, Schwarzbard was put on trial. The sufferings of hundreds of Jews were displayed like an open wound before the world. The Paris jury found itself in the same moral dilemma as the court in Berlin. They could neither acquit Schwarzbard nor condemn him. The conscience of the jury did not permit punishing a man who had avenged the death of hundreds of thousands of his innocent brethren, including his parents. But neither could it sanction the taking of the law in one's hands in order to uphold the moral standards of mankind.

The ingenious legal minds found a compromise similar to that in the trial of Tehlirian: "The perpetrator is insane and therefore must go free."

The man in the street the world over, who had the same natural sense as the animals in the fables of Aesop and Lafontaine, must have understood the lesson of this anomaly.

After the Schwarzbard trial, I wrote an article in which I called Schwarzbard's act a "beautiful crime." I deplored the absence of any law for the unification of moral standards in relation to the destruction of national, racial, and religious groups.

Gradually, the decision was maturing in me that I had to act. I knew, however, that I needed an appropriate forum. To be heard, one must raise one's voice in a proper setting, and I was only a young doctor of law preparing for a career in the Warsaw courts. I had already, as a student, published a law book. I started to work hard and published another book every year. They were well reviewed, and I soon gained a following and influence.

In 1929, I was made deputy public prosecutor of Warsaw. Other appointments quickly followed: secretary of the penal section of the Polish Committee on Codification of Laws, where I worked on the Polish penal code; representative at the International Bureau for Unification of Penal Law, which met every year in a different capital of Europe; secretary general of the Polish Group for the Association of

Penal Law. I was soon on friendly terms with the highest judicial authorities and leading intellectuals of Western Europe. I submitted papers to all these groups' conferences. There were solemn opening speeches, dinners, and receptions with delegates whose chests were half covered with decorations.

I finally had a forum for action, but I was encountering obstacles. In October 1933, an international conference for the unification of penal law was meeting in Madrid.[14] On the agenda was the problem of crimes creating danger for several states. Proposals had to be submitted as to which crimes should be included in this category, and which of them should be made international offenses.

I felt the time was ripe for me to put before the conference my idea, which had been maturing for so many years. Now was the time to outlaw the destruction of national, racial, and religious groups. I thought that the crime was so big that nothing less than declaring it an international offense would be adequate, and that it should be done by international treaty or convention. Hitler had already promulgated his blueprint for destruction. Many people thought he was bragging, but I believed that he would carry out his program if permitted. The world was behaving as if it were ready to acquiesce in his plans. The Polish government was negotiating a nonaggression pact with Germany. In the circles of the League of Nations, my friends were making sarcastic remarks about the pact, which they thought would undermine collective security. Now was the time to establish a system of collective security for the life of the peoples.

I moved fast. In September 1933, I sent a second report on the same subject to the secretariat of the Bureau for the Unification of Criminal Law. I formulated two crimes: the crime of barbarity and the crime of vandalism.[15] The first consisted of destroying a national or religious collectivity; the second consisted of destroying works of culture, which represented the specific genius of these national and religious groups. I wanted to preserve both the physical existence and the spiritual life of these collectivities.

In my report I pointed out that world conscience finds its expression in protecting mankind from such evils as slavery, trade in women and children, trade in drugs, circulation of obscene publications, piracy, and even the destruction of submarine cables. All these acts were already outlawed by civilized nations, which undertook to punish them by international treaties. Is not the destruction of a religious or racial collectivity more detrimental to mankind than destroying a submarine or robbing a vessel? When a nation is destroyed, it is not the cargo of the vessel that is lost but a substantial part of humanity, with a spiritual heritage in which the whole world partakes. These people are being destroyed for no other reason than that they embrace a specific religion or belong to a specific race. They are destroyed not in their individual capacity but as members of a collectivity of which the oppressor does not approve. The victims are the most innocent human beings of the world. They are the innocents of whom my mother sang to me in Nadson's songs.

I sent the report to Madrid and asked my publishing house, Pédone, which was the publisher for the League of Nations, to publish it. It was circulated among many important institutions around the world.

I was ready to go to Madrid for the big fight. And then one evening my phone rang. A justice of the supreme court, my associate at all international conferences, was on the line. He was the chief delegate to the Madrid conference. In a friendly voice but with tones of embarrassment, he informed me that the minister of justice opposed my going to Madrid. He also referred to articles which appeared in the influential anti-Semitic paper G Warszawska [Gazeta Warszawska], which had attacked my proposal for outlawing acts of barbarism and vandalism. In an article being widely discussed in Warsaw, the newspaper wrote that I was acting solely for the protection of my own race. The article stressed that I was public prosecutor and implied that people might get the wrong impression that I was acting in the name of the government.

That same night I dispatched several letters to my friends in Western Europe, asking them to support my published proposal. I was glad I had taken the initiative to print it in advance of the conference. Thus I prevented it from being suppressed. My proposal was discussed by the conference, and naturally it was tabled. They would not say yes, but they could not say no.

Although I could not win the battle in Madrid, I had at least started a movement of ideas in the right direction.

CHAPTER TWO

The Flight, 1939

ON SEPTEMBER 6, 1939, I WAS walking through the blacked-out Marszalkowska Street in Warsaw to the railway station. It had been only six days since the Nazi armies had attacked Poland, but already the country's defenses were disintegrating. The Luftwaffe struck simultaneously at various points around the country, especially the railway stations. The meaning of the blitz was made clear to every Pole—not through a definition in the dictionary, but by the ceiling of the state and of private life falling over his head.

Nazi tanks rolled onto Polish highways from the west, north, and south. In the kind of self-destructive act that affects not only individuals but nations as well, the Polish government in 1938 had helped place the Nazi war machine at its southern borders by endorsing the dismemberment of Czechoslovakia, from which Poland claimed the district of Cieszyn.

An order had been broadcast half an hour previously by the Polish authorities that all able-bodied men were to leave Warsaw immediately. I obeyed. My way was lighted by houses burning like candles at various points on the street.

When I entered the train station I found an ocean of human heads. It was impossible to see people's bodies, they were pressed so tightly together. Their eyes spoke with a glow of excitement and anxiety. I had with me only shaving material and a summer coat over my arm. It was easier for me to make my way through the crowd down to the platforms, from which trains used to depart.

After hours of waiting I was carried on the top of a storming crowd and thrown into a train compartment. I fell like a heavy bundle amid the other passengers. In the light of the night, already paling with a hesitant dawn, I found a corner seat and started to study my companions. There was a woman with a child in her arms who soon fell asleep, exhausted from hours of crying. Another young woman constantly repeated a man's name to herself: "Stasio." Was she taking leave of him in her mind, or imploring God to keep him alive? A man on my right was leaning on me with all his weight. I could not see his face, but I could discern a heavy golden watch chain across his vest and I could hear his heavy breathing. There were people sitting on the floor, and more were trying to get into the compartment. Those already within protested loudly.

The September sun spread its playful rays over these wretched bodies. It seemed strange to me that the sun was the same today as on all other days. The difference in the lives of all these people between yesterday and today was so great, and still nature did not take cognizance of it. Is nature cruel or endlessly clever? It does not pay attention to things it has seen from time immemorial. The same sun shone on the hooks perforating the lips of countless prisoners who were thus attached to chains in the hands of their Assyrian conquerors five thousand years ago. How impersonal the sun can be!

The train moved slowly and cautiously, like a tired old man. We passed the gardens of the suburbs and villages, the emerging gold of ripe rye fields already visible behind them. For a while a feeling of unnatural ease entered the compartment. Somebody took sandwiches from a bundle and offered them to the woman with the child. The natural gregariousness of the Poles was returning. "Two Germans—an army," goes the proverb. "Two Poles—a parliament."

Suddenly, a powerful detonation made the train tremble. Somebody screamed, "Everyone lie on the floor!" We obeyed. Another detonation, closer and more powerful, followed. Then a commanding cry made us all shiver: "The train is bombed, leave the train!" We began jumping out through the doors and windows. Cries sounded in Polish, "*O Boze*" (O God)—"*O Jezu*" (O Jesus).

I lay with my body pressed to the ground. The earth was refreshingly cool, and it gave my burning cheeks unexpected relief. The noise of the planes started to die away. There was a minute of ominous silence, as if the world were holding its breath. Somebody cried and groaned. A frog jumped over my head. Cautiously, I turned my eyes in the direction of the train. It was divided in two, and something burned between the sections. The locomotive was stretched on the slope like a dead black horse.

A short distance away there was a forest, and I entered the shadow of the trees and heard many voices. I sat under a tree and tried to think. The forest was full of people, all excited, all talking at once, running here and there.

These people now came to live with the animals in the forests. They even envied them, because the animals were at home, superior to the people in their feeling of safety. Certainly nobody planned to kill all the animals at once. I felt exhausted; a sharp pang of hunger nagged me. I had not eaten in twenty-four hours. In the midst of my thoughts about food I fell asleep heavily, dreamlessly. I must have slept many hours.

I awoke at sunset. It was cool in the forest, and the sky was an angry red. I could not tell whether the redness came from the departing sun or from a burning city somewhere far away. Now I felt rested and much stronger. The sharp tension was gone, though my hunger had increased. I had to think quickly and resolutely: where to obtain food and which way to go. The balance of the first day of my exodus was clear to me. I had survived the bombed train, but I had lost one day. Time is especially precious in flight.

At the outskirts of the forest I saw a small group of people gathered around a smoking fire. Something in my stomach commanded me: go there, they are cooking food. When I approached the group, a middle-aged man in a blue beret with a friendly smiling face greeted me cheerfully: "One more empty stomach, sit down, we will feed you too." A couple with their child, a little girl, and a big stuffed valise were in the center of the group. Somebody dug potatoes from a neighboring field. Our hostess was boiling them with pride and an air of cheerful responsibility. The fire was small so as not to attract planes, so the potatoes had to be cooked slowly. Meanwhile, we tried to suppress our hunger with conversation. We felt instinctively that the conversation of hungry people should not be too serious. We engaged in small talk, almost like the conversation at a cocktail party. From time to time someone suggested with hopeful impatience that the potatoes might be ready. A knife stuck in the resistant potatoes dispelled these premature hopes. Never in my life had I witnessed such a slow boiling of potatoes. Finally they were ready. With the grave mien of an ancient priestess and the eye of an impartial judge, our hostess took out the potatoes and counted them. She announced that everyone would receive one potato and a half. We ate them with our hands, slowly and deliberately, fully aware of their lifesaving value. Then the hostess opened the valise and offered a sandwich to everyone. Instinctively, we all looked at her little girl and said, "Thank you, no."

After the meal, the conversation turned to the question of where we should go. Despite having met only a few hours ago, we talked like old friends. Our common hunger had drawn us closer. Some argued that there was no sense in going too far from Warsaw because the Nazis would soon retreat from Poland. England and France had declared war, they argued, and would soon invade Germany. I did not agree. I remembered my conversation in London with my English friends during the Munich crisis the previous year. The night after Neville Chamberlain flew back from meeting with Hitler in Godesberg, I dined with Justice du Parcq of the court of appeals, in the Reform Club. Lord Simon, the chancellor of the exchequer in Chamberlain's cabinet, entered the dining room late and was approached by Justice du Parcq, who was eager for news. When my companion returned to the table, he said, "We are negotiating with Hitler because we are not prepared for war. We will not be prepared to meet Hitler's challenge maybe for two or more years."

I explained my views and urged my friends to start at once. We must walk at night and rest during the day in the forest to avoid the strafing planes, and head to the south of Warsaw. Let us go in the direction of the city of Siedlce. We will have to avoid this city and the railway station because it is an important center of communications, and it will certainly be under heavy bombardment. In the area of Siedlce we can make further plans. One man said that I was right because Siedlce lay in the direction of Romania. One way to save our lives was to cross the Romanian border and then go to France. I answered that there was also another avenue of escape: Lithuania was neutral, and from there it would be possible to go to Sweden. Furthermore, we were closer to Lithuania.

I arose and several men elected to join me. We thanked our hostess for the potato dinner and started to walk south. I suggested that we avoid the highway, where there were many vehicles, which would impede our flight. We would use the side roads between the peasant villages and thus be able to obtain food from the farmers.

We were a group of five men. In the next village we woke a farmer and persuaded him to drive us in his horse and cart to the nearest village for a good price. His wife would not allow him to undertake a longer voyage for fear of being lost or having his horse requisitioned by military authorities.

I lay on the hay in the cart with my companions fast asleep beside me. One snored and disturbed my thinking and rest. The best remedy against snoring is to become accustomed to it. Indeed, when he stopped for a while, I even missed it. I was making plans for getting out of the country. My instinctive preference was Lithuania and Sweden. The former minister of justice of Sweden, Karl Schlyter, was an old friend.[1] He would facilitate my entry if only I could reach a point where I could send a cable abroad. It was also clear to me that I must see my parents before I left. They still lived in Wolkowysk, in the eastern part of Poland, some eight hours by train from Warsaw. This distance now seemed insurmountable. My parents, I thought, would be worried about me. They knew my life was in danger. I must appear and show them that I am alive. I did not have much hope of persuading them to go with me abroad. But I must see them. I must, I must . . . With this decision, I fell asleep.

In the middle of the night we reached our destination. The farmer woke us with several shouts. As I was leaving the cart, one of our group started to play on the greed of the farmer. "Listen," he said, "why don't you take us from here to the next village? We will make a new arrangement. You will still have time to return home before daybreak." The farmer scratched his head, thought for a while, and asked: "Will you give me the same money for the next trip?" We agreed, and again we were listening to the monotonous trotting of the horse over the rough Polish road. But the farmer was more clever than we. The next village was only several miles away, a much shorter distance than the first. We had to leave the cart, pay the farmer, and continue our journey on foot.

Walking by night is not one adventure but many. Every object seen at night produces two images. One comes to your eyes in the most mysterious form and assumes the shape and dimension of something completely different from what it actually is. A cart seen from afar looks like a horse, a house like a hill, a small river with the moon reflecting in it appears as a huge lake. I enjoyed this game of double reality on my night walks across Poland. I kept my mind busy by trying to guess what the nearest object before me really was. This game was especially rewarding on dark and moonless nights.

At dawn, exhausted after a night of walking, we knocked at a window of the house of a farmer. We were hungry, and opened "negotiations" about breakfast. I was tired, both physically and mentally. In my new nomadic life, I was hungry for a glimpse of sedentary life. I walked out with the farmer into the yard and looked around with curiosity and envy. I wanted to see again how people live when they have a home.

The farm was beautiful, especially when it was awakening to morning life. Through the open door of the barn I saw two horses quietly chewing their food. From time to time they chased the morning flies from their backs by hitting them with their tails. In the yard, the farmer's wife was milking the cow. Noisy chickens tried to remind everybody of their morning hunger. A dog walked in the middle of the yard with the assurance of a guardian and protector. There was a strong smell of manure and animal sweat mixed with the fresh morning air. Somewhere a bird hesitatingly started its morning chant, and then stopped as if it didn't want to disturb the "busy folk."

There was so much basic logic and peaceful interdependence in all these lives placed within one framework of yesterday, today, and tomorrow. And I was a man without a tomorrow. I ate breakfast in silence and thought of the farm where I was born and raised.

After breakfast we asked our host to hide us for the day in one of his hay barns. I could not sleep and kept thinking of my childhood on our farm in eastern Poland. The similarity became more striking every moment.

While I lay in the hay that memorable day, I reviewed nearly thirty years of my life in terms of feelings, dreams, actions, and struggle. But I was still in the hay and there was no time now for bitter or sweet memories. I must survive and continue my fight.

It was already darkening when my companions began to get up. The farmer came in and cautioned us against getting too close to the highway because, as somebody had told him, German tanks were seen there in the morning. The detonations of fallen bombs were heard in the vicinity, he reported. We asked him how far we were from the area of Siedlce. "You are already in the vicinity of the city, and therefore you should be careful," he warned again. The Germans must have known that the remnants of the Polish army and many civilians, including government authorities, were moving this way.

We walked for about an hour in depressing silence. Suddenly, a huge searchlight bathed us in a sea of light. We instantly fell flat near the road. When nothing happened over the next hour, we arose and cautiously moved on. We decided to change direction and to go first east and later south.

This proved to be a wise decision, because a great massacre took place the next day in the area of Siedlce, claiming the lives of countless Jews.[2]

We were rested and able to walk fast. The rumors conveyed by our last host gave our steps a strong sense of urgency. At dawn we reached a forest and met a small group of escapees. We got acquainted and decided to spend the day together. We found a clearing among the trees and settled there. I looked over to my new companions. With the old companions I spoke little—there was no time to speak because we either walked or slept. Among the new group was one man who dominated all. He told us that he was from Lodz, the manufacturing center of the country, where he owned a big textile factory. Some thousand workers toiled for him. Several weeks before the war he had sent textiles abroad. Essentially he talked to himself, expressing his fears and hopes. When he reached a neutral country he would contact his creditors, he said. Then real life would start again. He looked at us, hoping to find confirmation here in the dark unknown forest where we were all suspended between life and death.

I had never liked his city, Lodz. It was the most unhistorical and impersonal city in Poland, a city without a face. It had only a body. One had the impression in Lodz that no street had a specific character. The houses were attached to geometrical lines informally, like barracks. There was not an attractive building in the whole city. The people never talked about literature or art, as in other cities. They talked about textiles, invoices, foreign exchange. They tell the story that two men were discussing textiles in a cafeteria in Lodz when a stranger entered. A dispute arose between the two men as to the kind of material in the newcomer's suit. Unable to agree, they approached this man and started to feel his suit, pulling at it and yanking at the sleeve and yelling to each other. The stranger fled, thinking the place was some sort of madhouse.

The man from Lodz proved to be kind and most helpful in organizing the breakfast. He led several of our group to the neighboring field to dig potatoes. We dug a hole, started a fire, and baked the potatoes. When we finished our meal, we realized that we had really been playing with fire. A telltale pall of smoke had risen into the sky over the forest. Hunger had dulled our sense of danger.

To heighten our misapprehensions, my companions reported that, while coming back to the forest, they had noticed several unoccupied military vehicles and a field kitchen parked along the road. Fearfully we wondered if the German soldiers were searching the forest.

The place where we sought refuge was one of the many old forests in Poland. The trees were immensely thick. Many were covered with running pine tar. Under the trees, broad-headed mushrooms were waiting to be picked. Usually they provided delicious food, but now nobody bothered with them. A subdued noise of bees and flies provided a musical counterpoint in this quiet world of aroma and coolness.

We went to sleep in the shade of the trees. A strong detonation and the noise of a falling tree awoke us. More detonations followed. We dispersed and I lay on the trembling earth listening to the groans of the wounded trees. Somebody was hit. I distinctly heard his cries. Then another man cried, and a third. Apparently many were wounded. As the trees around us were falling fast, I thought the best thing was to lie still. To combat fear, I concentrated on studying the grass before me. Several ants were carrying tiny loads to an ant hill they were building. Their movements were not coordinated, and I distinctly saw how they were meeting time and time again, and then retreating at the same angle. I decided to resort to superstition. I said to myself that nothing would happen to me if the ants met a third time and then retreated at the same angle. They did. I relaxed, having obtained much-needed security in the midst of the falling trees and the wounded people.

After the bombing was over, we discovered that three of our companions had been killed, among them the man from Lodz. We did not have shovels to dig a grave for them, so we put the bodies together and covered them with leaves and branches we had gathered. Then we went wordlessly to another corner of the forest and began to wait for night. We did not speak or look at each other until the time came to continue our march.

When darkness set in we walked east and wondered when and where we should turn south. We needed to consult somebody from the vicinity.

The road inevitably led to some village. Before us we saw a long file of other escapees. We started a quiet conversation and found out that we were going in the right direction. We also obtained radio news. A bespectacled young man told us that the Allies, who had declared war on Germany, had done nothing more. The French were still hiding behind the Maginot Line.[3] "Poland has been left alone," he said bitterly.

"The Polish government is heading toward Lublin and must be now close to the Romanian border," another voice reported from the darkness of the night.

"We must expect any day," somebody said, "that Russia will enter Poland from the east. This is inevitable in light of the agreement between Germany and Russia of the 23rd of August 1939. They must have divided Poland; Russia always wanted our eastern territories and the district of Lwow."[4]

We were all hungry for conversation and ripe for complaint. It started quite naturally.

"How stupidly our government behaved these past years," a woman's voice interjected. "In the League of Nations we helped to break up the system of collective security; we made a nonaggression pact with the Germans; we helped dismember Czechoslovakia; we spoiled our relations with Lithuania. We remained without friends. A great deal of our national energy was spent on suppressing minorities: the Jews, Ukrainians, and White Russians. We introduced a ghetto in our universities for Jewish students and obliged them to sit on special benches in the lecture halls. All this we were doing instead of working day and night for our defense, for the consolidation of our nation, and for improving our international position."

In the light of the night, I could distinguish only the pallor of her face, but we all felt the bitterness of her indictment.

"We like to call ourselves the Irish of the East," she continued. "This is, I presume, because we love national liberty. But we did not much prove that we also love individual liberty. By having had Paderewski as our prime minister and then Piłsudski and his successor General Śmigły-

Rydz, we proved to the world that we are a nation of musicians and generals.[5] We got our independence in 1918, and already in 1926 we permitted Piłsudski to establish his dictatorship. It is true that Piłsudski was a national hero and was basically a man of good intentions. It is also true that every dictator becomes somewhat of a god to himself and demands the entire nation should abide by his divine power. We disgraced ourselves before the world by permitting Piłsudski to throw the leaders of the opposition party in jail and then to condemn them for sedition. We even sacrificed our courts to Piłsudski. A dictator craves first your body, then he reaches for your soul."

"Don't you dare to attack Piłsudski!" a man protested. "He was the greatest patriot Poland ever had."

"What you fail to see," the woman continued, "is that an entire nation cannot depend for its life on one man. Nations have collective minds that grow by the force of many great individuals. If you put all your eggs in one basket, what happens to the eggs if the woman who carries the basket stumbles? What happened to Piłsudski's heritage after his death? He was succeeded by small dictators, by confusion and corruption. Now we are all paying the price for having delegated the government to one man. We are now a nation on the road, like the wandering Jew, whom we used to blame for all evils."

"Every Pole is patriotic," a voice protested. "In Westerplatte near Danzig, in the first days of the present war, Polish soldiers stopped Nazi tanks by throwing themselves in front of the advancing tanks while they had a belt of grenades around their waistline."

"Did they save the Polish army, or did they save the nation by this heroic act?" the woman asked.

These people were intelligent and saw things clearly. Although the situation was desperate, there was no fear in their voices. There was much defiance and much self-questioning. The younger people seemed to be tired of sleeping on mattresses and telling jokes in the cafeterias. Most of the escapees in the new group didn't speak at all. They seemed to be devoured by doubts, longings, and uncertainties. They suffered like all of us, from hunger and thirst, and thought frequently of their homes.

We continued our march and talked quietly. We were all stirred and could not easily close up the sources of our thought. The conversation was like percolating water. Everyone was tormented by things they had long repressed.

"I was a teacher in a grammar school in a village in the Carpathian Mountains," one man spoke up. "I came to visit my sister in Warsaw and was caught in the war. I do not know what our government could have done about it, but I assure you that I had to teach hungry children. They were not stupid. One morning I brought into class some buttered sandwiches and fed each pupil. Their eyes shined, their voices became stronger, and they did much better in their addition exercises in mathematics. I learned that meals were served in the homes of this village only once a day. The sole meal consisted mostly of soup and a slice of bread and was served at the end of the day. I tried to move the hours of my classes toward the evening. That failed. Next I tried to move the meal hour toward the morning. I could not succeed. The school inspector did not agree to change the hours, and the mothers could not afford to cook special meals for the children. You know how peasants are quite set in their ways. When the book *The Grippe Is Raging in Neprava* appeared, I was amazed how weak the reaction was against this indictment of poverty.[6] The author, as you know, a schoolteacher like myself, wrote about the peasants being deprived of salt for cooking, about splitting matches in four parts to use them four times."

"Do you really believe a book can stop poverty?" somebody asked sarcastically.

A story that had been recently told to me by a friend came to mind. My friend had been invited as one of two hundred guests on a special weekend train hired by the American ambassador. They traveled to the south to one of the bigger states and were lavishly entertained by one of the Polish aristocracy. The food discarded at this party could have fed the hundred children of the village school for many months, I told myself, and improved their addition exercises. Another story came to mind. At one of the big estates, after luncheon, a horse walked into the dining room of the castle and stopped before a table, and every guest gave him a piece of sugar. The guests applauded the horse and its imaginative owner.

Only several days earlier I had been recalling my mother's songs about the poor and innocent. Now, I thought, all these wretched people are cleansing their consciences in the most difficult hour of their lives. Another terrifying thought came to me. The conscience of humanity is like that of a dying man. All his sins invade his mind in his last hour, at once, when he is powerless to repair them!

One night a problem arose. We were approaching a big river. We could cross it best by following the highway, which led to a bridge. We might use the bridge, provided it had not been bombed out of existence by the Luftwaffe. We decided to follow the highway, which was already occupied by a retreating column of the Polish army. Marching beside military vehicles was not very dangerous at night, and it gave a sense of direction. Besides, we had no choice. The column was advancing slowly and stopped at frequent intervals. My feet were aching.

At one of the stops I climbed onto the front of a vehicle and took a seat beside a sleepy soldier. He did not move or speak. The night was not dark, and I could see how his gray, tired face matched his worn-out uniform, as though both were made of one piece. I looked at the cadaverous horses, which apparently had not been fed properly for many days. There was no conversation in the column, only the monotonous knock of the wheels against the highway.

I have seen retreating armies. Usually they do not have spirit, but they still maintain the promising noise of life. Even the soldiers of a defeated army are excited by their exploits and past dangers. They like to share these experiences with one another and usually excel in telling exaggerated tales of the miracle of their personal survival. But the men of the Polish army in 1939, with few exceptions, were defeated without battle.

They were like loose limbs of a body whose brain was paralyzed. Although individual attachments sometimes fought successful battles on their own, there was no central command. This was the most demoralizing of military misfortunes: defeat without battle. This was also the deeper meaning of the blitz, which consisted in cutting all liaisons in the army and rendering it immediately headless.

By becoming headless, it also became thoughtless. Every army, like every corporate body, has its own way of thinking. It has its own logic, which is different from the logic of other bodies. One cannot argue that one type of logic is worse or better than others. It is different. I first realized this during my own military training in Grodno. Several of us in my company had university degrees. We had a tough sergeant who was especially eager to prove his superiority to intellectuals. With a very serious mien he scolded us for not following the logic of the drill.

"You are not in a university here. You must think." This meant to think as the army thinks.

To my mind the column moved without plan or thought. For this reason all soldiers must have the same wooden face as the soldier next to me. In the army, the spirit is collectivized: one is like the other.

At our next stop the soldier next to me awoke and asked me to leave the vehicle. He was not even amazed that I was there. I marched again beside the column. From the pallor of the sky I sensed that day was approaching.

Soon we reached the river, and the column stopped in uncertainty. Only one narrow beam still arched the width of the river. The rest of the bridge was bombed out. We were told that pedestrians could risk crossing if they walked carefully. In the light of the dawn, the mutilated bridge looked like a dying monster. It hung high in the air, tattered with broken girders, and below it the water had a muddy color. We decided to try crossing over the poor remnants of the bridge. Only one person could cross at a time because the iron beam trembled, even under the weight of one person. It was possible to maintain oneself on the beam by holding on to the girders. But both parts, the beam and the girders, were of questionable reliability. Merely envisioning the passage in these conditions made us shudder.

We had no choice and were ashamed to show fear. We even tried to outdo each other in bravado. It was cold and we could easily blame our shuddering on the icy wind that swept upriver.

One of our companions began the crossing. Before he stepped on the plank he crossed himself and said a prayer. His movements were like those of a cat. We watched him to learn by his experience. Our fate depended so much on his success. We saw him arrive safely on the other shore and wave to us. I was the next to cross. I held my breath and tried to think of only two things: the beam below my feet and the hanging and twisted girders. I excluded from my consciousness the muddy waters below. They simply ceased to exist for the moment. It seemed to me that I could hear the beating of my pulse. A few more steps and the far shore would be under my feet. In danger a man becomes a human animal and acquires the highly developed senses and protective instincts of all other animals. Never did mud look so beautiful as the mud that greeted my boots when I stepped off the bridge.

We moved now to a large clover field, at the end of which we saw a house. A knock at the window brought an unusual reply: "We have no food and no place to sleep." Then the window came down with a bang. We followed the road to the next village.

After another hour's walking, we found a typical peasant house. There was only one room, a quarter of which was occupied by a huge stove. The rear of the stove was indented from above. I knew from my childhood that this was a most favored place in the family of a peasant. Everybody wanted to sleep here in the winter. The floor was of hardened earth. The Polish knew the secret of cementing the earth by a special process. They could not afford wooden planks to make a floor. There were wooden benches along the walls, and hundreds of flies "zim-zoomed" around the dirty windows. Children's faces, pressed together in curiosity, gazed at us from the corner.

"I have no milk, as our cow died two winters ago," the house's owner explained. She continued: "We have been trying to get one this summer but did not have enough money. You cannot collect enough money by selling eggs. I could sell the chickens, but then I would have no eggs."

This financial puzzle was familiar to Polish peasants, especially in a disaster, as when a horse or a cow dies. The whole summer this poor family had been eating potato cake baked in oil, from their own plant seeds, with a mixture of onions. They had not enough bread. Now the hostess was offering to share her small supply of potato cake with us.

We were very hungry and accepted the offer. Then we asked the woman how much money she needed to buy the cow.

"Thirty zlotys."

We made a quick calculation among us. If she did not buy the cow at once, she would be unable to do so later, because the first consequence of the downfall of Poland would be the devaluation of money.

We handed the woman one hundred zlotys, to which everyone contributed. We advised her to buy a cow as soon as possible because the cows might be requisitioned if she waited any longer. She looked at the money with bewilderment. Here was the realization of her innermost dreams. The money was offered by those who lost both their dreams and their reality. The Polish eagle on the bank notes was mortally wounded. It was bleeding, but it could still save a poor woman's hungry children from starvation.

When the woman put us up for the day in her barn, we fell asleep with the feeling of having performed our most constructive deed since leaving our homes. We also felt we had paid part of our moral debt to the unknown peasants who had built modern Poland with their sweat and tears.

CHAPTER THREE

The Flight, 1939–1940

THE DISASTER THAT BEFELL Poland continued in the midst of one of
the most beautiful Septembers in the country's history. Usually the rains
start that month, transforming the bad roads into a porridge of loam and
mud. This would have impeded the onward movement of the Nazi
tanks. But the weather was on the side of the Nazis. The sky was immac-
ulately blue in the daytime and full of stars at night. They twinkled
indifferently at our fate. The only help we received was from the Great
Bear, which marked our way eastward and southward.

In the daytime the planes controlled the sky with a terrifying furor, and
they continued to rain their relentless fire and destruction. We were exhausted from hunger, thirst, and animal-like fear. The earth that helped
our parents raise us did not want us any longer. We were her rejected
children.

People persisted in their grim determination to retain their human
patterns. It was not easy. With the disintegration of the state as the
outward symbol of social order, all other institutions—customs, family,
currency, property, morality—were affected. They were dying hard. It
started with the physical appearance of the men and women. Because
the order to leave the cities applied only to able-bodied men, there were
more men than women among the escapees. This order was mysterious
to some people, who thought it might have been inspired by a skillful

fifth column. Indeed, what sense was there in emptying the cities of able-bodied men while defending some of them, like Warsaw, until the end of September? The mayor of Warsaw, Stefan Starzyñski, who directed the defense of the city until he was imprisoned in a concentration camp, became a legendary hero.[1]

Most of the women who left Warsaw alone went to provincial towns in the east to join their families, from whom they had been separated. Some left the cities with their husbands or boyfriends. Their appearance changed rapidly. Soap and hot water were rarely available, so the chance to wash became a festive occasion. When the sun was shining warmly we quickly washed our underwear and socks and dried them in the sun. There was no possibility of shaving. Long beards became common, a fashion by necessity. The men acquired the look of members of a robber band. Only their eyeglasses were the reminder of a previous civilized status. Generally, men did not openly resent these outward changes. Women were different. When their lipsticks started to disappear they confessed that they felt undressed. During the first days they were all preoccupied with keeping their stockings intact. The disappearance of perfumes made them conscious of the natural smells of their bodies. They were exhausted by marches, hunger, fears, and constant escapes from bombing. While talking with men they tried to keep an unusual distance. Something essential to their existence as women was dying rapidly in them: this was the coquettish side of their femininity. Still they looked with pity and bewilderment at the barefoot peasant women who brought the smell of the barn with them as they served us food.

One night we slept on a floor covered with straw in a deserted police station near the road. There were some twenty or thirty of us. Some of the men and woman had met on the road in recent days and formed quick friendships. They needed each other for mutual protection. Under cover of night, thrust into an intimate closeness by the blind will of fate and disaster, they sought comfort in love. They did not mind the dismal surroundings or the lack of privacy. Yet their subdued love had the imprint of theft and guilt. Perhaps they were also moved by resentment at having been hurt so much and fear of being hurt tomorrow even more. Where are the psychologists who claim to know so much about human nature? Have they analyzed the depths of the sentiment that throws a man and a woman into each other's arms through fear of death and suffering? What is the human meaning of this so-called act of creation in the face of the impending destruction of the agents themselves?

The next morning, some of the women had deeper and more expressive eyes. We all knew how these new eyes had been born; we were their midwives.

Theft entered our community of nomads. One morning a man found a strange pair of shoes near his sleeping place. The purpose of the replacement was clear from the holes in the soles of the shoes. The owner of these shoes had arisen an hour earlier to obtain possession of the sleeper's precious, hole-less shoes. The dispossessed man could not fit into the ones left as consolation and had to beg for rags, which he rolled around his feet. We all sympathized with the victim, but he looked so comical in his improvised shoes that we could hardly repress our cruel outbursts of laughter.

As we moved farther south we noticed that there were fewer bombings. One day they ceased altogether, and we decided to walk more during the daytime. On this flight from our own country we discovered how beautiful some of the landscapes were.

A man rushing from place to place in a train or car has no time to absorb or digest his impressions. They make no permanent imprint on his memory. One must stop to look at a beautiful spot, if only for a short time, and then look again. Every man who learns to look becomes the possessor of an enchanting collection of pictured memories for his entire life. I could always charm out of my past, in full and fresh reality, the blue beauty of Taormina, the coquettish island of Margareta in Budapest, the misty cocktail of rain and sunshine on the seashore of Amsterdam, and the angular majesty of the Trocadéro in Paris.

The changing views of valleys and hillocks bathed in sunlight reminded me of a prostrate beauty who was trying to hide her face in the long hair of her forests, to cover the shame of defeat and rape. The rivers were silently carrying her tears. I felt I was conveying greetings and at the same time saying farewell to my country. For some of my fellow citizens it was more an intellectual concept than a palpable reality. But to love a country one must see it in its rich nakedness, like that of a cherished woman. It is not enough to love a country through the elaborate mirror of institutions and history.

One day we heard that the Russians had entered Poland. This explained to us the recent days' ominous silence in the sky. I would have to make the necessary adjustments in my techniques of escape. I was already in the province of Polesie. The peasants here, who are called Poleshuks, speak the White-Ruthenian language. They are poor and suspicious. Often their numbers are decimated by disease, the most common of which is a sickness called *kołtun*. The hair becomes matted with blood and sticks to itself like a wig. The peasants heal it with an extract of plants.

These peasants looked at the unexpected visitors from Warsaw with curiosity and hostility. It was impossible to rely on them very long for shelter and food. I decided to stop at the small towns, whose inhabitants, part Polish and part Jewish, appeared to be more tolerant of us. The Christians there could not define their ethnic origins or nationality. They referred to themselves very simply: "We are from here." This made their geopolitical views remarkably simple. I felt that I must be prepared to settle in some place until the trains started moving. By train I could reach my parents' city, and then move on to Wilno. I heard on the radio that this city, called Vilnius in Lithuanian, had been promised to Lithuania in an agreement between the governments of Lithuania and Russia. If I reached Vilnius before it was taken over by the Lithuanians I would find myself automatically in a neutral country. This was the plan, but I still was far from carrying it out.

I was aware that I must move cautiously. I still wore my city clothes. Combined with my eyeglasses, they gave me the look of a big-city dweller. It was rumored that the Russians were stopping people, examining their hands for proletarian traits, and questioning them about professions and past activities. Some were arrested while they crossed a bridge leading to a town near Kowel, an important center of communications.

A few miles from Kowel we decided to break up our group; everybody would go on his own. Near the bridge was a police post with several Russian soldiers in command. I had been staying for several days with a Jewish family in another town. My hosts advised me to buy peasant clothes and leave my city clothes with them. When I got to the other side of the bridge, I could send somebody for my city clothes.

When I looked at myself in the mirror several hours later, I saw a bearded peasant. I was doubtful about keeping my eyeglasses. They had expensive rims and could easily raise suspicions. I decided to change their rims and took them to the optometrist in the town. Next day I started out and was stopped by a Russian soldier near the bridge. He asked who I was and where I was going. I answered in White-Ruthenian, a language I spoke well in my childhood, that I was taken from my village by the Polish army and was returning home. The answer did not appear satisfactory to him.

"What is the name of your village?"

"Ozerisko."

"What is the name of the town nearest your village?"

"The town of Wolkowysk."

"You are not going in the direction of your home; you are going toward Kowel. Your home is northeast."

"I know it, but I have been dragged by the army south and would like to take the train home from Kowel."

It did not appear right to him. He asked me to show my hands. He found them too smooth for the hands of a peasant.

"But I work as a secretary in my village office. I went to school and I know how to read and write. You can telephone my village office and find out."

"There are no telephone connections now."

"I am not responsible for that," I said. He ordered me to go into a room behind the office and lie down on the straw. I had to think fast. I knew that if I were not released soon, all would be lost. I knocked at the door. The soldier appeared.

"Listen, you came here to liberate the peasants and workers, to bring them bread and liberty. I have not eaten for two days. If you cannot give me liberty, give me a slice of bread."

He looked pensive.

"Are you really hungry?"

"Yes, I am very hungry."

He thought hard. Some time later he brought me a piece of bread.

"In my village we used to eat bread with onions and salt," I said. "But this bread tastes very good."

I started to devour it like a hungry wolf. I was playing the part of a man who had been traveling for a long time, although I had eaten a leg of chicken only two hours earlier, given to me by my host in town.

The soldier said nothing, but he was thinking, looking at my clothes and then again at my hands.

In the middle of the night a peasant fell heavily, like a bundle, next to me on the straw. He had been pushed from the office.

"Why did they put you here?" he asked me.

"I do not know."

"Where are you from?"

"Ozerisko."

"Where is it?"

"District of Wolkowyski."

I became silent, and he soon resumed his questioning.

"Do you have a family?"

"A wife and four children. And you?"

"I have two children."

"In our village it costs ten zlotys to christen a child. How much does it cost in your village?" I asked.

He did not answer. So it dawned on me that he was put in my improvised cell to find out who I really was.

I started to snore. My neighbor woke me up.

"Do you know what time it is?"

"I have no watch. Let me look through the window. I will try to guess." My watch was conveniently left with my clothes in the town.

A silver line was visible in the sky. "It will be daybreak soon," I said with a broad yawn, typical of the peasants around my home. My neighbor went on talking.

"These Bolsheviks will destroy us. They will take away our food and make soldiers of us."

"I think we will have more to eat now," I replied.

Silence. I could not sleep, and while appearing to look at my boots with the stubborn stupor typical of White-Ruthenian peasants, I secretly studied my companion's face. In the pale morning light it looked different. His head was square, with a strange haircut that I seldom saw around Wolkowyski. I tried to recall whether I had said something I should not have. And then, as if he realized he was losing the game, he said,

"There are many Polish officers who are dressed like peasants. They are trying to escape captivity this way."

I said nothing, only yawned and scratched my head with indifference.

Then he looked at me a long time, as if he were making a decision. I feigned sleep while the beating of my heart increased.

When I opened my eyes, my neighbor was gone. Later the door opened. The soldier came in, called me into the office, and said only one word, a command in Russian.

"*Prochodi*"—"Go on."

I moved slowly. I could not show excitement or hurry. I was the typically phlegmatic White-Ruthenian peasant. The soldier still watched my movements.

When the bridge started to disappear behind me, I sighed deeply. I knew I had escaped a danger equal to what I had experienced in the bombed train and in the bombed forest.

From what I knew of the Russian police, from people who were arrested in Russia, a great deal depends on the personality of the questioning officer and the behavior of the person being questioned. For the most part, however, the result of the questioning depends on pure accident. My experience as a prosecutor turned out to be of great value and may have saved me. This episode remained in my memory for many years as a lesson in self-control and caution.

I was now in the province of Wolynia, in a little town difficult to describe in terms of American or Western European conditions. There are many hundreds of such towns in Poland and western Russia. For centuries they were inhabited predominantly by Jews. The Russian tsars established this area, the so-called Pale of Settlement, as a place where Jews could live. They could not live on the land, however, but only in towns. By bribing the police, however, many succeeded in living on farms in spite of the law.

The life of the dwellers of these little towns revolved around the synagogue and the marketplace. People of the elder and middle generations used to spend a great part of their life in prayer and religious studies. Since they prayed in Hebrew, a language they understood, their prayers carried an immense intensity, expressing despair, hope, and struggle. One could see a man's whole life in his prayer. The Jewish religion is the only one in the world that is based on a covenant between the individual and Yahveh, his God. It is a personal, bilateral, quasi-contractual relationship that brings a man face to face with his God. The Jewish God enters into such bilateral relationships with all members of the Jewish religion. The Jew owes obedience and promises to live righteously according to the covenant, which has explicit socioethical content. It is an ethical as well as a religious obligation that he undertakes. Only when the covenant is violated does a Jew expect punishment or suffering. Because of this special bilateral relationship, a Jew could defy Yahveh, receive punishment, and still retain his religion without becoming a heretic. After all, Yahveh chose Israel as his standard bearer and therefore he might punish the Jews, but he would never completely renounce them. After having argued out their dispute, they would become reconciled. This specific I-Thou relationship carried great importance.[2] The individual Jew did not disappear in the mass of his coreligionists but could develop his individuality. Bordering on fatalism without ever becoming blindly fatalistic, this relationship helped the religious Jew to face the supreme test of death with more calm. The Nazis took advantage of this philosophical attitude: nowhere in the history of mankind did six million people die so calmly, without causing their killers any unnecessary inconvenience. The exception, the uprising in the Warsaw ghetto, cannot change this historic fact.[3]

Much of a Jewish man's time was spent in the marketplace, a quadrangle in the middle of the town. (Sometimes he would delegate these functions to his wife and spend the whole day praying and studying the Talmud.) Once or twice a week this spot would be filled with carts, horses, and peasants who brought their produce for sale and came to buy salt, spices, kerosene, and agricultural products. The noise was unbearable, but it was music to both parties because there was profit and excitement in it.

By and large, the standard of living was very low. The Jews lived on practically nothing. They were undernourished all week in preparation for the solemn Sabbath dinner Friday night and the big Saturday noon meal. Since these two meals were holy, nobody in the town was permitted to be hungry on these days. All types of charity existed to prevent a desecration of the holy Sabbath through hunger. It was forbidden to use fire on the Sabbath, so on Friday afternoon, every family would carry a big pot to the bakery, with potatoes, meat, and soup. It was put in the oven until Saturday noon. Then this traditional meal, called *tscholent* (it is even mentioned in Heine's poetry), was brought home from the bakery and consumed with holy solemnity and good appetite.[4] It was usual that if a poor man had no meat for Sabbath, his pot would be opened and good people would secretly put in a leg or a wing of chicken, or even a solid piece of meat. After the tscholent meal the parents would invariably take a nap, and the young would gather in the forest or in the library to heatedly settle the most controversial issues of mankind. Late in the afternoon the entire community would take a stroll, dressed in their best Sabbath clothes.[5]

The feeling of social solidarity and mutual help was immensely strong. Everybody was known by his first name; sometimes people were called by their first name plus the occupation of one of their parents, for example Chaim-the-son-of-the-shoemaker.

A classic story in Jewish literature is told by the writer Leib Perez in "Higher Than the Sky."[6] The rabbi in a town used to get up in the middle of the night, dress like a peasant, and chop wood. He would bring the wood and some milk to the home of a sick widow, and then light her fireplace. When another rabbi was referred to as being as exalted as the sky in his personal charity, the first rabbi was said to be "higher than the sky."

The Jews spied on each other to find out the real degree of poverty so they could help the destitute discreetly. They read newspapers in Yiddish and sometimes in Hebrew, and as each was too poor to buy a paper for himself, they would organize in partnerships for the purchase of one paper, which would then pass through several hands. Learning was respected. Young men studying the Talmud were supported by free meals provided by various families in town. This type of help was considered honorable for the giver and made him feel he had a personal stake in the life of the scholars.

There was a great feeling for the continuity of the life of society, with possibly small changes; but changes could not be avoided. Children were enrolled in religious schools early, sometimes at the age of four. At five or six they could recite parts of the Bible in Hebrew. The more capable young men would dedicate themselves completely to religious studies.

Shortly before World War II, the nonreligious schools started to outnumber the religious schools, and parents tried hard to obtain at least a lay education for their children. During this time a substantial number of children, especially in the larger towns, studied in lay schools. The older generation complained but was reconciled to the part of lay education that was studied in modern Hebrew. Everyone spoke Yiddish, a language based on a middle-German dialect that adopted many expressions from Hebrew, Slavic, and other languages. The language developed a rich literature. Some of the schools used Yiddish as the language of instruction, and some used Hebrew. Medium-sized towns developed schools in both languages.

It was amazing how rapidly Hebrew, a dead language, was revived, and how skillfully Yiddish was refined through literature and poetry. These wretched and insecure people had a unique capacity to absorb and digest culture. It went straight into their bloodstream. In their cultural ability and receptivity there was a great deal of resemblance between the Jews and the Armenians, who, in 1915, lost more than a million people by genocide in Turkey.

Almost every Jewish family had relatives in America. They had gone, in the time of the tsars, to escape military service or to look for employment and build a new life. They maintained regular correspondence, inquired about the local inhabitants, and sent dollars home. This money smelled of the sweat and tears of young men and women who were lonely and dejected in their new lives in Brooklyn or the Bronx. The families left in these little European towns thus had an additional allegiance: brothers and sisters and parents kept strong emotional ties with those who left, not sparing them advice, at least as to eating kosher food, not working on the Sabbath, and of course marrying the right girl or boy.

This was the general background of my new surroundings. I walked into a little Jewish home, told them that I was escaping from the Nazis, and asked if I could stay in their house several days. I had to use my intuition and explain my case as fast as I could. The housewife referred me to her husband, and I saw that the situation could get complicated. I put in several Hebrew quotations as I talked, and won him over. There is a Jewish religious tradition regarding hospitality, especially in time of danger. My host sent to the nearby village for my clothes. Several hours later I took my first bath since I had left Warsaw, and soon I was drinking tea from a samovar with the new family, with jelly for my tea pushed toward me from all sides of the table at once.

My host was a baker. It gave the house an inviting feeling of warmth and sent the smell of bread into one's bloodstream, bones, and heart. But it also excited my appetite, which by then was big enough to ruin even a prosperous bakery.

My host asked if there was validity in the reasoning of the Jews who were escaping from the Nazis. "Why, there is nothing new in the sufferings of Jews," he argued, "especially in time of war. My grandfather used to tell me stories about pogroms by Kosaks. The main thing for a Jew to do is not get excited, and outlast the enemies. A Jew must wait and pray. The Almighty will help, He always helps."

"Have you ever heard of a book written by Hitler called *Mein Kampf*," I asked, "in which he boasts that he will destroy all the Jews like rats?"

"No, I have not heard of this book," the man answered, "but even if I would read it, I would not believe that he meant it. How can Hitler destroy the Jews if he must trade with them? People are needed to carry on a war. I grant you some Jews will suffer under Hitler, but this is the lot of the Jews, to suffer and to wait."

"But this is a different war," I insisted. "It is not a war to grab territory so much as to destroy whole peoples and replace them with Germans. It is like Assur, which you remember from the Bible, who destroyed many nations and settled their lands with its allies." I led him through familiar history, but still he objected.

"In the last war, 1915–1918, we lived three years under the Germans. It was never good, but somehow we survived. I sold bread to the Germans; we baked for them from their flour. We Jews are an eternal people, we cannot be destroyed. We can only suffer."

Many generations spoke through this man. He could not believe the reality of genocide because it went against nature, against logic, against life itself, and against the warm smell of bread in his house, against his poor but comfortable bed. He was firm and serene. There was not much sense in disturbing or confusing him with facts. He had already made up his mind. He had a private, bilateral covenant with God. When he was born this contract devolved on him from his father. He was ready to take his punishment if he were to violate this covenant, if he were to behave unrighteously; he would not complain about it. Punishment was a just consequence of transgression. Sometimes it could be forgiven, sometimes not; but it must be taken with calm and dignity. When we left the table late that evening, I was too tired to argue any more. My host's philosophy was clear and simple and, last but not least, integrated.

That night I was thinking again—deeply, penetratingly, across the brain and back. Late in the night, or early in the morning, I heard a chant. It became louder and louder. Somebody was praying: it was the baker. His voice reminded me of the voice of someone familiar. The chant was like a personal tale, an intimate story told to somebody in confidence. It was as if all the contents of the soul went up through his throat. Later there was a half silence as if his heart wanted to rest for a while, or maybe it was listening to itself. And then again to a crescendo: persuasion, solicitation, a delicate murmur of explanation. Silence again. And then—do I hear anger in his tone? Is he arguing with God? Is he—threatening his God? What is it? It dawned on me that I was listening to a dialogue with God, based on the covenant. All Jewish prayers are dialogues. How could they be otherwise? The baker had his own covenant, a contract for life and righteousness. A covenant must be defended, argued, explained. He was doing it this day, from the very moment he entered consciousness at daybreak.

At sunset Friday I was sitting at the Sabbath meal with my host and his family. Everybody had washed especially for the occasion and put on solemn clothes. The hostess said a prayer while lighting the candles. The worry that had shown in her face receded. She moved about with an air of solemnity, self-assurance, and discreet kindliness, maybe even with holiness. Two big white rolls covered with a white cloth stood before the host. He said the prayer and gave everyone a share of the white bread, and we then consumed it with a prayer. The meal ended with songs and a prayer of thanks. There was serenity in this ceremonial meal. The participants seemed like completely different persons; their movements had acquired rhythm and subdued dignity. Their faces were radiant.

They talked little, saying only the necessary words, as if they did not want to give away something very precious: their patrimony. This was where my host changed from a poor baker to a king.

After dinner I stepped onto the front porch of the house for a while and looked at the four rows of houses around the huge quadrangle of the marketplace. All the Jews in the town were having their rendezvous with the queen Sabbath. Bright lights shone through their windows. They spoke of thousands of years' determination to hold on to an age-old belief that justifies their lives, outside of which there is no life. In the clear sky, myriads of stars twinkled. Every person on earth must have thought that the stars were in cahoots only with him. But most of all, it seemed to the Jews in this town that the stars twinkled for them and said: "The Almighty is glad that you are fulfilling the covenant tonight."

There were such kingdoms in every Jewish house in this little town. In each there reigned, for twenty-four hours, a man who yesterday had been hunted, undernourished, destitute, insecure, and humiliated, a human being of yesterday.

Next morning my host's son, a youth of about twenty, entered my room. He was obviously disturbed. He started in bitterly: "I do not understand this attitude of my father and of all the people like him in this town. Their reliance on leaving everything to God is good for only one thing: the last moments before death. They would all make marvelous corpses: disciplined, obedient, they would all move like one and die silently, in order and solemnity. Of course, they would blame themselves that everything happening was due to their own sins."

I replied, "It is difficult to change the thinking of many generations at once. One must fight for one's own life: this cannot be taught by words, but by life itself, as a small duckling learns to swim. The instinct of life is a very good advisor. In the pogroms earlier in this century the Jews organized councils of self-defense. Some of them fought: even the Jewish children participated in self-defense. When the farmers came with their carts to villages to kill and to carry off the pillaged goods of the Jews, the Jewish children put bottles with kerosene in the straw of the carts and set them on fire. The horses ran, and the killers too. More than one pogrom was prevented in this 'childish' way."

Six years later, when I was in Nuremberg working on the Nazi trials, the excited face of the baker's son came compellingly to my mind when I read the following affidavit relating to the murder of the Jews in Dubno, in the same area where I talked with the boy that memorable Saturday morning. The affidavit was made out by Hermann Graebe on November 10, 1945, and it described a mass execution at Dubno that took place on November 5, 1942.[7]

> Now we heard shots in quick procession from behind one of the mounds. The people who had got off the trucks, men, women, and children of all ages, had to undress upon the orders of an SS man, who carried a riding or dog whip. . . . Without screaming or crying, these people undressed, stood around by families, kissed each other, said farewells, and waited for the command of another SS man who stood near the excavation also with a whip in his hand. . . . At that moment the SS man at the excavation called something to his comrade. The latter counted off twenty persons, and instructed them to walk behind the earth mound. . . . I walked around the mound and stood in front of a tremendous grave; closely pressed together, the people were lying on top of each other so that only their heads were visible. The excavation was already two-thirds full; I estimated that it contained about a thousand people. . . . Now already the next group approached, descended into the excavation, lined themselves up against the previous victims and were shot.

Two weeks passed. My hosts told me that the first train since the Soviet entry would leave the next day. There were still Polish conductors on the trains, they said, and no arrangements had been made yet for the control of passengers. No tickets would be required, because there were no such things as printed tickets.

I had seen in my life many changes in territorial sovereignty: in August 1915 my hometown was taken by the Germans, in 1918 it was no-man's land and then became Polish, in 1920 the Poles and the Russians entered, and some time later the Russians left and the Poles returned.

Now this game was on again. I knew from experience that in this part of the world it took time to establish control. Now I would have a chance to squeeze myself through during the general confusion. I decided to go.

Accompanied by the blessings and good wishes of my hosts, I was pressed into a train like a sardine. It was a freezing November night when I came to the city of Wolkowysk, where my parents and brother lived. A problem arose: to go at night into the city, where I was bound to be stopped by Soviet soldiers, or to wait until early morning? There must be curfew hours in the city. I found that there were—and I had to wait. But where?

I hid in the men's room of the station. When the clock struck six in the morning I moved out. This was my city and I had to sneak into it like a thief. My steps sounded frighteningly loud to me as I walked through the side streets to the house of my brother, who lived closer to the station. I had to avoid the main street. I knocked gently at the window, holding my breath, and then pronounced my name against the frozen glass.

I heard the joyful cries of my mother as she answered, gently crying my name in a diminutive form. My father said, "God, he is here with us!" In a moment I was holding my parents tightly in my arms. I looked for a long time at their faces, kissing away their tears. Then I greeted my brother and my sister-in-law. I wanted so much at that moment to become a child again, a carefree, happy child as in the golden days of riding horses without permission and tearing my trousers while picking cherries. Because my brother's children were still asleep, I could successfully take their place for a while. So strong was the desire to be protected by the memories of my past, to forget the sad framework of the present. Maybe this was a subconscious escape from the disasters of my mature age, or a child's search for parental protection. We all laughed a little sadly over my recollections of childhood scenes.

I inquired gently about my parents' health. Shadows appeared on their faces: they did not want to discuss it now. I guessed the answer.

After breakfast I was put to bed. When I woke up I would have pancakes, as in earlier times: pancakes with sour cream or—I would have a choice—with jelly. Let us close out the outside world for an hour, for a day, for whatever time may be granted. Let us close out the armies, bombings, police, the hunt for human beings, the grim changes of history celebrated on a red carpet of blood. I plunged into the warm bed, but I could not fall asleep at once. As I lay under this familiar blanket with its dear old-fashioned print, I made a quick balance sheet of the total disaster, peacefully and without resentment.

The castles I had built rapidly and successfully lay overturned by the typhoon that desires to be called history. All was covered with a deluge of water. Above the water I could see only the loving faces of my parents. In the far distance a blue cloud looked at me challengingly. It seemed to be the symbol of my hope and determination to outlaw the destruction of human groups. The blue cloud was like an ocean to me, that I should not fear the deluge; since time immemorial water has been the symbol of creation. These two sources of security were left to me: my parents, whom I might lose if they decided—as I feared—that they would not flee with me.

Late in the afternoon the conversation inevitably had to lead to some decisions. I saw how weak my parents were and how dangerous it would be for them to travel. My father argued, "I have been living in retirement for more than ten years because of my sickness. I am not a capitalist. The Russians will not bother me." My brother put in: "I gave up my store and registered as an employee before it was taken over by the new government. They will not touch me either."

I read in their eyes one plea: do not talk of our leaving this warm home, our beds, our stores of food, the security of our customs . . . We will have to suffer, but we will survive somehow. What did I have to offer them? A nomadic life, a refugee's lot, poverty. The question resolved itself: I would continue as soon as possible to Lithuania—alone.

I stayed another day. I tried to live a year in this one day, to borrow time from the future, to absorb the whole soul of my home. I looked intensely at their faces as if to imprint them as they were then on my memory forever.

When their eyes became sad with understanding, I laughed away our agonizing thoughts, but I felt I would never see them again. It was like going to their funeral while they were still alive. The best of me was dying with the full cruelty of consciousness.

I told them of my plans to go to Sweden and then to the U.S.A.

My mother interrupted: "Three years ago I prevented you with my tears from going to America, and now it seems to be the only solution."

"My brother in America could help you," my father said, "but I am sure you will make your own way." He added reassuringly, "And you know I believe in you."

We were at the table. My mother put down her fork and spoke again. "You realize, Raphael, that it is you, not we, who needs protection now. Of the seven of us—you, your brother, your sister-in-law Lisa, our two grandchildren, your father and I—of all of us only you do not live the life of love. You are the lonely and the loveless one. Still, you have been carrying the burden of your idea, which is based on love. You have had our support and love from afar all these years, and now it may be cut off altogether." She sighed. "We know you will continue your work, for the protection of peoples. Unfortunately, it is needed now more than ever before."

I knew what she was driving at in emphasizing my loneliness. I was even prepared to quote Goethe's *Hermann and Dorothea*,[8] as I had done before on such occasions: "Take a wife so that the night might become the more beautiful part of your life." But she interrupted me, and put me to shame: "In the past you used to walk out with jokes every time I discussed your marriage. Mothers want their children to marry, because as the givers of life they know the significance of married life. They want also to convey the protection of their children, to another woman, to a spiritual sister in the mission of love. We are not eternal, any of us."

A tear fell from her eye onto the napkin.

"Please, Raphael," she continued relentlessly, "in the past you did not have time. You wrote a book almost every year. But are you sure that every book is more important than a friend, a spiritual companion, who could help you develop the life of the heart? Your goal is to bring the world closer to the life of the heart—there must be a place in it for a congenial, intelligent woman."

I got up, put my hands gently on her soft hair, kissed her tearful eyes, and said, "I know how right you are, Mother, especially now. Recent events have been so drastic that perhaps I must make a decision on this too." And then I added, half-jokingly, "Maybe I will be luckier now, as a nomad, than I was as a member of a sedentary society."

The evening of the last day came cruelly and quickly. I had decided to leave the city at night by cart. Some food was prepared hastily and put in a bundle by my mother's trembling hands. We moved almost mechanically, determined not to show too much feeling. To take leave? What a difference from previous occasions. My father had always kissed me before with great heartiness; Mother kissed pensively, as if to deny the finality of my departure.

When I left them I took with me the image of those dear faces—solicitous, loving, and concerned but calmed with the happiness that we were all still alive. I had fulfilled my desire: I had seen my family. Neither the German nor the Russian army had stopped me.

Did not Confucius say, "When love is at stake, yield not to an army."

CHAPTER FOUR

A Refugee in Lithuania, Latvia, and Sweden

I ARRIVED AT VILNIUS several weeks before the Lithuanians took over the government.[1] The city was full of refugees. They intended to enjoy the benefits of neutrality, which were expected to fall on the city like manna from the sky.

Meanwhile, Russian troops were dismantling machines in some of the factories and printing shops. They were buying everything in the stores: watches by the dozen, shoes, trousers, shirts, hats, underwear, violins, nails. Their hunger for consumer goods seemed insatiable. Rumors spread that they were delaying leaving the city in order to acquire even more. This was their second chance to buy, as individuals, in a large consumers' market since their war with Poland in the summer of 1920.

Russian women, accompanying the army, bought embroidered night-gowns that they mistook for evening dresses. They wore them in one of the fashionable restaurants with their male companions. It was the talk of the town many months after they left Vilnius.

On the whole, the Russian army appeared to be engaged in an eco-nomic occupation rather than a political one, although propaganda outfits were not missing. One morning a Russian political commissar was standing on a corner talking to a passerby. "We are leaving this city— we are handing it over to the rightful owners," he announced. "We do not want anybody's territory. We made an agreement with the Germans because it is useful to the proletarian revolution."

"How is that?" he was asked.

"The British wanted the Germans to fight us, but we turned the tables on them," he replied. "The Western and the German armies will fight each other until they destroy each other, then we will come and take over."

"How do you know that one side might not be stronger than the other?"

"We have our information. The Germans have more arms now, but the Western allies have more money, and they will buy arms from America. It will be a long, exhausting war. We will be neutral for many years—and when the time for world revolution comes in Europe, we will take over without one shot."

He spoke confidently. He reflected the age-old dream of nations: to see their rivals destroyed in mutual conflict while they accumulate the political or economic benefits of their own neutrality. To emerge as the happy heir to the ruins of other nations—what is simpler than this? Sometimes the plan succeeds temporarily, but history usually catches up with the schemers.

Polish refugees roamed the city, and there was seldom one among them who was inwardly quiet. They worried about the wives or sweethearts they had left behind German lines. A new trade was developing: sending professional smugglers to Warsaw to escort people to Vilnius. There were several links in the chain of this trade, with a special price established for each service. At this time the ghetto was not yet established in Warsaw, and it was easier to smuggle people out of that city. The first persons rescued from Warsaw had already appeared in Vilnius. They were sought after avidly for conversation and information.

The refugees also worried about preserving the substance of their Polish currency, which they carried all day in little sacks hanging from their necks down to their belts. The physical safekeeping of the notes did not prevent them from losing value by the hour, however. The refugees also bought all sorts of consumer goods that they could later convert into new currency.

The black market on Rudnicka Street prospered almost officially.[2] Gangs of smugglers carried Polish notes inside cheese and butter to the other side of the Russian zone and imported dollars inside the soles of their shoes. Polish zlotys were still legal tender in the White-Ruthenian section outside Vilnius and in other parts of former Poland. Therefore Polish currency was exported from Vilnius and dollars were brought in. They were bought from poor Jews, who often received them in letters from relatives in America.

The refugees worried also about immigration visas. They wanted to know where to go from here. Some wrote to relatives and friends abroad; others turned to black marketeers. A new trade sprang up which provided visas to many countries at all prices, in dollars. Refugees were living in practically every house in Vilnius. Through the thin walls of my room I was constantly hearing the words and phrases "dollars," "visas," "Honduras," "Ecuador," and "Guatemala," and "just arrived from Warsaw," "caught near Bialystok." Sometimes I heard the word "noodles," which had come to mean "dollars." These people argued passionately among themselves for refuge and life. They were fighting on new lines of defense.

Several days after arriving in Vilnius I sent some cables abroad. One was to Karl Schlyter, the former minister of justice in Sweden; the other was to Count Carton de Wiart, president of the International Association of Criminal Law and former president of the League of Nations.[3] We had worked together for many years at international conferences. I informed them of my intention to go to the U.S. and asked whether they could arrange for my temporary entry into Sweden and Belgium. I sent another cable to my old friends the Pédones, a mother and daughter who owned a great French publishing house. I let them know I was alive and inquired about the fate of my manuscript on international payments, which I had sent them from Warsaw several weeks before the war. I made it clear that publishing this book would help me establish myself at a university. I also wrote a letter to Professor Malcolm McDermott, at Duke University in North Carolina. He was making a survey of the administration of justice in Europe, including Poland, for the American government, and I had been assigned to assist him on his visit to Warsaw in 1926. A friendship had developed between us, and we had even cowritten a book on the Polish criminal code, which was published in 1939 by Duke University Press.

I went to the University in Vilnius to visit friends. No arrangements had been made to open the academic year, but certain seminars were active for the faithful postgraduates. Bewildered, hungry professors were not sure of their own tomorrows.

I visited the criminologist Bronislaw Wroblewski in his home. His wife was a painter. They were both sitting in an unheated room. They had divided what food they had left into small equal parts and were partaking of it once a day. The professor's face was the color of a wax doll's, and his eyes were like cold glass, staring beyond me expressionlessly. Where was he looking? He feebly patted a huge dog who was so exhausted from hunger that tears ran constantly from his eyes. Mr. Wroblewski told me that the dog understood the situation: the food would be divided every day among the three of them, and they would eat it rapidly and in silence. The dog never touched the portions left for his friends, even if they were not in the room.

I tried in vain to shake the professor's apathy. I suggested that once I arrived in Sweden I might try to get him a visa. He would not listen. "This is my city and I want to die here." He spoke about death as something as close and concrete as an article he might write for a magazine or a lecture he had to deliver. A deeply moral man, he foresaw the end of all morality for at least a hundred years. "This is the most violent and amoral of all centuries," he kept saying. "Whenever the war ends, human beings will not regain their lost moral standards but will continue to behave like barbarians even in peacetime."

I replied, "We are in a century of transition to a different type of culture, and to different values in government, economy, and all forms of thinking and feeling. We see the changes only dimly now. We sense them rather than understand them fully." I sat silently for a moment, patting the poor dog.

"In all periods of transition," I continued, "moral standards break down. This does not mean that we should accept it passively—we must try to set the standards up again. We must even raise them more forcibly. We cannot disregard the changes; we must take them into consideration."

"Weren't you stopped in 1933 when you tried to establish your new definitions for the international crimes of barbarity and vandalism?" the professor interjected.

"I will try again," I said. "I might be stopped again, and then I will do it again." I could see he was skeptical. "Men carrying ideas are like the Cleopatra cells in botany. These cells of the seed go first into the soil, but they are destroyed, and while dying they pave the way for other cells which develop into a plant."

Wroblewski shook his head. He was a broken man with a broken faith. I had retained my optimism in the midst of the deluge. We spoke different languages.

At a later date, free abroad, I inquired about Professor Wroblewski. I was told that he had been attacked by his dog while out walking him one day. The dog had gone suddenly mad and mortally wounded him.

I took many long strolls in Vilnius. Many years earlier I had attended a gymnasium here, the equivalent of an American high school and junior college. This beautiful city is the ancient capital of the Polish-Lithuanian kingdom. A marriage between the Polish Queen Jadwiga and the Lithuanian King Jagiello extended the romance between the two rulers into a personal union between the two states. This romance seems to have brought to the history of Polish-Lithuanian relations some of the ingredients of marriage: love combined with hatred.

I climbed the mountain in the city suburbs and looked at the expansive view around me. Nothing on this mountain, with its calm serenity and purity of air, betrayed the depressing atmosphere below. It gave me a literal as well as spiritual bird's-eye view, which I very much needed at that time. Not only could the entire city be seen from here but also the valleys, hills, forests, and lakes stretching peacefully to the far horizon. If only people and nations could make the effort to remain together for a while in such harmony.

I suddenly remembered that it was on this mountain, years ago, that I had had my first date with a girl. I thought of her brown, girlish school uniform and the freshness of a delicate cheek that I touched timidly with my lips. I recalled so vividly then, as I do now, her enigmatic look, as if directed to some distant vista. I remember how I wanted to kiss her on her mouth and how this desire was stifled by something in me that I could not understand.

The people cheered. Neutrality was finally here. I went the next day to the military commander to request permission to go to Kaunas, the capital, where I could be in close touch with the consulates of foreign countries. He advised me to wait patiently.

A letter arrived from my parents. They wrote about how happy they had been to have us all together again. Everything was all right—the usual subdued optimism with ill-concealed worries. They never wrote about sad things, but I could always read between the lines. An escapee from Warsaw had stopped at their house and told them that he was my friend and colleague. They invited him to stay in our home. He would come soon to Vilnius and in appreciation of their hospitality promised to bring a package of cakes baked by my mother, and a jar of jelly.

As announced, Benjamin Tomkiewicz arrived, in high boots and with innumerable cakes. He brought with him the tender climate of my parents' home and the familiar smell of my mother's oven, which radiated from the cakes.

The freshness of our common yesterdays and professional life in gay Warsaw came back to us. It was a feast of nostalgia, interrupted only by my friend's frequent sighs. He was an unhappy man, and I tried to divert him. He had left behind his old mother, with whom and for whom he had lived. A brilliant lawyer and a professional pessimist, he tried to convince me that the situation was very bad and that we would never again be so happy as we had been in Warsaw. I was well aware of this; I had already crystallized my new opinion about personal happiness.

"There is no sense in reminiscing about the past," I told him. "The big lawyers' fees, the idle talk about our endless professional wisdom, that expensive furniture, the country house will never return. Should they ever come my way again, I would not let them cross my threshold. They never made me really happy, they only intoxicated me for a while. As a public prosecutor and a lawyer I served power and enjoyed false prestige. I really lived only when I was fighting for an ideal. I will devote the rest of my life to my work—outlawing the destruction of peoples."

"It sounds good," he said dubiously. "I wish you luck. But why can't you have both?"

"You know that's impossible," I said. "I would be stopped by my own greed and instinct for power, which this way of life must stimulate. You cannot serve two gods at the same time. An ideal, like an ancient god, demands constant sacrifice, undivided loyalty, complete integration, and self-denial."

I felt suddenly that I was giving a sermon to an intimate friend, and I stopped in embarrassment.

One week later I boarded a train to Kaunas. I wanted to be closer to the Swedish consulate, as I expected a visa from Sweden. I stopped by the house of a lawyer to whom I had been directed by friends in Vilnius.

My host's family was in Switzerland. He had free time and, like most lawyers, liked to talk in monologues. I experienced a reenactment of my life as a lawyer in Warsaw—a Kaunas edition. How many times had I heard stories about court cases that always turned out to be of interest only to the lawyer telling the story: the difficult case, the big fee, the devastating impression on the judge, all due to an original insight in the law . . . The other lawyer appears to be listening, but in fact he is only preparing his own story about a more complicated case involving even more legal ingenuity and resulting in a bigger fee.

When lawyers become rich or tired of collecting fees they go into politics. Sometimes they do both at once. Occasionally they embrace lost causes and deliver fiery speeches in court. On these occasions the whole profession takes credit for their idealism. My advice is not to quarrel with lawyers: they do not overlook details in a fight. One must take them rather as they are. Although they wield considerable influence on society, they lack on the whole a social conscience and passion and are therefore unable to effect larger changes in history. Occasionally it is even possible to use lawyers for good causes if one is able to show them that they had the idea before anybody else, or that this cause will make them even more important than they were. I have had many difficulties with lawyers in my lifetime, and only the fact that I am a lawyer myself has permitted me to overcome the obstacles they put in my way.

For the first time since leaving Warsaw I lived among people who were not refugees themselves. They were unaware of their future status. I was compelled to compare my present way of living with theirs. When I was on the constant run, escaping from actual dangers, I called myself an escapee. But now that direct and immediate danger of losing life and liberty did not threaten me, I became a refugee. Now I was threatened with the disintegration of my personality through idleness, apathy, loss of self-esteem and assertiveness, and, last but not least, constantly eating at somebody else's table. Dante, who was a refugee from his native Florence, described how bitter the salt of another's bread tastes and how hard it is to go up and down another's stairs.[4]

When I had met refugees in the past, I was more depressed by their mental state than by their physical condition. A refugee is, first of all, a state of mind. Refugees who have been especially active in cultural fields lose the earthly and people-conditioned elements of their inspiration. The native landscape is no longer available to the painter, the white birches to the poet, the forms of local injustice to the statesman, even the local diseases to the physician. He becomes like a broken pencil and cannot reunite the lost values of the past with the confused and hostile values of his present state of dispossession. The refugee status is the *capitis diminution*, the fall of modern man, sometimes the giving up of spiritual life and creation. He becomes a ghost. A nonintellectual is better off, because the value of physical work is more universal in nature. The twentieth century, marked by violent social and moral changes, is the paramount century of the refugee, living with one lung and one kidney. Their permanent impermanence, the suspension of their values and hopes, their gnawing uncertainty and longing for normalcy gradually ravage their souls.

There were three things I wanted to avoid in my life: to wear eyeglasses, to lose my hair, and to become a refugee. Now all three things had come to me in implacable succession.

I knew I could change my refugee status only through my spirit: by continuing my intellectual work and by enlarging the concepts of my world—awareness of the oneness of the world, despite its desperate division at that time.

A letter arrived from the Pédones, my Paris publishers, with the first galley proofs of my book. It was like a ship with food supplies to a starving demon. The Pédones wrote to say how happy they were to publish my book and also to help me as a friend of the family. They sent me copies of my 1933 Madrid draft on outlawing acts of barbarism and vandalism as international crimes. I started to work on improving the text. This resulted in new proposals to outlaw genocide, which I made in 1944 in my book *Axis Rule in Occupied Europe*; in 1945 at the London Conference of Prosecutors, when I included genocide in the indictment at the Nuremberg trials; and since 1946 before the United Nations General Assembly.

I paid a visit to Mr. Zalkauskas, the president of the district court of Kaunas. I had met him and his wife at the conference on Unification of Criminal Law in Copenhagen in 1935.

"How could it happen so quickly?" he asked me when we were sitting in his office. "How can a state disappear in three weeks?"

At that time the question sounded to me like "How could Mr. X die yesterday when we dined together only a week ago?" There was no way of explaining it to him, because Europe was divided at that time into two groups: those to whom it had happened, and those to whom it had not happened yet. It happened to Mr. Zalkauskas some time later. When I was in Chicago in 1951, working on ratification of the Genocide Convention, a man knocked at the door of my room in the Hotel Morrison at 5:30 in the morning. He apologized for the early hour; he was working as an elevator man in a hotel until late at night, and he could come to see me only at this time. It was Mr. Zalkauskas.

In Kaunas I met, through Mr. Zalkauskas, men and women in the government and society of the capital and obtained an insight into the life of this nation, which had successfully built late independence between the two wars.

The Lithuanians were basically a democratic people. They did not have their own aristocracy. The Lithuanian gentry was of Polish origin and was looked on with suspicion as too friendly to Warsaw; it was not permitted much influence. The Lithuanians developed as a nation of farmers—hardworking, economical, attached to the soil, stubborn, religious, prosperous. They had a great understanding of agricultural cooperatives.

However, a combination of the bureaucrats and the military gradually developed into self-appointed "mavericks" of the nation. This was the line of evolution from Premier Woldemaras in 1927 up to Premier Merkis in 1939–40.

Culturally and linguistically the nation was remarkable. The language is the only one in Europe that has preserved its vivid connection with ancient Sanskrit. It dates from the time when the Arians controlled the part of the world from the Baltic to the Mediterranean and the Indian Ocean. It was intriguing to read on restaurant signs in Kaunas the same names as in the ancient records of Hittite kings. From my philological studies, before selling my soul to the devil spirits of the law, I knew some Sanskrit and Lithuanian. I now bought a dictionary and began to read a newspaper every day, moving gradually from the headlines to the contents. It was rewarding and helped me to appreciate the people among whom I lived, and especially their culture, which had such ancient antecedents and still preserved its vigor.

I visited Professor Karsavin of the University of Kaunas. A Russian by birth and culture, he had come to Kaunas after the Bolshevik revolution and taught Slavic literature. He was tall and erect, and had a handsome face adorned by a long ornamental beard and vivid eyes. He was the brother of the famous Russian ballerina Karsavina. Imaginative and scholarly, Karsavin was the theoretician of the Eurasian movement. He believed that Europe is only a peninsula of Asia, that there is a community of culture between them, and that this is especially true of Russia. Later, when I traveled through Siberia in 1941, I saw how much of Karsavin's vision was true.

The consulate of Sweden phoned that my visa had arrived. A consulate at that time was the god and supreme ruler of the race of refugees. They studied their gods, whose idiosyncrasies and habits of conversation they had learned from people who had already been received by them. The waiting rooms of the consulates were social meeting places for refugees. People would go there just out of habit. From there they would go to another meeting place, the cafes Monica or Konrad, where they would report to their friends that they had just come from the consulate and that their visas had not yet arrived. For a long time the real relationship between a refugee and a consulate was just—waiting.

The Swedish consul fixed a huge royal stamp on my passport and wished me luck. Next day I was on the train to Riga, the capital of Latvia, another neutral Baltic state, where I had to wait several days for a flight to Sweden.

There was more life in Riga than in Kaunas. The buildings had more majesty and the women more elegance. As a people the Latvians are related to the Lithuanians, but they are more volatile and worldly, especially in the capital. They are an independent-minded people, as proud and efficient as the Lithuanians. When I visited an old friend, Udrie, the procurator general (attorney general) of the Supreme Court, he was more outspoken than my Lithuanian friends had been, openly blaming the unskillful Polish foreign policy for the disaster of Poland. I have never heard from him since that conversation and do not know what happened to him when his country's neutrality ended.

The famous Jewish historian Professor Simon Dubnow lived in Riga. I paid him a visit at his home in Kaiserwald, near the capital. It was a frosty winter day, with a penetrating icy wind blowing from the Baltic Sea. White birds with black beaks flew over the trees around his house. As I entered his bright study, a fireplace with crackling wood logs was sending waves of heat over the room. The rosy face of the professor was friendly and animated. "You can't recuperate from the Baltic frost just with a fireplace. You should be warmed also inside." He offered me a welcome cup of tea.

"It is so pleasantly peaceful here," I remarked.

"The lull before the storm," he said.

"Where will it start, do you think?"

"Now that Hitler has swallowed Poland, he plans his next move while we sit here comfortably by the fireplace. It is strange how initiatives taken by dictators fascinate and even paralyze statesmen of democratic nations, and how easily they let them get away with such bold actions."

"It was the same with Napoleon for some time," I interjected; and from there I turned the conversation cautiously toward my plan to outlaw the destruction of peoples.

His reaction was vivid. "The basic value of your plan lies in the criminal character of the act," he said. "Obviously if killing one man is a crime, killing of entire races and peoples must be an even greater one."

"Killing an individual is a domestic crime—every nation deals with it through its courts and on its own initiative," I said. "But murder of a whole people must be recognized as an international crime, which should concern not just one nation but the entire world. Nations will have to cooperate to punish such criminals, to prevent future mass murders. Should such a thing start again, the nations would have to act. Moreover, the offender will face the judgment not only of his contemporaries but also of history."

"The most appalling thing about this type of killing," said Dubnow, "is that in the past it has ceased to be a crime when large numbers are involved and when all of them happen to belong to the same nationality, or race, or religion. These things must be discussed openly. Let nations take their choice whether they want to belong to the civilized world community. I have always felt that history must sit in judgment," Dubnow argued.

The great historian was evidently thinking about the judgment of history a year and a half later when he was led to execution by the Nazis. Friends told me that at this supreme moment of his life, he called to the people who saw him: "Write it down, write it down!" It was a historian's testament.[5]

The day before I left Riga my friends took me to the art museum. I remember distinctly a sculpture called *The Mother.* Love and forgiveness looked out from the statue's face. It still looks now at many sons and daughters who rush with the business of living so fast that they forget those who gave them life. But the mother always forgives. The next day, as I was flying to Stockholm through the icy air of the Baltic, I felt that I might be leaving this part of Europe forever, and that my parents would be alone in whatever danger might threaten them. But the vision of the Latvian mother seemed to urge me to ask forgiveness from my own mother.

When I got up next morning in Stockholm, I had a quick breakfast and went for a stroll to inhale and drink in the city. It is not a city that overwhelms one at once with its fast movements and lights, like New York, Paris, or Berlin. It grows on one slowly, steadily, and strongly. Some of the elements of its great charm are the marriage between city and water; the eerie coloring caused by the sun breaking through mist and fog and at sunset making the water reflect its dark blue on the snow; the sun playing on the ancient metallic green of the rooftops, conveying at the same time a feeling of antiquity and youth; the erect, shapely figures of men and women in the streets, like Norse gods in modern clothing; the attractive shop windows, especially the many bookstores, which bear testimony to a city not only well dressed but highly literate.

In one of these shops I bought a book to learn Swedish, and a smiling saleslady translated some of the numerous titles for me. I told her how I had learned Lithuanian from newspapers and a dictionary. She advised me to do the same here, but not to neglect to find a living dictionary with dimples, who would give more incentive to my linguistic studies. On the whole, the Swedes gave me the impression that they had come a long way from morbid Viking habits, and they were no longer thinking about heroic death but were thoroughly enjoying life.

The Swedes like to eat well. Innumerable eating places with shining casseroles on the walls served food by candlelight even in daytime. One can have one's own private *saga* at every table and devour endless pieces of *smorgos* before even looking at the menu. It is customary in Sweden for the smorgasbord to be free. One pays only for the main dishes. This almost gave rise to a diplomatic incident during the Finno-Russian war, when the Swedish government gave the Germans permission to travel over their territory to Finland. The Germans used to stop at the restaurant at the railway station in Stockholm, eat all the free smorgasbord, and then continue their travels. The restaurant protested, but to no avail.

On the whole the Swedes enjoyed their neutrality. There was none of the uneasiness that had underlain the strained temporary neutrality of the Baltic states. To the Swedes, neutrality came naturally. Sometimes they would try to justify it this way: "We fought wars, we built empires and lost them. Under Charles XII we went as far as Poltava. What is the use of fighting wars if one destroys values without creating anything permanent in their place? What is the sense in destroying cities and people? We will not participate in anyone else's madness." They liked to fortify this position of neutrality by quoting Chamberlain's statement after he flew to Godesberg in 1938 to settle with Hitler. He said then that at the end of war the reasons for war do not appear relevant any longer, because the entire picture has changed. I asked them if Chamberlain realized later what would have happened to England and the rest of the world if she had not seen the danger to her very existence. But I could not very well carry the argument much further, because I owed my own life to neutrality.

The Nazi occupation of Denmark and Norway on April 9 and 10, 1940, shattered Scandinavian solidarity. The practice of neutrality began to bother the Swedes' consciences. Their indignation was deep when it became known that before the invasion the German minister to Norway had invited distinguished guests, including members of the Norwegian government, to view a German film at the German legation. The guests were horrified to see in this film the German conquest of Poland with gruesome pictures of the bombings of Warsaw, accompanied by the caption, "For this they could thank their English and French friends." The presentation of this film was seen as a means of terrorizing the Norwegian government. When I heard this story it brought to mind the night of September 6, 1939—less than a year before—when I walked through the burning streets of Warsaw to the last train leaving the capital.

A letter arrived from Count Carton de Wiart, advising me that a visa awaited me at the Belgian legation. At that time I had intended to use Belgium as a transition point but had heard nothing definite from Professor McDermott of Duke University about an appointment. On this occasion I came to know the minister of Belgium, who expressed his sympathy over the disaster of Poland and deplored the waste of lives and human energies among the refugees.

On May 10, 1940, the Nazis marched into Belgium and Holland. At the same time they thrust toward Paris. Belgium was totally occupied within days. It was my turn to express sympathy to the Belgian minister: his country now shared Poland's fate, and the Count had become a refugee deluxe.

Several days later I visited the Polish consulate. The corridors were full of Polish refugees. Especially animated were the former officers stranded in Stockholm, who were flabbergasted by the sudden weakening of the Allies' cause. But as military men they did not forget to enjoy the sad rehabilitation of the Polish army's honor. "We were defeated in three weeks," they boasted. "Our allies collapsed in a few days."

My book on international payments had by now appeared in Paris. It was also printed in the professional Swedish press, and my friend Karl

Schlyter, the former Swedish minister of justice, suggested that I start lecturing on this subject at the University of Stockholm. I went to see the vice president of the university, Gosta Eberstein; we had a meeting of minds, and an invitation was extended. "In what language will you lecture?" he asked.

"In what language would you want me to lecture?" I said. "I know a little Swedish—I study it every day."

I tried my Swedish on him; he understood me but was not satisfied with my pronunciation. Friends telephoned a former actress, who agreed to work with me on my diction several hours a week.

I started preparing my lectures, drawing extensively on my book, which was in French and from which, with help, I translated excerpts into Swedish. Whenever a lecture was ready I read it aloud with my teacher. It went well: she was elated. When my lectures were announced I still did not believe that I could address an audience in Swedish after only a five-month sojourn in the country. Some three hundred persons came to hear me; many members of the faculty were also present, as well as the vice president.

The suggestion later arose that I publish the lectures in Swedish, and my first book in Swedish appeared before long under the title *Exchange Control and Clearing*.[6] To me this linguistic victory meant a great deal. It gave me intellectual self-assurance, and it helped me to rise spiritually from the "refugee" fall of modern man. But most of all I rejoiced in being able to add the understanding of a new culture to my intellectual treasury. I always remembered the words of Victor Hugo: "As many languages as you know, as many times you are a human being."

I dined often with Swedish friends. Swedish dinners are more formal than elsewhere in Europe. Much protocol attends the eating, and especially the drinking. There is an order in toasting: a guest must toast first the hostess, then the neighbor to the right, then to the left. One must not raise the glass higher than the upper button of the vest and one must look straight into the eyes of the person being toasted. A toast is always accompanied by the word *skall*, which actually means "skull." It is derived from the Vikings' ancient habit of using the skulls of their defeated enemies as drinking vessels. It would not be good policy, however, for a guest from abroad to comment on these historical reminiscences during a Swedish dinner.

The Swedes use titles that describe a person's professional and social status in detail. The wife of a cashier at a railway station would be called by her full title: "Mrs. Ticket-cashier-at-the-railway-station." Never mind that the title is long. What matters is its complete accuracy. This emphasis on titles seems to reflect an exaggerated seriousness that dominates behavior. When Swedes decide to have fun, it is a formal decision which is announced: "We are going to have fun."

Whoever may have thought that Sweden at that time was a happy country was mistaken. Bombs did not fall on the Swedes' heads, but their nerves were shattered by constant bad news. On June 20, 1940, Russian troops marched into the three Baltic states, Lithuania, Latvia, and Estonia, and quickly incorporated them into the Soviet Union.

I had not stopped worrying about the people in Poland. I wanted to find out what the Nazis were doing there. As a lawyer, I knew the significance of official documents for understanding policy. I knew I could read the intentions of the Nazi government only from legal enactments such as decrees and ordinances. A decree is objective and irrefutable evidence.

Central and Western Europe were almost entirely occupied. A New European Order was proclaimed. Was there any place left for non-Germans under Hitler's domination? Hitler was one of the few statesmen in history who proclaimed his intentions many years before he took power. Yet the statesmen of the democracies either did not read him or did not believe him. They were like my baker friend in the small Wolynian town who refused to believe Hitler's intentions because they were opposed to his old-fashioned thinking.

Yet Hitler's convictions—or rather idiosyncrasies—were very strong, because, as he writes in *Mein Kampf*, he formulated them in his early youth, especially in his Vienna days. He wrote: "I was repelled by the conglomeration of races, which the capital showed me, repelled by this whole mixture of Czechs, Poles, Hungarians, Ruthenians, Serbs, Croats, and everywhere the eternal mushroom of humanity—Jews and more Jews." He promised to destroy them like vermin.

I decided to follow his plans from my observation point in Stockholm. I had friends in a Swedish corporation for which I had sometimes acted as a lawyer in their businesses in Warsaw. I visited their office and requested a favor: to ask their branches to send them official gazettes from those occupied countries where they still operated. It was simple; the official gazettes were as public as the names of the countries. I started to read them, and I also found official gazettes of the German Reich in library collections in Stockholm.

From my reading, the following picture unveiled itself: Hitler advocated in *Mein Kampf* that Germany should not look for colonies outside Europe but within it. The only possibility for carrying out a sound German territorial policy lay in the acquisition of new land in Europe. This strategy, formulated in 1924, was formally carried out by the decree of October 8, 1939, six weeks after the attack on Poland. The western and northern parts of the Polish territories were incorporated into Germany, and arrangements were made to Germanize them, completely under the premise that one can Germanize only the soil, not the people. The Poles of this area would have to go. In the rest of Poland the people would be rendered headless or brainless, the intelligentsia liquidated and the bulk of the population organized mainly for physical labor. Denationalization followed by dehumanization. This would mean the death of the nation in a spiritual and cultural sense. As for the Jews, ominous signs pointed to their complete destruction in gradual steps.

The Nazis' first step was to identify the Jews through registration and through Star of David badges that they had to wear on their right arms. The law defined who was a Jew, and this definition was incorporated in the decrees of the occupied countries. I was appalled by the decree that established the Warsaw ghetto in October 1940, which imposed the death penalty on those leaving the ghetto without permission. Why the death penalty? Was this just a way of hastening what was already in store for them?

The property of Jews was being seized. The people were rendered destitute and totally dependent on rationing. There was a decrease in carbohydrates and proteins and an almost complete exclusion of fats from the Jews' diet. They were being reduced to living corpses, their spirits broken, apathetic to their own lives. A special form of forced labor was introduced: all Jewish inhabitants from fourteen to sixty years of age were subject to it. Much of the labor, designated for "educational purposes," was economically useless except for the purpose of destroying the workers. Large numbers of them were dying.

In the peaceful library of Stockholm I saw an entire race being imprisoned and condemned to death. The dehumanization and disintegration had already begun; when would the hour of execution come? Would this blind world see it only then, when it was too late? The only help could come from America, which itself had been born out of moral indignation against oppression and had many times in its history acted according to these feelings.

My impatience to get to America was increasing. Although the United States was formally neutral, its expressions of human concern were warming Europe like the Gulf Stream. But I was powerless, caught in this pocket between Russia and Germany.

CHAPTER FIVE

From Sweden to the United States

AS 1941 STARTED, TWO events helped me break out of my Swedish isolation. My appointment at Duke University came through. Also, rumors had started that the Soviet Union might permit refugees to travel through its territory. My friends at the Polish legation in Stockholm, which was in contact with the exiled Polish government in London, told me that a rapprochement between the Allies (including Poland) and the Soviet Union was possible, and that relations between Russia and Germany were steadily deteriorating. One of the conditions for obtaining a Russian visa, they told me, would be a Swedish passport for stateless persons, as Russia did not yet recognize the Polish government in London.

There was a feeling in Stockholm among the refugees that now was the time to go to the U.S.A., because in the summer "something" might happen again. Through the first two years of the war the world seemed to be acting like a bear: sleeping in the winter and running wild in the summer.

I wrote to my parents that the door to the United States seemed to be opening. They replied—in one of their last letters to me—urging me to go. Emotionally, I was in a Hamlet state of mind. I felt I would be leaving my parents on a powder keg, even though I could not actually help them from Stockholm. It was one of those struggles of the heart, difficult to live through and quite impossible to explain logically. As long as I was in

Europe, I had felt that I was watching over them. But it was only a geographical illusion.

On the other hand, it had been my strongest desire to go to the United States. From there I hoped I could explain to the Allies and friendly neutrals the real purpose behind the Nazi war policy. They had to be made to see that this war was being waged by the Nazis not only for frontiers but for the alteration of the human element within these frontiers. This alteration meant that certain people were to be annihilated and supplanted by Germans. Their destruction would be irrevocable and their cultures erased forever. I realized that the real issue at stake in the war was civilization not as a propaganda slogan but as a palpable reality.

The Nazi plan was so outrageous that nobody would believe it in time to try to forestall it. It was not the first time in history that Poland had been subject to genocide. Exactly seven hundred years earlier, in 1241, the Mongols had overrun Russia, then Poland, Silesia, and Hungary. A great part of the population of important Polish cities was slaughtered: Lublin, Sandomierz, and Krakow, where thirty thousand Polish boys and girls were carried off by the Mongols and sold in the Russian city of Vladimir. The Polish countryside was devastated. When the Mongols retreated, the population losses were so great that the Polish duke Leszek had to import people from other countries, especially Germany. He wrote in 1287: "Since our land has been depopulated by the sword of the enemy, since it has been soiled with innocent blood, and left untouched by the plow and uncultivated, we desire to colonize it and reconstruct it with other inhabitants and farmers."[1]

At the same time, Hungary was subject to one of the greatest bloodbaths in history. Here, too, the slaughter was systematic and calculated. Because the Mongols wanted the Hungarians' clothes free of bloodstains, they made them undress before they shot arrows into them. They burned merchants over slow fires to make them confess the hiding places of their possessions. The Mongol women participated in the slaughter. They cut off the noses of good-looking Hungarian women and trained their children to kill Hungarian children. This was done by putting the native children in a row, facing the Mongol children, who had sticks in their hands. At a signal from their mothers, the Mongol children clubbed the heads of the Hungarian children. The invaders also practiced sexual cannibalism: they cut off the breasts of beautiful women and ate them.

The Mongols' intention to destroy the Hungarians was evident in the game of hide-and-seek played in Hungarian cities. Hungarians who had managed to survive would flee into the countryside or hide among the corpses during the invasions. After retreating into the forests for a few days, the Mongols would swoop down again upon the cities and kill those who had crept back to their homes in the belief that they had been spared. In this way the Mongols succeeded in completely emptying the cities. When they retreated from Hungary, plans for repopulating the country had to be devised as well.

This decimation of the peoples of Poland, Hungary, Silesia, and Russia was perhaps one of the most outstanding cases in history of multiple genocide.

Russia was controlled by the Mongols for more than two hundred years. At the first invasion the people in the large cities were killed mercilessly. A usual practice was to burn the churches after people had taken refuge in them. The Mongols later established a controlling government of the Golden Horde in Sarai, on the lower Volga. Their invasion had such a deep impact that the Russians subsequently adopted their taxation system and even their postal system, which used horses. The administrative techniques of the Mongols were successful because they brought able administrators from China, which they had previously invaded. As Russia had no central government, only quarreling princes, the Golden Horde played the princes against each other and subjected what remained of the population to confiscatory taxes and tortures. This long period of suffering and sorrow is perhaps the basic source of Russian fatalism. It certainly helps to explain the melancholy of Russian folklore and literature since that time.

While I was in the Stockholm library comparing the Nazi and Mongolian invasions of Europe, I could not help thinking about the attempt to save Poland and Hungary from the Mongols by what was called at that time the "Western world." These comparisons did not augur well for the present. Pope Innocent IV protested to the Mongols at the time, but German and Austrian princes quarreled with the pope and could not organize any common action. The prince of Austria even invaded Hungary instead of helping her. In addition, as the *Cambridge Medieval History* reports, in 1248 Innocent advised Mongol envoys to Rome that the Mongols should attack Vatatzes, the Greek Orthodox king of the Nicaean Empire.[2] I wondered if the tragedy of Western division and disunity would repeat itself in the face of this new barbarism.

I started to say goodbye to my Stockholm friends. The Ebersteins gave a dinner for me at which I committed a regrettable faux pas. I was so dejected that at first I did not notice that my friends had decorated the table with small red-and-white Polish flags. My attention was discreetly drawn to this fact at the end of the dinner. I was ashamed and as grateful as a child who had misbehaved and instead of being spanked had been given a piece of candy.

I hurriedly assembled the necessary visas: American, Russian, and Japanese. The next morning I was flying to Moscow. We stopped for refueling at the airport in Riga. The wind was as icy as it had been on my flight to Stockholm a year earlier. The square face of the Russian officer was impassive as he looked at our passports. All airports and railway stations have a peculiarly impersonal atmosphere. This time I was grateful for it. I had a passport and a duly issued Russian visa, and still I was seized by uneasiness, a feeling bordering on fright.

When boarding the plane I looked instinctively to the southwest, in the general direction of the town where my parents lived. What were they doing now? Were they playing with their grandchildren or anxiously discussing their son, who was now on the first leg of his American odyssey? Back on the plane, we were told that we would be in Moscow in four hours. My fears, my thoughts of the past, were superseded by my curiosity to see and know the Russian capital and its people.

The day was gray; so were the refugee passengers' faces. So too was the face of Moscow, toward which we descended early that afternoon. There were more inspection formalities, more cool glances at our passports; not one word was uttered, not one smile wasted on us.

Intourist, the Russian government travel office, handled our arrangements. We were driven to the hotel, an old-fashioned building with a cold lobby and long, unfriendly corridors. My room was huge, with a high ceiling. Had it been smaller I might have felt less lost. I lay on the bed and tried to warm up my frozen thoughts. I began thinking of the people of this city. I wanted to see ordinary men, not soldiers, not policemen. As human beings they must have daily worries like everyone else. The concerns of ordinary men—food, clothing, health, shelter—are common to all mankind and have a quality of holiness. I wanted to talk with a Russian mother or child, a grandfather, a student, a railroad man. I hoped to meet some such person when I went down to dinner. The hotel dining room was dimly lit. Guests in uniform occupied many tables. They all seemed to reflect a collective anxiety. I had seen such faces before, in my own country just prior to the Nazi onslaught.

Lonely people in any hotel feel miserable, but in some cities they become aware gradually of a certain communication with strangers. An occasional smile, a tentative greeting, make one feel a part of the human community. Here there was no room for a smile. Looking around the large dining room, I realized that the world situation was indeed tense, that I was a foreigner, from a land conquered and occupied by my present hosts. At that time I failed to understand that smiles could be completely regimented, even banned.

After my grim dinner I tried to sleep but could feel myself being bitten. I threw back the blanket, turned on the light, and found myself covered with fleas. Attempts to remove them proved unrewarding. At last I dressed and spent the rest of the night on top of the blanket. The 1917 Revolution had not abolished fleas.

Next morning I strolled to Red Square, in front of the Kremlin, and looked at the pointed domes of St. Basil's Church at the corner. The domes mesmerized me. I had often seen them in books as a child and had fallen in love with them then. I think that the Russian nation in its more colorful youth must have fallen in love with them too. St. Basil's is not only overwhelming as a structure, but it is also enveloping as a concept.

What is so captivating about its spirit? It is basically a fantasy, a playhouse, a toy for children that, by a caprice of history, became a reality for adults.

I went around the Kremlin walls and looked down at the Moskva River. Ivan the Terrible and Napoleon had looked down from here too— perhaps with the foreshadowing of doom—but so too had Tolstoy and Chekhov, possibly with more hopeful sentiments for mankind. The Kremlin was especially dark this gray day. The Moscow sun tried to pierce the clouds and mist. I wandered through the streets, watching the people. I could see that their old-fashioned coats, which had been "turned" years before, had obviously been old at the time they were carefully altered. The men's caps were shabby, the women wore no hats, only babushkas, and their stockings were thick above their scuffed shoes. They resembled people who had been unemployed a long time. Their movements were slow, their faces showed concern, preoccupation, heavy responsibility, as of men and women who had long carried a sad burden. One could see the effects of war, though there had been no fighting here as yet. I saw almost no young people, which gave the streets of Moscow a dreary aspect. Not until several days later, beyond the Ural Mountains, did I see any Russian children.

We refugees, several hundred of us, traveled by the Trans-Siberia railroad, and the trip from Moscow to Vladivostok was to take us ten days. We traveled four to a compartment, in seats that converted into narrow berths at night. I shared a compartment with a couple from Poland and their two children, a boy of seven and a baby about a year old. At the time the baby represented one of my greatest trials, as it cried incessantly and always at the exact moment that I was dropping off to sleep or, worse, trying to concentrate on a thought.

In the dining car I met two ladies, a mother and a daughter who were refugees from Berlin. We became friends, and they invited me to come to their compartment. On my first visit there, to my consternation I discovered in the corner of the compartment a cradle with a blond baby in it. This one, however, belonged to the race of noncrying babies. On later visits I learned that it was the illegitimate child of the daughter, begotten in Stockholm. Maybe this is why the baby was quiet: it wanted to gain acceptance from the outside world.

I watched Russia through the window of the train, as if trying to unveil its face. Although the train did not stop at most of the dreary little stations, I was able to catch their mood, a deep melancholy. There were intervals of many hours between stations when I saw only deep snow and occasionally the thatched roofs of a distant village. After we crossed the Ural Mountains we stopped at a station that is still pressed on my memory. It was here that I first saw Russian children. Dozens of them with pale faces were calling to us, *"Chleba! Chleba!"*—"Bread! Bread!" We had no bread with us, but I had some candy, which I threw to them. Their swooping movements, as they tried to catch the candy pieces, reminded me of hungry pigeons.

We left the children and continued into Siberia. The railway stations became more interesting to me, as they increasingly revealed Asiatic faces among the railway personnel. More Russians came on the train during this part of our journey. They were friendly and willing to talk, and we could discuss with them their work and lives. There was an enthusiastic young schoolteacher who tried to explain to me the special privileges accorded to volunteers for work in Siberia. My knowledge of Russian was very useful to me as the schoolteacher dwelt eloquently on the marvels of Siberia. He told me with pride that Siberia was the backbone of Russia. "Look at Novosibirsk when you reach it," he said. "It is the wonder of our industrial cities."

The schoolteacher's enthusiasm seemed to come as much from nationalistic pride as interest. I asked him what he thought about the legend, so widely spread in Siberia, that Tsar Alexander I, who chased

Napoleon out of Russia, had never died but was still walking the plains of Siberia disguised as an old pilgrim under the name of Fedor Kuzmicz. "Do you think," I asked him, "that the feeling that Russia is unconquerable gave rise to this legend?" He looked pensively out the window at the wide Siberian plains, as if searching for Kuzmicz, and said, "At this moment in our history, that is the way we feel."

I used to come to the dining car and wait until a Russian passenger sat alone at a table, then I would take the place opposite him. Looking out the window, I would say casually in Russian, "What an interesting countryside." From this the conversation would usually follow quite naturally. Russians seem to feel most gregarious and communicative when they eat. My dinner companions talked freely, and I learned much about developments in Siberia. The unity of Asian and European Russia, as in the Eurasian theories of Professor Karsavin in Kaunas, materialized before my eyes. Russia was amassing its industrial potential in Siberia. I was told that foundations had been built on which factories transported from west of the Urals could be placed. It became clear to me why Moscow had reminded me of a besieged city: the Russians apparently expected a Nazi attack on European Russia and were concentrating their defenses in their "Far West."

The station in Novosibirsk was as active as the Gare du Nord in Paris or Victoria Station in London. It took us almost an hour, after pulling out of the station, to reach the city's outskirts. The buildings were large and new. There was life pulsating here that left Moscow far behind.

It was a brilliantly sunny day when we reached Baikal Lake, one of the largest lakes in the world. It is equal in area to all of Switzerland, and like that country it is surrounded by mountains. Obviously there could be no bridge across such a huge lake, and the train had to wind its way along the shore. My thirsty eyes drank in the unbelievable beauty of the blues in the lake, in shades ranging from opalescent to dark marine, apparently produced by the rich minerals at the lake's bottom. The changes of tonality created a symphony that was almost hypnotic. I keep this blue symphony in my treasury of visual memories and recall it whenever I feel a thirst for beauty.

We descended from the mountains into the valley. Our train stopped at a station called Birobidjan.[3] The inscription on the station was in Russian and Jewish letters, the first of its kind I had seen. This was the famous autonomous Jewish republic established in the late 1920s. Learning from the conductor that we would stop here for a time, I got out to stretch my legs.

Two men in the station were carrying a Jewish newspaper, the *Voice of Birobidjan*.[4] They looked shabby. They wore high boots, their caps pulled low on their foreheads. They spoke in Yiddish while leaning over the rail to look at the passengers. They had evidently come to the station because they were curious to see people from the outside world. Dylan Thomas speaks in one of his poems about the pleasure people derive from hanging around stations and watching trains. This common hunger for social contact is especially acute where small populations are scattered over wide areas. Thus the melancholy of railroad stations is almost universal. It was clear that the once hopeful experiment, the Jewish Autonomous Republic of Birobidjan, was not a thriving success. It began when Stalin was the commissar of minorities, a position that ultimately carried him to the top of the Soviet hierarchy. The Soviet government had planned to concentrate Jewish life in this area and transform the bulk of Russia's urban Jewish population into an agricultural society. Birobidjan now survived mainly as a handful of displaced people cut off from their roots.

The last stop of our trans-Siberian journey was Vladivostok, a city of asymmetrical houses that climb haphazardly around a steep mountain. At the time it was covered with snow, which was gradually melting under the caressing sun of the Pacific. The buildings appeared to have been constructed with little regard for beauty. We were taken to an office, where we lined up before several dozen secretaries who examined our passports for what seemed many hours. Then we were taken to a small, ugly hotel farther up the mountain. After a dreary dinner I went to my room, undressed, and got into bed. Once in bed I discovered many relatives of my old enemies from the Moscow hotel. I again slept fully dressed on top of the covers.

After a day or so in Vladivostok we were driven to the foot of the mountain where the harbor was located, and jammed into a small Japanese boat that was to take us to the Japanese port of Tsuruga. On the entire trans-Siberian trip I had seen some of my fellow refugees only at mealtimes. This cramped sea voyage gave me my first real opportunity to see all of them at close quarters. There were several hundred of them altogether. They looked worn out and tense, as I too must have looked: tired from the long trip and apprehensive about all that was happening. One old gentleman in particular epitomized our disintegrated state. He had been a senator in Poland, a distinguished banker from a well-known banking family. He had become completely disheveled, his nose was always running in a most remarkable way, and he constantly sought me out to ask, "What do you think is really happening? What is the significance of all this? What does it mean?" He seemed to believe that there must be logical explanations for this illogical, chaotic situation. Or maybe he was voicing his protest at having ceased to be an individual, at having been lumped into this mass of humanity floating on the choppy Japanese sea. To add insult to injury, our boat, which we dubbed Floating Coffin, ran into many storms on the three-day journey. We were called on day and night to help remove the water that seeped constantly into the lower deck.

Landing at Tsuruga under a bright April sun was a great relief. My first act was to go to a barber for a shave. The Japanese barber put on a mask in order not to breathe into my face. What a change, after three days of such close proximity to running noses and other physical expressions of angry humanity.

We were free of each other until the following week, when we were to embark at Yokohama on our American journey. I decided to spend the rest of the day in Tsuruga, then to go by night train to the old capital,

Kyoto. I walked most of the day around the quaint port village of Tsuruga. It was the blossom season, when Japan is so beautiful; for the Japanese, seasons are so much a part of the cultural and religious life that hardly a conversation is started, or letter begun, without their being mentioned.

I was joined in a restaurant by a young couple whom I recognized from the boat. They appeared relaxed and happy, in contrast to how they had looked, along with the rest of us, on the Floating Coffin. As we lunched I noticed that the waiter and waitress came to us only at moments when we were not talking to each other. I asked the waiter if this was deliberate practice, which he confirmed. I found this delicate custom extremely pleasant. How many times in a restaurant in Warsaw, London, or Paris had I been deeply engrossed in a conversation when the sharp voice of a waiter had rudely interjected the subject of vegetables or dessert.

In the evening I traveled to Kyoto in the company of my new friends, whom I had converted to the idea of staying with me there instead of going to Tokyo. In Warsaw I had read about Kyoto, Japan's capital until 1868, and I considered it the city most interesting and genuinely representative of Japanese culture. When we arrived in the middle of the night the hotels were full; we had not taken into account that this was the cherry season. Finally a hotel agreed to accommodate us in its lobby for the rest of the night. We slept uncomfortably, but breakfast later in the morning compensated for all our inconveniences: a large cherry tree in full bloom overhung the terrace where we ate, its shadows casting a trembling mosaic on our tablecloth, interspersed with the gold of the brilliant morning sun.

Kyoto had almost no modern buildings. Many people in the streets were wearing kimonos. They would stop before each other, bow slowly and gravely, and continue their leisurely pace. We strolled throughout the wide city, coming at last to a famous old cherry tree that faces a huge Buddha on a public square. This great tree is over five hundred years old, dead now except for a single flowering branch which people from all around come to admire. Balding gentlemen among the tree's visitors stop at the Buddha to water their heads under its flowing fingers, which is supposed to make new hair grow. I was not yet eligible for this benefit.

I attended a theater performance, which was preceded by a tea ceremony lasting for about an hour. The entire audience of three or four hundred people sat in a huge room with bare walls, on the ground floor below the theater itself. Before us were simple wooden tables, also bare. The profound silence would have been unimaginable in a European gathering of this size. A cortege of geisha girls entered the hall. One by one they approached our tables and bowed. We responded in kind. Each geisha put a napkin before each guest, then both parties bowed again. The first servers disappeared. Another group of geishas came in, each carrying a cup that was placed before each guest. Then came the spoon-servers. Another cortege appeared with little teapots. When they left, still another wave of geishas came to pour the tea. They all seemed to be different; each had on a uniquely patterned kimono that never seemed to repeat any other. Since the preceding day I had been prepared to accept all possible onslaughts of beauty, but this one surpassed my imagination. The graceful walk of the geishas underlined the variegated pageantry of their magnificent dresses. I understood only then the rule of Japanese aesthetics: repetition must be avoided.

The tea was green and bitter. I did not enjoy it. I looked at the faces of the Japanese around me. They were drinking the tea as if it were part of a sacred ceremony, with expressions near to ecstasy.

Japan as a whole and Kyoto in particular are dedicated to the tea ceremonies, which take place for the most part in small teahouses serving only four or five people. The rooms are remarkably simple and almost completely empty of decoration. The tea drinkers release their souls into a world of meditation where purity, harmony, and mutual charity prevail. Here they forget their cares, their political troubles, and the drabness of their daily lives.

The tea ceremonies were started in Japan in the fifteenth century by the Zen sects. The monks gathered before the image of Bodidharma and drank tea from a single bowl.[5] Gradually this became an institution among all classes of Japanese, a symbolic source of spiritual as well as physical strength.

At the theater, I did not understand the play because of my ignorance of the language. But I was impressed by the fact that the performers moved around very little on the stage, conveying through expressive facial and bodily tremblings the impression of torture and pain. The serene faces of the audience that I had seen in the tea ceremony downstairs were now completely transformed by the intensity of their identification with the actors. This contrast was my first real glimpse into the duality of Japanese culture, a duality that exits in all cultures and all human beings but seems especially pronounced in this country.

As I was walking late that night through the quiet streets of Kyoto I came to a district with many lights. These were the geisha quarters. I saw couples approaching the houses; the women would kiss the men goodbye, and the men would enter the houses. I was later surprised to learn that most of these were married couples.

The following day I saw the castle of Nijo, which had been converted into a museum. To get to the castle one must cross over a high, arched wooden bridge which affords a beautiful view of the surrounding park. This bridge's planks rub against each other as one walks over them, producing the chirping sounds that give it the name Singing Bridge. It was explained to me that the bridge was designed in this way so that the castle could be warned by the shrill chirping that enemies were approaching.

Several centuries ago, Japan was the scene of internal warfare among the feudal lords who lived in such castles as this. Here too there was a marked contrast to the tranquil tea ceremonies. There is so much harmony in the nature of Japan—the union of aesthetics and botany is so perfect, the adulation of flowers is so deep—that one would be inclined to expect a bucolic type of human being always to have dwelled in this land. The historical realities are different. The duality of human nature that is so striking in Japan permitted not only internecine warfare but also one of humanity's most atrocious cases of genocide, which occurred here in the seventeenth century.

At that time there were about fifty thousand Japanese Catholics, converted by Portuguese and Spanish missionaries. The white man carried to the Far East his god in one hand and his merchandise in the other. Before long a competition developed among the missionaries of various Christian denominations, but the competition for trade was even sharper. British and Dutch businessmen were afraid that the Portuguese and Spanish would monopolize Japanese foreign trade. They told the shogun, the military dictator of the empire, that the Catholics were paving the way for the invasion of the country by the Spanish and Portuguese.

A persecution started early in the seventeenth century and lasted almost two hundred years. It is estimated that during this period all the Catholics in the country were destroyed. Such a persecution must have had an impact on the persecutors themselves—two hundred years of cruelty with all possible outlets for the imagination cannot leave a nation unaffected.

An edict was published stating that it was a serious crime to be a Christian. When Christians, who were called Kirishitans, were found on board ships, the whole crew was executed. In 1629 a technique of discovering Christians was introduced. In the course of yearly census-taking throughout the country, the government clerk ordered all members of a household to trample on Christian holy pictures. This practice continued into the nineteenth century.

In March 1650, near Nagasaki, seven Christians were so skillfully sewn through the middle that three continued to live for four days, and one lived for seven days. There were cases of children as young as five being sentenced to life imprisonment for being Christians, and dying in prison some forty years later. A favorite technique was burning alive: fire was built far enough away from the victim that he was consumed only slowly. Other Christians were held over glowing coals and slowly turned so that they were roasted on all sides. Christian children were ordered to hold glowing coals in their hands.

Most of these records come from Japanese literature itself. Catholic Christians were reported to have been dipped in water heated to over two hundred degrees; they were buried alive so that only their heads protruded, making them objects of ridicule until they finally died. At night, corpses of the victims were thrown before the doors of the Spanish and Portuguese missionaries to make people believe that they ate human flesh. The sign of the cross was burnt into Christians' foreheads. They were undressed and put in thin rice sacks before the public. They were dragged by large iron hooks put in their ears, and they were compelled to stand in freezing water until they died. Nailed to their own walls, they were sometimes—although seldom—crucified, but this was usually avoided to prevent glorification.

There were cases wherein water was poured through a funnel into the mouths of victims, a board was placed on them, and their tormentors stepped on them so that water and blood came out of the ears, eyes, and other body openings.

Most of the extreme persecution began after 1627 when, in the province of Arima, the Christians were driven by persecution and high taxes to revolt. They shut themselves up in the fortress of Shimabara, where they held out for two months. Most of them were massacred, and the rest were subjected to more gradual liquidation, as described above.

Thirteen Portuguese missionaries were caught and sent back to Macao with these words: "While the sun warms the earth, let no Christian be so bold as to venture into Japan. Let this be known to all men, though it were the king of Spain in person, or the god of the Christians. . . . Whosoever shall disobey this prohibition will pay for it with his head."

Abundant correspondence confirms that this genocide was encouraged by the Dutch and the English. The Catholic bishop of Japan wrote in 1609 to the king of Spain: "I wish to communicate to your Majesty the calamities and ordeals which the Dutch cause us. . . . They are everywhere in the seas and they will not rest until they have destroyed the commerce between the Portuguese and the Japanese and consequently Christianity in this Empire." The bishop also complained about British intrigues. He wrote that an English captain had shown a map of the world to the emperor and described how Catholics were driven out of many parts of it. Whereupon the emperor answered, "Therefore, if I chase them myself, it will be nothing new."

In 1615 and 1616, the English were given a special charter for shipping privileges. There is also a report that in 1615 the Dutch had started up a large trade and were teaching the Japanese how to make artillery. In this report the Dutch are called the "main cause of the persecution of the Christians." This prolonged persecution isolated Japan from much of the Western world for several centuries, despite the temporary inroads made by the British and Dutch at the expense of their European brothers, until the warships of Commodore Perry forcefully reopened its doors to Western influence.

Japan entered this marriage with Western culture more than reluctantly. This became increasingly clear to me as I traveled from Kyoto to Yokohama. Through the train window I could see the tiny rice plots divided by narrow irrigation ditches. I did not see any large agricultural machinery, only simple, age-old hand tools and an occasional horse or ox. How could a huge tractor fit into these garden-size fields? This was the way Japanese agriculture had been practiced for centuries. The marriage with the industrial West hardly seemed to have touched the countryside.

As we came into Yokohama I was struck by the sudden emergence of the West. The city bustled with activity, the shops displayed modern wares, and the huge buildings were a flagrant contradiction to the humble rice fields of yesterday. I hired a rickshaw and toured the city. The rickshaw itself seemed an anachronism in this island of modern civilization. I was amazed at the deftness of the rickshaw boy, who ran through the city with graceful speed. At first I was uneasy at using a fellow human being as a horse, but gradually this feeling disappeared, as the pleasure provided by an institution so often overrides the social injustice on which it is based.

After touring the port, teeming with ships of all sizes, I returned to my hotel. The dining room was decorated with beautiful flowers. There was a typical impersonal cheerfulness in the surroundings, a cheerfulness without the participation of the individual Japanese soul, which remains inaccessible. A Japanese smile does not indicate warmth or personal feeling; it is generally intended only as an invitation to another person to approach.

In a shop in the hotel lobby I marveled at a display of beautiful kimonos. One robe held me captive. I looked at it for a long while, finally deciding I could not buy it because of its cost. I left the shop, then reentered and spent more time looking at the robe. I left again, with a heavy heart, still thinking about "my" kimono. Finally, capitulating to its beauty and craftsmanship, I entered the shop for a third time and bought it—or rather, the robe bought me. My capture by the vivid Japanese color was a symbol to me of my temporary surrender to this foreign culture, a surrender everyone who travels will understand.

From sunny Yokohama I took a streetcar into Tokyo. When I was well into the city I left the streetcar and joined the pedestrians thronging the streets. It was lunchtime, and I found myself in front of one of the buildings owned by one of the great family corporations that control a great part of the economic interests of Japan. Each morning this building, and others like it, swallows large numbers of the population of Tokyo, disgorging them at lunchtime and again in the evening. Clerks scurry antlike to down a quick "bite" and run back to work, where they disappear into the leviathan's huge stomach. I saw no one strolling, out for the pleasure of a walk. They all, without exception, seemed to be propelled by some hellish machine, but in their faces could be seen a certain order, discipline, and submission to something bigger than themselves.

I went to the Imperial Palace, inhabited by the Emperor Hirohito, who was still the "god" of Japan.[6] Like the Kremlin, it bore witness to an enigmatic life behind its walls whose power was felt by all outside. Unlike the Kremlin, the Imperial Palace was built of wood, with curved, overhanging roofs and numerous pagodas. The quiet in the vast palace park only increased my feeling of the power of the god in residence.

I returned to Yokohama with my head full of contradictory impressions. I tried to sum up Japan in my mind. I clearly saw two Japans: the old one based in Kyoto, with its historical traditions and rural economy;

and the new Japan, with Tokyo as the center of industrial power—an octopus with a huge head and a small body. I saw Japan disfigured, in the throes of transition.

From my hotel terrace, watching the lights of the harbor, I could hear the subdued voice of Yokohama. The word "subdued" fits Japanese life so well; one can almost feel the controlling power of a superior will. The individual, while striving for personal happiness, retreats voluntarily and surrenders to a controlling force, either religion or the state. The murmur of the ocean, mixed with the whisper of the breeze through the cherry blossoms, lulled me to sleep.

The next day we embarked on a ship bound for the United States. The ship, *Heian Maru*, was modern and beautifully equipped, very different from the pirate boat that had brought me from Vladivostok to Tsuruga. A cheerful crowd waved goodbye from the dock as the ship tore itself loose from the shore's embrace.

The voyage was restful and uneventful. Two passengers, however, attracted my attention because they represented such different Japanese outlooks. One was the famous Christian leader Kagawa, who spent his days in the lounge, earnestly discussing world problems.[7] Behind the self-assured attitude of a builder of world amity one could sense his worry: the condition of the world was grimly attested to by the numerous refugees aboard, all of them halfway around the world from their point of origin. The other was a young Japanese naval officer who was at my table in the dining salon. After several days of table conversations, I expressed my concern over the unbalanced structure of the Japanese economy and wondered aloud what would happen if this condition continued.

"We will have to conquer new markets for raw materials, and new areas for colonization," the officer told me.

Another night, over coffee, he said earnestly, "Australia is remarkably well suited for colonization by Japan, I think." I felt it might be impolite to ask him how the Japanese would get into Australia, but he continued, with a tone of injury in his voice, "Our territory is as small as California in the United States; Australia is larger than all the United States, and still it is inhabited only by 7 million people. We have 80 million." Then he added, "The Japanese climate is like Australia's." His eyes looked past me into an imagined future, and I understood then that he was clearly expressing a collective thought, not just a personal one.[8]

We arrived at Vancouver at night. The ferric lights of the city drew all the passengers up on deck. I felt that this beauty was at the same time an augury of security. This was finally the New World.

We stopped at Vancouver until the following day, and I set out the next morning to visit the city. The friendly Canadians advised me what to see. A stranger on the street took me to the main courthouse and introduced me to the presiding judge. Another stranger took me in his car to Vancouver Park, which has pavilions of plants from all over the world. It was a refreshing spring day, ideally suited to strolling around a fresh new city and marveling at the world. Europe and Poland were very far away.

That night we sailed to Seattle, Washington—our final port. The American sun was shining bright on my pillow the following memorable morning. I was too excited to understand its reality. When we got off the boat we were asked to go down to the customs. My valises were lined up on the table, and the friendly eyes of a huge customs officer looked first at them, then at me.

"How was it in Europe?" he said. "Very bad?"

I felt that there was great compassion in his voice. It seemed strange to me that this unknown man in his green uniform was really concerned with me and the people in Europe.

I told him where I came from. Our conversation was chatty and informal rather than official, and my passport was examined not with cold glances but with a feeling, it seemed to me, of friendly curiosity. Was I reading too much into the words and attitudes of these officials who seemed so unexpectedly humane?

The huge customs official gave my valises a superficial examination, then told me, "I'm from over there myself. My mother still lives in Shannon." Then his big hand landed on my shoulder and squeezed it warmly, and his deep voice boomed out, "Okay, boy—you're in!"

CHAPTER SIX

First Impressions of America

APRIL–JUNE 1941

ON APRIL 18, 1941, I WAS sitting on a graceful terrace flooded with sunshine, facing a garden in which red and yellow roses fought coquettishly for my attention. In the distance I could see a hanging bridge cut the clear air with its shining steel. There were mountains in the background with snowy peaks that seemed to warn the vain roses of their mortality. An enveloping feeling of peace and dreamlike reality was everywhere. It was my first day in the United States.

Only an hour earlier I had been introduced to my hosts by a fellow passenger from Poland. They had asked me to spend the day at their Seattle home before taking the night train to Durham, North Carolina. Their invitation had been extended in a natural manner, without flowery phrases, like most of the countless kindnesses I have experienced since that day in this country.

"Is this industrial America?" I asked my hosts, pointing to the paradise around me.

They laughed. "Wait until you see our factories! But they don't necessarily abolish the gardens and roses. The more our industries grow and spread, the more we remove our private lives from the dust and noise. How could we survive otherwise?"

My hosts treated me with as much kindness as if I had been just rescued from the Nazi gallows. They fed me luncheon, compelled me to take a nap, and then drove me in their car over the city and the surrounding area. That evening they drove me to the station, and I boarded the night train.

I slept through my first night in America deeply and peacefully. In the morning I watched the mountains on the horizon from the glass-domed observatory and felt that they spoke the language of primitive power, unlike anything I had seen in my recent travels.

The passengers on the train seemed to have a self-assuredness, which also appeared to me a sign of strength after being so long with frightened Europeans and retiring Japanese. The equipment of the compartment was magnificent compared to that of the European or Japanese. The cars were larger, airier, cleaner, and more comfortable. It occurred to me that the transportation facilities of a nation mirror its wealth, as the appearance of the passengers reflects its health.

When I arrived in Chicago after one and a half days of continuous travel, I was told that this was only half the way to Durham. It was then I realized that America is more than a country, it is a continent. In Europe, in the same amount of time, I would already have passed through several countries.

In Chicago I sent a telegram to Professor McDermott at Duke University, telling him I was on my way. I stopped over in Chicago for a day, and my first feeling in walking around the Loop was of a man lost in a noisy, hostile, perspiring crowd. I could not stop to look at the buildings for fear of being overrun by these hordes. I went into a drugstore and sat down at a counter. While waiting for my order I tried to make conversation with my neighbors. The one on my right only grunted "Huh!" very loudly, and the man on the other side paid no attention to me whatever, keeping his nose in his soup.

I had no idea, during this brief stopover, of the elegant lakefront Chicago I would see three months later. But I never really lost my first impression of having been inside the stomach of a huge industrial whale, and this was perhaps the more real Chicago. That evening, I boarded another train and continued my travels.

As much as I was impressed by the rigor of the Rocky Mountains on my way from Seattle to Chicago, I was more mesmerized by the dreamy quality of the Appalachians. They were like angelic lords that had descended to earth for the delight of man. At times the train made such complete and rapid loops in the mountains that I felt as if they were dancing around me, and that I was on a tremendous carousel.

The train stopped at Lynchburg, Virginia, and here I saw for the first time, in the rest rooms of the station, the inscriptions "For Whites" and "For Colored." These intrigued me, and I innocently asked the Negro porter if there were indeed special toilets for Negroes. He gave me a puzzled look, mixed with hostility, and did not answer. After seventeen years in the United States I understand now that he must have thought I was making fun of him.

As the train moved south I kept thinking about those inscriptions with all the naïvete of a newcomer. I remembered that in Warsaw there was one Negro in the entire city. He was employed as a dancer in a popular night club, where he pounded the floor with both feet as if to destroy it. Everyone enjoyed his dancing and tried to invite him for drinks. A feeling of curiosity and friendliness prevailed toward this lonely black man in Poland. But toward the Jews, I could not help thinking, there was not the same friendliness; there were three million of them— in the trades, in the professions, in other work—and their competition was felt.

In the afternoon, a day and a half after leaving Chicago, my train arrived at Durham. Professor McDermott was waiting at the station. He always had an air of confidence-inspiring friendliness. I felt that the lapse of five years since I had last seen him had not changed our relationship; our feelings about world events were of such a similar quality that we would be able to resume our conversation just where we had left off. Durham was a lively, bustling city smelling of tobacco and human perspiration. There were gasoline stations on the corners, cars crowding bumper to bumper, people moving along without looking at each other and yet somehow never bumping into each other or knocking each other over. People greeted one another in a casual, friendly manner: "Hiya, John!" "Hey, Jack!"

In the car my friend kept inquiring about my travels, but when he saw after a few questions that I had tears in my eyes, he stopped.

"This is our university," he said after a little while, as we drove along a beautiful winding avenue. We crossed a little bridge over an artificial lake. At the end of the avenue I saw a huge quadrangle of high buildings, clean-cut and dressed in stony dignity. The smell of fresh-cut grass on the lawns and the coolness of the shade from the old trees was soothing. Young men and women moved about the campus with a remarkable ease. The boys wore white shirts open at the collar; the girls wore no stockings—they had on light summer dresses and carried many books and even more smiles, which they distributed generously.

There was nothing of the European university atmosphere of worry, nothing of the suspicious concentration of the Russians, the impenetrability of the Japanese in these faces. One could read them like open books.

"This is where you will live," Professor McDermott told me, leading me to a room on the first floor of a dormitory.[1] The bed was already made up. The professor sat for a while, and we talked about the war and my trip. Then he said, "I'll leave you now until six o'clock. There is an alumni dinner this evening with the university president, and I promised that you would speak."

"What?" I asked, utterly astonished.

"You will address the dinner," my friend replied calmly.

"In what language?"

"In English, naturally."

His unperturbed face both reassured and frightened me even more. I had a fairly good writing knowledge of English, but when it came to conversation I had only technical terminologies to call on, or a few simple phrases. I did not know the language of everyday living, and even when I talked with my friend I relied often on innuendos, significant pauses, and a little coughing. I could deliver a lecture in English on law or economics, perhaps, but I could not talk freely about simple things like human beings and human feelings.

A man possesses two languages within his native tongue: the language of his childhood and of daily life and objects, and the language he requires in his profession or trade. These languages are different not only in words and expressions, but above all in mood and feeling.

I tried to explain this to my friend, but to no avail. "Do you realize," he said, "that if you were to take a plane from here to Stockholm, you would complete your round-the-world trip in less than a day? The fact that you have just arrived from Europe and Asia is more interesting than the quality of your language. I will sit behind you and whisper in your ear any words you may need. Why don't you rest and wash up now and I'll come to pick you up before six."

I was here only an hour and already expected to make a formal dinner speech to the most important body of any university! I decided to take a shower and then sleep over any linguistic worries. There was no time for preparation.

My friend was a good psychologist. When I walked into the huge dining room filled with people, I felt as I had felt at Stockholm University when I delivered my first lecture in Swedish. I felt I had to conquer all those good smiling people and prove to my friend that he had been right in giving me this unique opportunity.

After the introductory remarks, which I found very pleasant to listen to, not only because they were flattering but because they were mercifully long, my fatal hour arrived. I plunged into my speech. I had jotted down only a few sentences to start myself off; as to the rest, I relied on God and the linguistic lend-lease my friend had offered. When he had first proposed this loan of English words I could not understand how I could explain to him which word I needed if I did not know the word. But he listened attentively, and every time I stopped he gave me the word he thought would fit in. Usually he guessed correctly—I think.

I started by explaining Hitler's plan of not only conquering new territories but actually destroying whole peoples. I referred to examples of history, how America had tried in 1915 to save the Armenian people from genocide and had made other efforts to help oppressed people in many parts of the world. I saw in the audience an elderly lady with shining eyes and a benign smile. In my mind I decided to concentrate my speech only on her, and thus establish a personal equation for my appeal. Looking at her directly, I said: "If women, children, and old people would be murdered a hundred miles from here, wouldn't you run to help? Then why do you stop this decision of your heart when the distance is five thousand miles instead of a hundred?"

To my complete surprise I was stopped by a thunder of applause. From that point on, I felt that the deepest communication had been established between me and these people of North Carolina.

The president of the university, Dr. Flowers, sat next to me.[2] He was genuinely interested in world affairs, and he told me that I had clarified many questions for him. Many people came to me afterward to express their feelings. I did not know how much of this was hospitality toward a stranger and how much was due to a real desire to fight for justice. But I was sure that this warmhearted community would be a good partner in my struggle.

Since I had arrived at the university near the end of the semester, no teaching schedule had been set up for me. I had time to look around and to plan. Later I was introduced to the dean and my colleagues on the faculty and was installed in a pleasant office overlooking the park. Every hour I would hear the cheerful noise of the students changing classes. It made me feel that we all belonged to one big family. The students often stopped in my office to chat. When I was taking a rest on the porch in front of the law school they would invite me to sit with them under the trees.

I was genuinely interested in them. They were refreshing. I was accustomed to the type of student in Europe who was class conscious and highly nationalistic, and who considered physical work a personal degradation. With few exceptions, European students had harbored the feeling that they were born to do something exceptionally important, if not for the world, at least for their own country. Every one of them was a human being plus something supra-natural, vague, and, of course, vain. The American student is more natural. He has little sense of mission, neither personal nor collective. He would be ashamed to admit class-consciousness or excessive nationalism. He might even overdo his attempts at objectivity toward his own country. When I spoke to students about belligerent European traditions, they said, "What about our Marines in Nicaragua? Do you know how we got the Panama Canal?"[3] Unfortunately, this objectivity seems to be gradually disappearing from the minds of American students.

The American student's most interesting quality is his curiosity. This is probably due to the fact that the high schools in America are of lower quality academically than those in Europe: I believe this makes the American student feel that there is always something new to discover that he should have learned in high school, when he could have been organizing his mind and knowledge.

My colleagues on the faculty were friendly and curious too. We often discussed the differences between the European and American legal systems. The European mentality, which works with concepts rather than experiences, molded a legal system that was rigidly enclosed in abstract codifications. On the other hand, the experimental nature of American thought preconditioned a legal system mostly based on the evolution of court decisions. This permitted constant growth through departures from previous decisions that had ceased to reflect the new situation. Accordingly, legal decisions are usually studied in American law schools, not codes and theory alone, as in Europe. This is called the "case" system, which puts on the student the obligation of preparing himself daily for the classes in order to be able to recite a case. The European student (unless he is a member of a seminar) is more passive all year: he may or may not attend classes, and usually he starts worrying only before examinations, which are oral. On the whole, an American student works harder on the college level than a European one. This is also one of the reasons European students have had the time to be in the forefront of many political movements, while in America this has been left largely to professional politicians. This is also connected with the fact that American life is more fluid than European: it registers more quickly social, economic, and even moral changes. The American constitutional system permits peaceful adjustments to uphold the basic order under all circumstances, and thus prevents revolutions.

I liked to drop in from time to time at the office of Judge Thaddeus Bryson, who taught North Carolina statutes.[4] He was an old man with a handsome, dreamer's face, somewhat of a mystic. He had a Polish first name, given to him by his parents to honor the Polish hero Thaddeus Kosciuszko, who came to these shores to fight for American independence.[5] Once, Judge Bryson looked at me significantly as we were talking together, then lowered his voice as if to give his words more weight: "I have no doubt that you were saved from the European holocaust for a special purpose," he told me.[6] "It is bigger than you are, or than any of us—wait and you will see." He repeated this several times but did not explain precisely what he meant, and I departed in a state of embarrassment. I have often thought of his words, however, and have somehow been strengthened by them in my singleness of purpose in the midst of many of the difficulties I have met.

The vice president of the university, Mr. Dwyer, whom I met the night of my arrival, became enthusiastic about the story I had to tell. When a request for a university speaker came, he recommended me. I visited many towns in the state and told the same story to Chamber of Commerce meetings, to women's groups, to gatherings of young people. At the end of most of my speeches people would come and say to me, "I am ashamed that we are standing idle and watching innocent people being slaughtered," or, "When Hitler finishes with Europe, he will turn against us anyway—so shouldn't we intervene now?"

I bought a white suit with white shoes and white socks, all of which I wore with a dark silk tie, in order to attend the dinners I was invited to. I was rapidly initiated into such local customs and had to keep a sharp eye out not to offend anyone. I noticed that men never tendered their hand to a woman first, never kissed their hands on greeting them as they did in Europe. At the seating ceremonies I learned to size up the dimensions of my neighbor lady, and to gently push the chair far enough under her to let her occupy it comfortably. I learned other table manners with considerable difficulty. In Europe we ate holding the fork in one hand, the knife in the other. In America I saw that one first cut a piece of meat, then put the knife on the plate, shifted the fork to the other hand, and ate with it. This did not fit well into my notion of American economy of movements, as it slowed down the eating process considerably. But it had one potential (though not always real) advantage: it allowed more time for conversation. In Europe, conversation, especially among intellectuals, is in terms of ideas and concepts, intermingled with facts if these are amusing or otherwise interesting. I noticed that at campus dinners people spoke mostly about facts, and would show impatience and even change the subject if I would introduce a more conceptual theme. I complied with this form, but with all due respect to these really good people, I still remember some of my dinners there as the most tiring rituals I have sat through. I could never understand why it was important for a gathering to know what kind of refrigerator or vacuum cleaner was the best, or that someone's boy had spilled ink on the rug.

One day Professor McDermott asked me if I would like to drive with him to Washington. Never having been to the capital of my new host country, I welcomed the opportunity. I also wanted to visit the Polish Embassy and several friends whom I had met in 1937 at a Congress of Comparative Law at The Hague, and with whom I later corresponded.[7] I was particularly eager to see John Vance, who was law librarian at the Library of Congress.[8]

We started out early one morning. I was interested in the North Carolina tobacco fields and the well-built highways by which Americans traveled. We passed through innumerable little towns, which I could hardly distinguish from one another—they were all alike to my eyes. So were most of the houses. In one Virginia town we found an inscription on one of the houses which said: "Washington slept here." This was the only difference I could see between this house and all the others from Durham on.

It occurred to me that the comparative shortness of American history is evident above all in the uniformity of its small towns and main streets. With few exceptions, towns and cities simply had no time to evolve an individuality or to have imprinted on them the variations of the centuries. The practical American, who knows the shifting nature of his young nation, makes a virtue out of this freedom from history—it permits him to make quick adjustments and to move in a flexible, down-to-earth manner from one phase of life to another.

The youth of the American nation impressed me refreshingly when we got to Washington, D.C. There seemed to me little trace of the torturous imperial sumptuousness, such as one sees in London, Paris, Berlin, Vienna, or Moscow, in the manor-like simplicity of the White House. Its style seems to say plainly, with a democratic graciousness, "We just started from here." There is great power and spirit in this architectural understatement. I was impressed by the subdued elegance of Sixteenth Street and the park-like extravagance of Massachusetts Avenue. The monuments, especially that of Lincoln, told their story with what seemed to me a grand simplicity without being grandiose. In the way Lincoln is seated there is no artificial feeling of a pose struck to impress and terrorize posterity: there is above all a feeling of humane and contemplative loneliness. The offices and government buildings had an impressively unpretentious working atmosphere. The capital city of America seemed to me more American in mood and setting than any other city in this country.

After a visit at the Polish Embassy, we drove to the Library of Congress. John Vance was as outgoing and full of verve as ever. Slender, with a moustache and sideburns, he had vivacious brown eyes and a voice that conveyed a peculiarly deep concern for men and the world. He played the guitar and sang songs from his native Kentucky. A good lawyer and very competent librarian, he also had a touch of the poet and artist. He brought his guitar on trips to foreign countries and played it with abandon at small parties, making friends who never forgot him.

Now Vance seemed to feel that he was personally responsible for the liberation of Europe and for the restoration of Poland as a personal gift to me. He meant it sincerely, and he made all my worries his own. He introduced me to Colonel Archibald King, of the military government division of the War Department. Colonel King had long practice, dating back to World War I, in preparing legislation to regulate the behavior of American army personnel in foreign territory.[9] He was trained in American and British law, and like every lawyer was dedicated to the concept on which he based his work and thinking, and which he served so skillfully all his life. He was adept in the Anglo-American experimental legal system, and he believed that lawyers of other countries were also basically decent and dedicated. To make him understand the concept of genocide I had to move him a little, unfortunately, from this position.

I started by telling him that law in Germany had become a different species from what was assumed. It was no longer an ethical function of distributive justice but a system for enforcing whatever was deemed useful to the state.

"The Nazis," I told him, "do not recognize the principle accepted by other countries and inherent in the Hague Conventions, that wars are directed against sovereigns and armies. In their opinion, wars should be directed against subjects and civilians—in other words, against peoples. In 1935 one of the theoreticians of National Socialism, Alfred Rosenberg, wrote in his *Myth of the Twentieth Century* that 'history and the mission of the future no longer mean the struggle of class against class, the struggle of Church dogma against dogma, but the clash between blood and blood, race and race, people and people.'"[10]

"Then the Germans are officially rejecting the Hague Regulations," Colonel King interjected.

"Not officially," I said, "but unofficially. They cannot do it openly as long as German prisoners are in the hands of the Allies."

I explained, in terms he understood too well, the German laws and decrees of occupation that were perpetrating this genocide on European peoples. "It is not a problem of preventing isolated and wanton atrocities even on a large scale, as occurred in Belgium or France in 1914. Hitler intends to change the whole population structure of Europe for a thousand years—which means virtually forever. Certain nations and races will disappear completely or be crippled indefinitely. Even in the case of German defeat, the Germans have it planned that these remaining nations will have to lean on Germany to stay alive. The Germans are trying to defeat and destroy not governments, but peoples. They know that if a people is destroyed, there will be no governments or, with partial destruction, such weak governments that Germany will not have to fear them. If this Nazi plan succeeds in Europe, you might as well write Europe off for future planning or policy consideration in your relations with the rest of the world."

"This is completely new to our constitutional thinking," the colonel said. "I would like to study this whole problem further."

I told him that I had scheduled a series of lectures on the subject at Duke University. The colonel replied that he would like to attend these lectures, and that they would be of vital interest to the War Department.

Back on campus, I put myself to work more intensively. I translated the Nazi decrees into English and wrote an analysis of them. I wanted to secure a regular flow of such decrees from occupied Europe and suggested in a letter to Vance that he might get them through book dealers in neutral countries—Portugal, Switzerland, or Sweden. In this way I hoped to build up in the Library of Congress a center of documentation that would be helpful in explaining the "war on the peoples" behind the current European "war on the armies."

Vance invited me to address the Annual Convention of the American Bar Association on the subject of totalitarian control over foreign economies.

One morning in June 1941, when I opened my box at the university post office, popularly called the Duke Station, I found a letter from my parents, in a tired envelope. It had been en route more than two months. "We are well," they wrote, "and happy that the letter will find you in America."[11] It was written on a scrap of paper, perhaps a quarter the size of normal writing paper. The quality of the paper spoke eloquently of the extreme poverty in which they were living. Something within me told me that in this letter they were saying goodbye. I chased the thought away, as I would a mosquito, but it came back to me in the evening as I walked through the campus. Despite my parents' efforts not to alarm me, their letter had a tone of subdued despair. It was the last letter I ever received from them. Several days later, on June 24th, I turned on my radio during breakfast, and the words of an impersonal newscast fell on me sharply, cutting deep into my flesh: "The German army has invaded Eastern Poland."[12] There was no way to turn my back on these words. They were heavy, like lead. Like destiny. They meant burning villages and columns of bluish-brown dust rising quickly after artillery shells had fallen on the ground. Like a wounded animal, the earth in my town of Wolkowysk cried out for having been desecrated for the third time in this century. The blood of men and of animals is red; the blood of a town is yellow-brown tinged with blue, and it mounts skyward, as if complaining to God of the folly of men.

In 1915 the German army invaded my hometown: in 1920 when the Russian army moved through on its way to the capital, and in 1939, when I was bombed out from smoking Warsaw. Now, through barking radio words, they invaded my refuge on the Duke campus. What would happen to my family now I could realize only through a shudder. Why did I have the foreboding of a farewell in the three lines of their letter?

The Duke campus was smiling that June morning. "Have you heard the news about the Nazis invading Poland?" I was asked on all sides when I walked into the Law School building. My expression gave them their answer. "Sorry," they said, and moved away in silence, my colleagues and my students.

Several days later, when the North Carolina night was paling, I woke, covered with deep sweat. I had had a dream in which my mother's face came close to me. I didn't see her body, just her face, with her hair combed low on her forehead. Her eyes smiled through a thick mist of sorrow, as if she knew a secret I did not. I stretched my hand toward her face, to caress it, but she moved back from my touch, fading gradually, and I awoke. Much later I learned that during the Nazi blitz, which was as "blitzy" as real lighting, the largest area of the city, including the place where my parents' home had stood, was burned to the ground. The population, some twenty thousand people, was crowded into a few small houses near the railroad station. This happened more than a year before they moved my parents, together with others, to be gassed.[13]

Several days later I received a request from the vice president of Duke to address a Chamber of Commerce group in High Point. As I drove down the smooth highway to High Point, I had one fist clenched, mentally directing it in the face of an unknown Nazi. I was returning the compliment to the genocidal robot in a rage of feelings and words, which were powerful in High Point but which would have sounded weak in the town of Wolkowysk. I was ashamed of my helplessness in dealing with the murderers of humanity, a shame that has not left me to this day. Guilt without guilt is more destructive to us than justified guilt, because in the first case catharsis is impossible.

On my return to the university I spent the evening with McDermott. "You serve your cause by fighting for it," he told me. "This means you must be strong. Otherwise, how can you influence anybody? Keep your chin up." This was an order, and I obeyed. In North Carolina, a man is not fully dressed unless he wears a smile. I started to smile again, but the world lost its color for me for many months.

CHAPTER SEVEN

Alerting the World to Genocide

IN JUNE 1942, A TELEGRAM lay on my table that meant the beginning of a new phase in my life and work. The Board of Economic Warfare in Washington was offering me an appointment as chief consultant of the board. I wired acceptance.

I came now to a different Washington from the one I had visited earlier. The city was teeming with people and energy. People walked in the streets and offices with busy faces, talking a lingo that was born almost overnight. The words "commission," "report," "production," "appointment," "secretary," "typewriter," "boat," "plane," "Germany," "Japan," "London" repeated themselves in all possible combinations. Every day the trains and planes poured thousands of newcomers into the city from every corner of the country: in new military uniforms ready to report, and in civilian clothes to assume authority; businessmen, professors, lawyers, men and women, old and young. They all came to find out "how they could help" defeat the Axis. They offered services in many fields. I discovered a radio storyteller for children working as a personnel officer, and my secretary, alas, could not type. When I first saw her spelling I wondered whether she had decided to reform the language and to simplify it according to her own system. Even so, I was envied by my colleagues, who had no typists at all. The story goes that the candidates for typing were picked on early trains, brought to offices, and hired if they could only change a typewriter ribbon. Having obtained their personnel, chiefs of the offices fought to get assignments and battled for budgets to cover increased activities.

In my agency I found complete unawareness that the Axis planned destruction of the peoples under their control. My first attempts to educate my colleagues were discouraging. They were only politely interested. They were absorbed by their own assignments and were masters at switching the discussion to their personal problems. The issue I tried to bring up seemed too theoretical and even fantastic to them. "Have they already begun to implement their plans?" they would ask me. "For two years," I replied. Some answered that Washington would not believe it, and many still remembered the "atrocity stories" told about Germans in the First World War. I thought: genocide is so easy to commit because people don't want to believe it until after it happens.

I met Henry Wallace, the chairman of the board and the vice president of the United States, known throughout the country for his experiments in cross-breeding corn.[1] The cornfields of Iowa seemed to cling to him in all gatherings in the capital. His movements were angular, as if he had not yet fully emerged from the half-dreaming contemplation in which a field farmer is continually held by nature. A farmer never becomes a purely cerebral and extrovert type; there are too many mysterious forces in nature to permit him glib abstraction.

My friends advised me to discuss my forebodings with Mr. Wallace. As I talked with him for the first time, across a huge desk in his office in the Senate Building, I sized him up. I decided to go slowly. So I talked about the TVA Project that I saw in Tennessee. This project consisted of building a huge dam that provided electrical power to the adjacent agricultural settlements.[2] If nations having common rivers were to pursue common commercial exploitation of these rivers, they would be more eager to preserve peace among themselves; war would only undercut the common basis of their economy. Mr. Wallace warmed up when the word "agriculture," and our debt to the farmers of the world, were interjected into the discussion. Incidentally, I also mentioned that I was brought up on a farm and saw poverty among my own country's farmers.

With these words, I left his office. I dined later with Mr. Wallace in the house of a friend, and I tried to introduce his mind to my idea, but I could not penetrate the friendly fog of his lonely dreams that evening. I talked with Mr. Wallace on several other occasions. I explained my idea. I looked hopefully for a reaction. There was none. It suddenly dawned on me that these conversations were futile. Where in nature could he find such cruelty as we find in men? The earth is not destructive, but man has chosen martyrdom as his blinding guide. How could he believe in the finality of genocide, this man whose spirit was so deeply rooted in the perpetual regeneration of life in the fields?

I confided to a friend that I would like to approach President Roosevelt. The reply came quickly. I was asked to write a memorandum of one page. The president promised to give it his attention. For several days I worked on this one page. The first draft appeared good to me, but it sounded too flat, like a statement by an accountant. Clarity and fire were required, and it did not have enough of either. This one page for my idea was like the bed of Procrustes to me. How could I compress the pain of millions, the fear of nations, the hope for salvation from death onto one page? I suggested in this page the adoption of a treaty to make genocide a crime, the crime of crimes, that would have to be adopted by the nations of the world. Such a treaty would take the life of nations out of the hands of politicians and give it the objective basis of law. A declaration, which would later be questioned as a mere expression of hope, did not seem sufficient to me. It would lack the solid foundation of an international commitment. I was urging speed. It was still possible to save at least a part of the people. The Allies still had access to the parliaments of most nations. A treaty branding genocide a crime could still be enacted and applied by many governments. A warning had to be issued to Hitler concomitantly with the treaty.

The warning would state that the protection of the very existence of nations and races was the Allies' main aim. The demand for the rule of law should not be a mere propaganda slogan. To have ethical and political force, the rule of law must be given content in accordance with grim reality. How could the restoration of the rule of law be taken seriously when the destruction of nations and races and religious groups was not yet established as a crime under the law of nations?

I gave the page to my friend, who promised to give it to the president. The hours of waiting were agonizingly slow. Several weeks later my phone rang. My friend came running to my office: the president replied that he is aware of the danger but that he sees difficulties in adopting a treaty now. He urges patience. A warning will be issued later. Patience again. Was anybody in Washington able to use the magic eye of his soul and send over the ocean a warm look at the emaciated faces of the millions awaiting death? "Patience" is a good word for when one expects an appointment, a budgetary allocation, or the building of a road. But when the rope is already around the neck of the victim and strangulation is imminent, isn't the word "patience" an insult to reason and nature?

I was leaving the corridors of my office on Constitution Avenue. At that time of day, the cars moved slowly, as if at a funeral, it seemed to me. There were so many, and people wanted to get to their suburban homes for drinks and relaxation before dinner. My friends picked me up in their car. I sat silently and saw myself as in a procession of mourners, following the bodies of dead millions. I thought of a funeral of nations, but how strange that I was among both the mourners and the dead. How strange to feel the body alive while the soul was being carried to the grave. This was a conflict not between the Jewish people and the German, but between the world and itself.

That night I realized that I was following the wrong path. In a matter of such magnitude, where the lives of entire nations are involved, I should not rely on statesmen alone. Statesmen were messing up the world, and when it seemed to them that they were drowning in the mud of their own making, they rushed to extricate themselves. They lived in perpetual sin with history. But the people are different. In a democracy they are supposed to make the final decisions. At that time I had spent only a little more than a year in America, and I did not realize that this was true especially of this country. It became clear to me that I must appeal directly to the American people. But how?

On the dresser in a corner of my room were my valises, piled with documents on Nazi decrees of occupation with notes on every country. I had brought some of them from Stockholm, some I found in the Library of Congress, some were already included in my paper of 1941 before the American Bar Association, "Totalitarian Control over Foreign Economies."[3] All over Europe the Nazis were writing the book of death with the blood of my brethren. Let me now tell this story to the American people, to the man in the street, in church, on the porches of their houses, and in their kitchens and drawing rooms. I was sure they would understand me. I spent three days writing an outline. It consisted of an analysis of Axis rule in different fields, such as administration, law, economics, and the labor plan. Every American, I thought, will say, "I am from Missouri, show it to me." I will publish the decrees spreading death over Europe as an annex to this book. They will have no choice but to believe. The recognition of truth will cease to be a personal favor to me and become a global necessity.

After that I talked with George Finch, director of the International Law Division of the Carnegie Endowment Fund.[4] As he was reading the material while lounging in a soft chair in the sleepy Cosmos Club, I watched his face and read in it an approval of the plan of my book, even before he said yes. Finch already knew my collection of decrees of occupation, which I had submitted as reading material to the School of Military Government in Charlottesville, Virginia, that same year. He encouraged me to complete the manuscript and promised to start at once on printing the sections already finished. I worked feverishly.

The picture of the destruction of peoples peered at me frighteningly from the old and new material. Reports reaching Washington detailed the amount of calories allocated to peoples in different occupied countries. The Poles and the Jews were at the bottom of the list. Jews were walking skeletons in the streets. They were the ghosts of fairy tales come to life. Rumors ran through Washington that mass executions were taking place all over Europe, that the Jews were being deported for annihilation. But nobody could lay his hands on such reports. Were they being suppressed? The rumors kept recurring with ever greater intensity.

The impression of a tremendous conspiracy of silence poisoned the air. There was no escape from this feeling. No explanation of such a conspiracy was morally possible. A double murder was taking place. Were the Allies refusing to make it known that the execution of nations and races had already begun? Since time immemorial it had been customary that the fact of murder be denounced by the community. Even the most obscure and savage tribe would take immediate notice of a homicide. The red symbol of blood would make a savage tell his indignations to his fellows or to the stars. The ban of silence, if any, was placed on the lips of the condemned man.

The silence of murder started the day the first reports of mass executions reached London from Warsaw late in 1942.[5] It lasted until December 1944, almost two years. No acknowledgment was made of the death of a nation that had given the world the belief in one God, whose Bible was still read every Sunday in the Allies' churches. It was the murder of the truth: suppression of the notice of murder. In a way it was disrespect of death, which has its own dignity in the natural cycle of life.

My nights turned into nightmares. Dreams came incessantly and compellingly. Visions of my parents in these dreams became very realistic. I saw the interior of a train. A drab light was falling on people sitting on the floor. Among them was my mother, stony-faced, her eyes saying nothing, her mouth silent as ice. Where was she going? Was it her last journey?

In the midst of this turmoil I wrote feverishly. My health was deteriorating. Friends made an appointment for me to see a doctor. "Nervous exhaustion, high blood pressure. Slow down, rest, relax."

"And above all, don't worry," I heard him say, as if he were miles away.

I was embarking on a new crusade. But now I knew that my health was not going to be a reliable companion in arms.

CHAPTER EIGHT

The Birth of the Convention

THE NUREMBERG JUDGMENT only partly relieved the world's moral tensions. Punishing the German war criminals created the feeling that, in international life as in civil society, crime should not be allowed to pay. But the purely juridical consequences of the trials were wholly insufficient. The quarrels and other follies of the Allies, which permitted Hitler to grow and become strong, survived these proceedings and found expression in the Nuremberg Tribunal's refusal to establish a precedent against this type of international crime. The Allies decided their case against a past Hitler but refused to envisage future Hitlers. They did not want to, or could not, establish a rule of international law that would prevent and punish future crimes of the same type.

Genocide was included in the indictment of the war criminals in London in August 1945 as a war crime.[1] The Tribunal had thrown out this charge. It declared that it was bound by the Statute of the International Military Tribunal, which did not contain the charge of genocide. The Tribunal said, in fact, in its opinion as follows: "The Tribunal recognized in advance the superiority of a document signed by the Prosecution." The statute that created the legal framework of the Tribunal was signed by the chief prosecutor of the Allies on August 8, 1945.

It could be that this timidity in establishing future rules of international law is due to the Tribunal's military origins. It could not step outside its military limitations and the authority given to it by its founding document. Maybe members of the military tribunals asked themselves, with appropriate humility: How can we, a military institution dealing with a concrete war situation, promulgate principles for the behavior of the civilian world in times of peace? Maybe they also thought: The essence of democracy is civilian control of the military, and not vice versa.

The judgment of the International Military Tribunal can be reduced to the following points:

1) The German war criminals were punished for planning and waging a war of aggression.

2) They were punished for certain war crimes or crimes committed during the war on the civilian population of occupied countries.

3) They were punished for certain crimes committed against a civilian population during a war of aggression. These were called "crimes against humanity" and were made punishable only when they were committed in connection with other crimes that were subject to the jurisdiction of the Tribunal, namely crimes against peace, and war crimes.

In brief, the Germans were punished only for crimes committed during or in connection with the war of aggression. Crimes against humanity were not an independent category in themselves. They were considered crimes only when their connection with other crimes could be established. Thus, in order to punish someone for crimes against humanity, the following elements were necessary:

1) A crime against humanity had to be proven.

2) A crime against peace or a war crime had to be proven.

3) A connection between the concrete plan against humanity on the one hand and crimes against peace or a war crime had to be established.

4) All these elements had to materialize in the course of an aggressive war and not a defensive war.

5) War of aggression was not defined.

No precedent applicable to crimes committed in a defensive war or in peacetime could be found in the judgment. Still, one should note that nations that are attacked may also commit crimes against a civilian population. But on this point, the Tribunal was silent. This was in brief the legal situation after Nuremberg.

About six months before the Nuremberg Tribunal issued its verdict, I published several articles on genocide in *The American Scholar* in New York, in the *Belgium Review of Penal Law and Criminology*, and in the Norwegian magazine *Samitisen* (Modern Times). I attached to this article a list of points that outlined the workings of the Genocide Treaty through the U.N. It appeared to me that machinery for protecting national, racial, religious, and ethnic groups must be established through the world body. I sincerely believed that a modification of the proposal I had made in Madrid in 1933 could be enforced through the U.N. But I still hoped that the Nuremberg Tribunal would issue a verdict that could at least have some limited use as a precedent for bringing up the issue of a Genocide Convention in the U.N. This was the reason I went to Nuremberg in May 1946.

Even my most modest expectations were thwarted. I had to appeal directly to the U.N. In October 1946, I was sitting in the office of Otto Tolischus at the *New York Times*.[2] I told him the story of my hopes, disappointments, and plans. "Go ahead," he replied. "We are interested and will help." Eugene Meyer and Alan Barth of the *Washington Post* were close friends and well informed about the issue.[3] The *Washington Post* was the first paper in the world to write an editorial on genocide, on December 3, 1945.[4] I knew I could count on their support. Then I paid a visit to the *Herald Tribune*.

Time was short and I had to move fast. I knew that I could hardly count on the great powers to introduce the resolution to the U.N. Their agenda for the General Assembly was made up well in advance, and I could not lose time on policy changing decisions. Moreover, the nations would have to examine such a proposal from many angles, which might be and often were in conflict. I turned my mind to the small nations, thinking first of Norway. Armed with my book *Axis Rule in Occupied Europe* and with the opinion of the Nuremberg Tribunal, I sat in the lounge of one of the New York hotels and discussed the matter with Professor Frede Castberg, a member of the Norwegian delegation.[5]

As a professor of international law, he saw the issue clearly, but the timing was not favorable. He had to refer the issue to Oslo, and by the time he received an answer it might be too late to insert the item in the agenda. But Castberg told me that if some other delegation would propose to include it on the agenda, the Norwegian delegation would favor it.

I looked through the windows of a U.N. car at the Long Island landscape as it was undressing itself of its colors and leaves for the bleaching tonality of November. It was drizzling. Uncertainty was in the air and my excitement mounted. There was a great deal of animation in the corridors and in the Delegates' Lounge. This was the first regular session of the General Assembly. The general mood was favorable. The statesmen felt as if they owed an apology to the world for the holocaust [*sic*], and for past follies, frustrations, and the many crimes committed. There was an accumulation of constructive energies, which always follow a destructive period in international life. If there was not open enthusiasm, one could sense a latent open-mindedness about humanitarian issues.

I have always been able to sense the mood of an environment with all the elements of my personality. This was especially true this time, when so much depended on this fluctuation of collective feelings and on receptiveness to ideas. In brief, I felt the statesmen would listen. The main thing would be to find the right people. I would put my little boat under the favorable wind, which would carry me to the open sea of world affairs. I told myself, "In hoc signo vinces." In this sign, you will vanquish, Raphael Lemkin.

A friend introduced me to a young man who worked in the Secretariat, and he told me about the solidarity among the Latin American delegations. This led me to the conclusion that at least one of the sponsors should come from the Latin American delegations, which boasted an imposing membership of twenty-one states. My plan was to combine the support of a Latin American republic with that of a nation in Asia, which would attract through its culture and world position many other nations of the East. I will make a "marriage" between the West and the East for the sake of this resolution. If it was possible to create such a combination, the European delegations could not refuse to follow, especially after the recent holocaust. The nations of Africa, on whom genocide was practiced, would be very receptive. The Allies of the recent war would have to say yes, because they could not afford to be led but must themselves lead.

This was the plan in its entirety, and I started on it as rapidly as I could. First I wrote a draft resolution on the soft sofa in the Delegates' Lounge. Then I let it be mimeographed by the U.N. because it is easier to talk about a draft proposal with the document before one's eyes. The draft resolution modestly asked the U.N. to study genocide with the view of establishing it as an international crime, like piracy, trade in children, and slavery. I stressed that genocide had happened throughout history and inflicted great losses on mankind and culture. I thought the draft should not demand too much, so that the delegations might make it stronger. The main thing is not to frighten by too-bold demands.

When the resolution was ready I approached the smallest Latin American delegation, headed by Mr. Ricardo Alfaro, the minister of foreign affairs and former president of Panama.[6] Alfaro had a great name among international lawyers and liked a good fight for an idea. I told him where the Nuremberg Tribunal had left the idea, showed him my book *Axis Rule in Occupied Europe*, and gave him a reprint of my article on genocide from *The American Scholar*. He asked for twenty-four hours to study the material and made an appointment with me the next day in the Delegates' Lounge. With a smile that brought heaven and earth together for me, he signed the resolution and wished me luck.

The next country to be approached was Cuba. Its delegation was headed by Ambassador Belt, a man with a razor-sharp mind and a vivid imagination.[7] He called genocide a powerful concept and signed the resolution the next day.

In the Delegates' Lounge, I saw Mrs. Corbett Ashby, the former president of the World Alliance of Women, whom I knew from London.[8] She was enthusiastic about my idea.

With two Latin American signatures in hand I had the bold plan of obtaining the signature of India. This appeared natural to Mrs. Corbett Ashby. "Let us see Mrs. Pandit, the chairman of the delegation of India," she said.[9] We found her in a corner of the lounge surrounded by several grave-looking Hindu gentlemen. Indians, especially the older ones, always look to me as if they have just finished a conversation with eternity and are about to begin another. They look so only because they have their feet firmly on the ground and use their tremendous intuition to penetrate the present quickly.

Madame Pandit introduced me to a former judge and member of the parliament. I briefly explained my formula for the unity of mankind in diversity and the rule of law for the protection of national, racial, and religious groups against destruction. Through this protection, groups are permitted to exist and mankind is enriched—like a universal concert in which every nation plays its part.

"We in India live by this principle," she said. "We are many races and creeds. Still we have the concept of oneness. Our philosophers preached it, Gandhi worked for it. I will be glad to propose that our delegation act as one of the sponsors." As soon as Madame Pandit signed the resolution I rushed to the secretary general's office and deposited the document.

I was like an intoxicated man. There was not any time for contemplation. Action was required, deliberate, well-prepared, unfolding at one end and logically serving the following steps. I visited the newspaper correspondents in the U.N., and favorable reports began to appear in the press.

I had the ambition that in the steering committee the United States should propose that the genocide item be included on the agenda. The traditional help and concern of the United States for the peoples of the world, I thought, predestined America for this role. This country was settled by persons escaping persecution abroad. At the beginning of the present century, John Gray, the secretary of state of the United States, issued instructions to the U.S. minister in Romania to protest the persecution of minorities there.[10] He formulated his request beautifully and impressively: "This country cannot be a silent party to an 'international wrong.'" In 1910, William Howard Taft, president of the United States, denounced a trade agreement with the Russian tsar because of religious persecution.[11] U.S. leadership on the genocide issue thus made sense. I mentioned this to Adlai Stevenson.[12] A telegram was sent to Ambassador Austin urging him to propose the inclusion of the genocide issue in the steering committee. I knew that Austin was a deeply religious man.[13]

Congresswoman Helen Gahagan Douglas was a member of the United States delegation.[14] I had known her since 1945, when she was a member of the foreign affairs committee, before which I testified on the genocide issue. It was she who introduced me to Adlai Stevenson, who served as advisor to the delegation. Stevenson asked for literature. The next day we discussed the matter again, and he told me that he hoped that the United States would propose adding the genocide proposal to the agenda. An editorial promised by Otto Tolischus soon appeared in the *New York Times*.[15]

Mrs. Corbett Ashby was happy about these developments and organized a private gathering of women from many countries to visit the first session of the United Nations. This was the beginning of a fruitful cooperation with the women's organizations of the world on the issue of genocide. In this connection I met with two prominent women: Frances Perkins, who had been head of the Civil Service Commission in the Roosevelt Administration,[16] and Dr. Hanna Rydh, a Swedish archaeologist who was president of the World Women's Alliance.[17] Miss Perkins was clever and kind and wanted to extend her kindness to more people. This is, by and large, the personal creed of every American, especially of women in public life. Rydh traveled the world over, participated in excavations, and described them not only to adults but also to children. She ignited children's imaginations with the history of mankind and created in them a love for archeology. The history of genocide, especially in antiquity, is written in the pages of archeology. The murder of civilizations was not yet a fully told story. The impact of the concept of genocide could be greatly enriched if the cultural losses that occurred through assassination of civilizations could be brought before the eyes of the world. Of special educational value apparent to me are Dr. Rydh's books for children. Children start their education from the eyes, after which comes the education of the mind. If the children of the world can visualize, through pictures of excavations, the scope of assassination of civilizations through genocide, they might retain this in their memory and later be open to a richer understanding of the variety and value of human cultures. Dr. Rydh's enthusiasm for the issue of genocide was based not only on humanitarian considerations but on the craving of a generous mind for new vistas in scientific inquiry.

At this juncture I ought to state in all objectivity that in 1945 and in subsequent years the contribution of individual women and of women's organizations to the issue of genocide was considerable. There were many reasons for this. Women in general participate to a lesser degree in violence than men; they are more ready to oppose violence. As the creators and protectors, they guide men in their first steps in the world. They instill and develop moral feelings. They are children's first judges. Unknowingly, they are the creators of moral philosophy for the benefit of every human being.

After I had explained the issue, two Czechoslovakian women spoke: the deputy mayor of Prague, Madame Palantova, and a young resistance leader named Madame Walfora. They described in detail before these women how they were tortured under the occupation. This gathering decided to send one woman back to her delegation with a request for support of the genocide proposal. Within a few days I noticed growing interest among the delegates. I made contacts with the legal department of the U.K. and was assured of the interest of its more prominent members.

I felt that every step was constructive, every initiative well received. A hint of holy-like achievement entered me, for which I had been waiting for so long. My soul was frustrated through so many ordeals and setbacks, and so much indifference, hopelessness, thoughtlessness, and even cruelty. Now I had finally a chance to act. I did not realize fully that I was entering a new road.

The day of the steering committee meeting arrived. This committee consisted of the president and vice president of the Assembly and of the six committee chairmen. It is considered powerful because it approves the agenda of the Assembly. The president of the legal committee was Roberto, ambassador of Panama in Argentina. He had high hopes and assured me of the item's approval. He talked with friendly chairmen of other committees. When the item of genocide was reached, Adlai Stevenson asked for the floor and proposed in the name of the United States of America that this item be included in the agenda. But the Russian delegate opposed. I had expected unanimity, and this was a surprise to me. Most delegates supported the inclusion, and it was finally adopted.

I tried to understand why the Russian delegate kept saying in the steering committee, "*Eto ne nyzno*—it is not necessary." There was no other word of explanation. They must have had something on their mind. I tried to piece together my conversations with the Russians in Nuremberg, with the judge and prosecution. They listened then with considerable interest, even warmth, but nothing happened on genocide. Already in Nuremberg I was hearing rumors that after reoccupation of the Crimea and the Northern Caucasus the Russians had discovered that some of the people there had collaborated with the Germans, and that some of them were executed or transported to Siberia. Was this the reason for the Russian delegation's opposition?

The resolutions of the steering committee have to be approved by the General Assembly. I wanted to prevent the item from being controversial and facing another fight in the Assembly. The same evening, I called on Jan Masaryk, the Czech minister of foreign affairs.[18] We sat on a green plush sofa in his suite in the Carlyle Hotel. He was cheerful and warm, his brown eyes smiling straight into the bottom of my soul.

"The Russians have opposed the inclusion of the genocide item on the agenda of the Assembly, your Excellency." "I am sorry to hear it, but what can I do about it?" I suspected that the Czechoslovaks could be influenced by the Russians, but not vice versa. I had known the Masaryk family and it was still 1946, a little more than one year after Hitler's ovens, and little more than one month since the Nuremberg Judgment was handed down. "Your Excellency, I have studied the writings of your father, Professor Tomáš Garrigue Masaryk, who devoted his life to explaining the cultural personality of nations, not only to his own people but to the world at large.[19] When a nation is murdered, its culture goes too. The dead cannot write literature. Through its culture, the life of a nation continues, when the physical life of individual members is finished.

"If your father were alive, he would be fighting now for the Genocide Convention. I appeal now to his son, who is a continuation of the spirit of his father. Tell me first that you believe in this idea, that you are ready to fight for it. Then I will make certain suggestions."

"Of course I believe in this idea. I was very close to my father. We had our Lidice massacre; one does not forget these things easily."

"The Russians had Babi Yar and many other massacres. The blood of their children was removed from their veins to the last drop to provide blood for the wounded Nazi soldiers. The heart of all Slavic peoples is still moaning. The voices of the tortured are still trembling in the air. They complain to history. Nobody can escape its judgment."

"You are making a sermon. Better tell me instead what I should say, in your opinion."

"I am making a sermon to Vishinsky through you.[20] You do not need any sermons, Excellency. I think you should speak with Vishinsky. As the minister of foreign affairs, he should be able to understand that a Genocide Convention could not be considered an intrigue against the Soviet Union."

Then I added: "Both you and Vishinsky have a sense of humor. Why not tell him that penicillin is not an intrigue against the Soviet Union."

Masaryk took out his notebook and under the date of the next day inscribed: Vishinsky. Genocide. Penicillin. After showing me this note, he told me: "Give me your phone number. I will call you tomorrow in the early afternoon." He called and told me that he had already talked with Vishinsky and obtained a promise to support the Genocide Convention. In fact, in the 1946 Assembly, Russia cooperated fully and even made fiery speeches supporting the convention.

The Belgian minister of foreign affairs, Paul Spaak, presided over the Assembly meeting when it adopted, without one word of discussion, the resolution to include the item on genocide.[21]

The next step was to prepare for the meeting of the legal committee. Again I distributed among the delegates copies of my book *Axis Rule in Occupied Europe* and reprints from my articles on genocide in *The American Scholar,* as well as a pamphlet in French published by the French Ministry of Information. I gave copies to Monsieur Parodi, the secretary general of foreign affairs, and to Professor Henri Chaumont, the delegate of France.[22] Monsieur Parodi told me the next day that the French delegation was in agreement with the proposal, and added, "This is understandable, *n'est ce pas?*"

In the Delegates' Lounge I had a talk with the British secretary of state for foreign affairs, a professor of political science at the London School of Economics. He told me that he read my book during the war, that he shared my ideas, and that he hoped for the best outcome for the Assembly. The United Kingdom representative on the legal committee was the Attorney General, Sir Hartley Shawcross.[23] I had luncheon with him and we discussed the issue thoroughly. Sir Hartley used to come to the Nuremberg Trials for the more representative functions. The main work for the prosecutor for the United Kingdom in Nuremberg was done by a small and very efficient staff under Sir Maxwell Fyfe, later the house minister of the Conservative government. A brilliant jurist, he also wrote poetry. He was warm and imaginative and saw the value of the new concept.

Then I turned to Ernesto Dihigo, Cuba's delegate on the legal committee.[24] Cuba was a cosponsor of the resolution, and Mr. Dihigo intended to introduce it to the legal committee. Dihigo was learned, idealistic, and clever. The discussion started off well. After he introduced the issue the representative of India, which was another sponsor, took the floor. His eloquence, judicial leaning, and, last but not least, his Oxford accent made an impression.

Sir Hartley was at his best. "Let us not act like small-town lawyers," he pleaded. "Let us outlaw genocide now." Charles Fahy, the delegate of the United States and legal advisor to the U.S. State Department, declared that the United States "feels strongly about genocide."[25] The jurists were swimming in the sea of humanitarian enthusiasm. They were trying to outdo one another, and there were some sixty of them. The discussion promised to last some time.

One day in the Delegates' Lounge, an olive-faced, bespectacled man, tall and angular, handed me my book and asked me whether I was Raphael Lemkin, the author of *Axis Rule in Occupied Europe*, in which he had read about genocide. He told me with great simplicity that he had heard that I was in Washington and went there especially to meet me. At the Carnegie Endowment he was given information about me by George Finch, the director of the International Law Division.

"I am Judge Riad of Egypt. I am an advisor to the King of Saudi Arabia and a delegate to the legal committee." He must have been a lonely man who spent a great part of his life in thinking. Such people can be recognized when they walk. They do not integrate into their environment either physically or spiritually. When they walk, they appear to belong not here but elsewhere. Our conversation displayed in this man a treasure of knowledge, imagination, feelings, and wisdom. It was as if he had been waiting for this generous wind for many lonely years.

"The resolution in the legal committee must expressly demand the preparation of a treaty or convention against genocide. It is a beautiful concept. It is something worth living for. The word 'genocide' has so much appeal, so much force. I congratulate you warmly," he said, and his eyes shone. I knew that he cared about it more than anybody else in this building. I was beginning to have formal success, but Judge Riad gave me the first expression of spiritual congeniality. Through him I understood the scope of spirituality of the Arab mind: the Avicennas, the Ibn Rushds.[26] Devouring books and transforming each of them into a firmament of stars. Every thought a star and reality. The intensity of thinking and integration is tremendous. The feeling of responsibility and cultural sharing is limitless, and the observation capacity is great indeed. Above all that flies a lovely soul which loves mankind and is therefore lonely. Its universal interests, the encyclopedic knowledge, and the ability to learn still more, the belief in a cultural creation, is a special revelation of the human spirit. I learned to admire the complete equality in the treatment of cultures, in which they excelled over the intellectuals of Europe. They were more integrated in their cultural ideals than were many intellectuals of other nations. With these qualities in mind it was easier for me to understand the golden period of cultural and religious tolerance that adorned the tenth through the thirteenth centuries of the rule of the caliphs in Spain, and which has no equal in history. For tolerance based on religious and cultural indifference and weakening of beliefs, as we can see it in modern times, is not the real test. The Arab caliphs permitted themselves at that period a leap into the loving human conscience, which created a spiritual federation of minds and souls. Judge Riad believed that the real spiritual values of any period are never lost. "To a certain extent, if we work for it, we can only make this period live again through the Genocide Convention," he said without sentimentality, and his angular figure disappeared down the long corridor of the U.N., leaving a great void beside me.

Judge Riad became the spokesman for the Genocide Convention in the Arab world. He explained the concept and made impassioned pleas for the resolution and for the convention. He knew the great receptivity of the Arab mind. He knew its workings. He laid the foundations for this work, which found at every Assembly a generous spokesman for the Arab world.

A special subcommittee of the legal committee was set up to prepare the text on the resolution on genocide. Charles Fahy, the United States delegate, was the chairman, and the delegate of Chile was the rapporteur. The rapporteur was interested in the problem and was also a good draftsman. In the course of the subcommittee's deliberations, an attempt was made to delete the word "genocide" and to replace it with "extermination." Judge Riad pleaded: "A term is progress. This term describes the action, 'cide,' to destroy—and describes the subject which is destroyed, 'the genos.' Extermination can refer also to insects and animals. Extermination would limit the concept in scope of action. To exterminate a group means to kill all members of the group to the last. A group can be destroyed as a group even when the members are not all destroyed, but when the cultural identity is replaced by another one. This is the case when children are taken by force to another cultural group."

Judge Riad pleaded beautifully and eventually won. It was decided to preserve the term "genocide," but I realized how close I came to losing this fight. The subcommittee decided to include in the resolution a declaration that genocide is a crime under international law, a condemnation of this crime by all civilized nations, to prepare a convention on the prevention and punishment of the crime of genocide, and to present this resolution to the next Assembly.

One morning copies of this resolution were lying on the desks of all delegates of the legal committee. There was a solemn mood in the chamber as the delegates started to assemble. Genocide was the first item on the agenda. The chairman beat the gavel, and my heart started to beat too. The discussion was not too long. A feeling of accomplishment was visible on all faces. Some statements followed. It was voted unanimously. Several days later the resolution was approved unanimously by the General Assembly.

The first stage of the birth pangs of the Genocide Convention was over. I received congratulations from delegates, from friends in the United States, and from many parts of the world. Editorials, feature stories, radio broadcasts followed. The world knew what had happened, but it hardly knew how much more would be required before the convention was a reality, and how tremendous the opposition would be.

Now that the groundwork was laid, I could rest for a while. I said to myself, "It was not too difficult, was it?" When one finds oneself on the top of a mountain one is prone to forget the pain of climbing every step. But this was not the least of my worries. The fact is that the rain of my work fell on a fallow plain, only this rain was a mixture of the blood and tears of eight million innocent people throughout the world. Included also were the tears of my parents and my friends.

CHAPTER NINE

Geneva, 1948

ONE MORNING IN JULY 1948 I arrived at my office at Yale Law School and found a cable on my desk. Ambassador Perez Perozo, the Venezuelan delegate to the U.N., attending the session of the Economic and Social Council in Geneva, was writing to say that the council would take up the report on genocide.[1] The council's approval of the Genocide Convention would help its adoption by the General Assembly, scheduled to meet in Paris in September. It was clear that I had to go to Geneva at once. Every action at the U.N. must be prepared. One must know the distribution of sympathies and animosities in advance in order to get favorable results. I cast a melancholy glance at a page of my manuscript, interrupted by fatigue last night, on the destruction of the Moors in Spain. It was a shame to interrupt this work just when I was gaining insight into the atmosphere of this most intriguing epoch, which ended so tragically.

Through the open window an old oak tree, planted some fifty years ago in the Yale garden, looked quite indifferently at my disturbance. But the decision was made, not so much by me as by something inside me. Perhaps the Moors had in fact influenced my decision. I asked my secretary to attend to all traveling formalities. It was impossible to return before the end of the Assembly, sometime in the middle of December.

My chapters on genocide had to be submitted to the delegates either in the Economic and Social Council or in the General Assembly. Historical cases of genocide must be communicated to those who would decide the fate of the Genocide Convention. Let history make a plea to them. As a spokesman for the convention I must be strengthened by the voice of the past. Reading and rereading these cases of genocide always made me more articulate and determined. It had sustained me in the past, and I would use it again in Geneva and Paris.

Several days later I watched the lights of Geneva from the descending plane. I had not been here since 1938. A strange feeling enveloped me. In this city I had buried the hopes for a better world in the sentimental and confusing days of the old League of Nations. Here I had talked for days and nights to the perplexed minds of men who could not stir themselves into action to save the people of the world. Now I was going to the same city, to the same people, with the same type of plea. But, I said to myself, I might be better equipped now because the "voice of history" was in my valise. The blood of the victims of the last cases of genocide had not yet dried on the face of Europe and Asia.

The next morning while sipping a cup of chocolate and nibbling a croissant in the Hôtel Métropol, I saw Lake Leman and her big brother, the Mont Blanc, and felt more reassured. There was deep peace in that sight. There was also so much concentration, regularity, and steadfastness in the walk of the Swiss that it could not but help to communicate itself to me. Where do these people derive their strength? Does it come from their mountains, or from their concept of neutrality?

Soon I was walking through the corridors of the old League of Nations looking for the chambers of the Economic and Social Council. The same corridors, with less business and less-crowded elevators, with fewer officials running through the hallways. Symbolically, this building contains only a sideline of the activities of the U.N. It serves as a reminder of past errors and frustration and seems to echo with the speeches of the statesmen of the defunct League. A cultured cemetery of a dead world. Where are the lions of the League now? Where are Paul-Boncour, de Valera, the former presidents of the Assembly? Where are Politis, Venizelos, Sir Robert Cecil, Titulescu, Litvinov?[2]

Although I felt so much wrapped up in the present I could not escape these melancholy memories. Perhaps because of these I was feeling the inherent elements of destruction and rebirth that follow man at all times. The king is dead, long live the king. The League of Nations has gone; here is the United Nations. I would not have these thoughts in New York, but I could not escape them in Geneva.

In the chambers of the Economic and Social Council I met Ambassador Perez Perozo and other delegates to the council. Hastily I looked over the list of delegates with the ever-present questions in my mind: Who will be for, who will be against, and who does not care either way? Somehow I felt that something good might happen. The new surroundings gave me a new surge of energy and even aggressiveness. I made cautious overtures: The genocide draft? Oh yes, it is on the agenda. But the majority did not seem particularly interested. There were still two or three weeks before the council would take up the Genocide Convention. There was considerable time for planning and action. Some new friends must be found. New avenues for alerting public opinion must be sought.

While lunching on the terrace of the Palais des Nations, facing Mont Blanc with the sun smiling in my thick Swiss soup, I hastily made plans for action in Geneva.

I decided to go to see my friends at the Headquarters of the World Association for the U.N. Major John Ennals, the general secretary, was an old friend and a good fighter.[3] He might have some ideas: the Swiss press was not exposed yet to the Genocide Convention. It occurred to me that the delegates, away from home, were more lonely here than in New York and might have more time to listen to me. I might call on some of them in their hotels and talk about philosophy, art, music, Switzerland, and finally we were bound to come to the topic of genocide. And this happened.

I called on Ambassador Gilberto Amado, whom I had known for several years.[4] Amado always lived several lives. He was a professor of criminal law, a famous Brazilian novelist, and a connoisseur of good food and French wine who spoke freely and entertainingly about many subjects. Last year Pearl Buck had shown me a letter from him in which he answered her inquiries about the Genocide Convention.[5] "Lemkin," he wrote, "is a generous fanatic but we like his ideas and we are supporting them."

When I walked into his room in Hotel de la Paix, his square and full face was all smiles. Since he had a very short neck, it seemed as if his entire body was smiling. I was determined not to talk about genocide this time. I asked him about the novel he was writing. This produced a new wave of smiles and a fascinating story about a woman who was in love with a man whom she kissed by endlessly extending her lower lip. Amado called it the "long kiss," which is especially peculiar to Oriental women who engulf their man in a kiss. Since we were both professors, we mildly criticized a new book by another professor. Amado asked me what would happen to the Genocide Convention at this session of the Economic and Social Council. "Well, Mr. Ambassador," I replied, "that is for you to decide. Latin America is the reservoir of active humanitarianism. This is an issue which is very congenial to the Latin American delegates and I hope they will put up another fight." "We will see," he said. "We will have to sound out our friends." Rapidly I changed the subject, and after we had discussed Swiss food and French wine for a while, I closed my first visit.

The next day I visited the World Federation of the United Nations Associations. Major Ennals led me with an embarrassed friendliness from room to room. The Villa Rigot, which was donated to this association, was, to say the least, in a very bad shape. The walls were literally crumbling, and every visitor was cautioned on which chair he should not sit, through which door he should walk carefully, and through which he should not walk at all. Nevertheless, I was told, visitors would often lean against the wrong wall and suddenly find themselves in the world of the beyond, consisting of old chairs, piled-up boxes, and broken glass from which they would have to be rescued with considerable damage to their clothes and body. But spirits were high and the sense of intellectual adventure, even if mixed with occasional martyrdom, prevailed and helped to further the "aims and purposes" of the U.N. Everybody lived for and believed in his work, and even the secretaries did not mind being underpaid as long as they could type on the stationery of the association and meet interesting people from all corners of the world. Here I met the known Egyptian journalist who later became Egypt's ambassador to the U.N., Dr. Azmi, and the young Alaoui, a correspondent from Morocco, chief of the press to the king of Morocco.[6]

We went into the garden, which was the safest part of this institution, and sat on a bench, under a tree, in a lonely corner. It was nice and cool, and here I poured my theory into the ears of my captive audience. Azmi was a man who is credited with coining an Arabic name for culture. He proved to be interested in the development of concepts and in the coinage of new words. The term "genocide" intrigued him as much as his own creation in the Arabic language. He was a profound scholar. We discussed our two newly created words, in context with the ancient Egyptian theory that words precede things. "Words," said Azmi, "bring order into a system of thought." "Yes," I replied, "they help to crystallize our thinking. They become symbols for action, they are rallying points for past human experiences and a program for the future."

Alaoui listened attentively. He took out his notebook and asked whether I would mind if he wrote up our conversation as an interview for his paper in Morocco. I readily agreed. The issue is very simple and it can be better understood as an example of genocide perpetrated against the smallest nation. When Alaoui came to New York in 1957 as chief of the press for the king of Morocco, he repeated this conversation word for word while introducing me to members of the king's party. "Take, for example," I said, "a nation like Iceland, which consists of some hundred and eighty-eight thousand persons. This small nation has an original culture and defends it stubbornly and consistently; it has its own language, its own theater, four political parties, and a newspaper for every one of them. It has a very old Bible in its university library which I saw during my visit to Reykjavik. It has also one of the world's oldest parliamentary bodies, the Allthing. Suppose somebody decides to commit genocide on the Icelanders. Together with the 188,000 persons, an original culture would disappear from the world forever. A culture cannot be re-created artificially, like synthetic rubber. Practically then, genocide of a nation means the destruction also of its culture; it means, also, the impoverishing of world civilization."[7]

"Yes," added Azmi, "through genocide you have created a concept for the protection not only of the physical bodies but also of the collective minds of nations." With Ambassador Azmi I later worked on ratification of the Genocide Convention by Egypt.[8]

There were still three weeks before the Economic and Social Council would start discussing the Genocide Convention. I felt that the issue must be made important in the eyes of the delegates. Major Ennals organized two lectures on genocide: one in the building of the United Nations to which delegates were invited, the other in the summer school that the World Federation of the U.N. Associations was running for foreign students. A discussion followed each lecture. Interest was aroused by my historical examples, dating from antiquity through the middle ages to modern times. When questions were asked I did not refrain from reading aloud, in considerable detail, from my historical files. In this way I conveyed the impression that genocide is not the result of the mood of an occasional rogue ruler but a recurring pattern in history. It is like a disease that is congenital to certain situations and requires remedies. I was asked whether genocide had ever occurred in the Far East, and I quoted the case of fifty thousand Catholics who were destroyed in Japan in the seventeenth century. They were compelled to drink water until their bodies were completely bloated. Then all the openings of their bodies were closed with cement; they were made to lie down and then covered with planks, and carts with heavy loads, pulled by horses, were rolled over the planks. The bodies of the victims exploded with a strange mixture of water and blood. So perished fifty thousand Catholics.[9]

"What can you do to prevent such a thing from happening?"

"You do exactly what you do to prevent other crimes. We have to deal with this matter on two levels: national and international. Nationally, we must make it a crime in our criminal codes and punish it through national courts in the same way as we punish larceny and arson.

"On the international level," I continued, "we make every nation responsible to the world community, either by bringing up cases of genocide in the World Court of Justice in The Hague, to which all civilized nations belong, or in the U.N. The main thing is to make the nations of the world feel that minorities and weaker nations are not chickens in the hands of a farmer, to be slaughtered, but that they are groups of people of great value to themselves and to world civilization."

Although not one night passed that I did not think about the Genocide Convention and not one day elapsed when I did not do something practical for the convention, I still felt as though I were moving in a big void. I did not see around me persons with the fitting gleam in their eyes on whom I could rely. I knew that such a fight was unavoidable, and somewhere, somebody must be found who had power, imagination, and determination.

One night an unforeseen, almost miraculous event happened. I felt weary, tired, and empty. It was a windy afternoon without sunshine, with dust rising at every corner: one of those afternoons when you like nobody, neither yourself nor the world, not even the newspaperman from whom you buy the evening paper. I went to bed early but I could not sleep. I worried because I felt I was not accomplishing anything substantial, while the deadline for the discussion of the convention was looming ominously. Endlessly I turned in my bed from one side to the other. Then, suddenly, I got up and decided to dress and go out. It was 1 A.M. I crossed the little bridge on Lake Leman and stood there, looking aimlessly before me. I do not know how long I stood there without one thought in my mind.

Suddenly I heard steps behind me; I turned and in the light of the moon I recognized the delegate of Canada, Ambassador Dana Wilgress.[10]

"What are you doing here so late at night, Mr. Lemkin? Are you still worrying about the Genocide Convention?"

"At least I have an excuse for not sleeping," I replied. "What good excuse do you have for not being in bed at two o'clock at night, Mr. Ambassador?"

"I just can't sleep; it is as simple as that. I have often sleepless nights, then I go for a walk and sleep better later. Would you like to walk with me?"

"Gladly," I said. I joined the ambassador on a night stroll that carried us to many corners of the sleeping city, even to the deserted station, which was as empty as my mind had been earlier. My mind quickly started to function, however, when the ambassador asked me why I thought the convention was so important. This was my chance. Since I had never before talked as long with him, I asked him what was his main field of interest at the university. "History," he said. "And since history is endless," he added, "I am continuously reading history."

"Well," I said, "history might help us to answer the question which you asked me on the bridge, Why is the Genocide Convention so important? Genocide is an essential part of history; it follows humanity like a dark shadow from early antiquity to the present. The Assyrian kings practiced genocide on a large scale; they obliterated entire nations, sometimes for no reason other than that their victims refused to pay tribute after having been subdued. After that they themselves dictated to their scribes the most detailed descriptions of genocide they perpetrated. We are reading in these records how they boasted of having killed off the entire populations of great cities and how they drove into captivity scores of people; how they blinded, mutilated, skinned, and hanged—and all with the feeling of having fulfilled the command of their gods, who ordered them to do so in their dreams. No excuse before history ever occurred to them to be necessary."

"Do you mean," the ambassador said, "that they never considered those acts evil?"

"Not in the least. However, there were cases of genocide in antiquity when the conscience of the perpetrators became aroused and they finally refrained from committing these acts because they felt their wrong-doing."

In the empty streets of Geneva we were the only two persons walking and talking. I had my field day. I asked only that dawn not come too early. I spoke about the case of Mitylene in the fifth century BC. The people of Lesbos, of which Mitylene was the capital, rebelled against the Athenians. The Spartans were intriguing and making trouble for the Athenians, whose growing sea power they feared. The Athenians called a meeting of the Assembly to decide the fate of Mitylene. Cleon, a leather manufacturer, made a speech against Mitylene. He requested its doom. The Assembly decided to send orders to the military commander of the Athenians in Mitylene that he kill all the males and sell the women and children into slavery. The night brought better counsel. The Athenians felt that it would be too harsh to indiscriminately destroy the innocent and the guilty.

Next day another Assembly was called; another speaker by the name of Diodotus held the floor. "Anger, folly, and revenge are bad policy," he said. "We should find the guilty and punish only them. If we should bring wholesale destruction to all rebels, this would strengthen the decision of rebellious cities to hold out against us at any price."

"The higher culture of the Athenians prevailed," I told the ambassador. "After all, this was the time of Plato. The orders were reversed and new instructions were issued to punish only the guilty. Mitylene thus escaped the harsh fate of genocide through the voice of conscience strengthened by reason."

The ambassador made a sound that I thought promising; at least I understood that he approved of the new decision for life and justice. And so we reached the second bridge on Lake Leman; I was talking about the case of the Mongols, about religious genocide, and I came to speak about the Armenians. The ambassador remembered this case with many details. This gave me an occasion to change my role in the monologue. Now he was telling me about the suffering of the Armenians. Soon I knew in detail what the churches of Canada had done for the orphans in this horrible case of genocide. I let him talk, and I suddenly felt as though he was trying to win *me* over to the Genocide Convention.[11]

When I accompanied him back to his hotel he told me it would be very good for *us*, and I distinctly heard this saving phrase *"for us,"* to win the support of the future president of the Assembly in Paris. He was Wilgress's personal friend, Dr. Herbert Evatt, the minister for foreign affairs in Australia, now sleeping innocently on the third floor of the same hotel.[12]

"I will arrange an appointment for you with Dr. Evatt tomorrow morning, rather this morning—wait for my call in your hotel. And don't worry, Dr. Lemkin, this is too big a cause to be lost; it is simply a matter of getting the right people to do the right thing at the right time."

At six o'clock in the morning I entered my hotel; I plunged into the big metal Swiss bathtub and stayed there, dreamily, for a long time. I was afraid to move for fear of waking up and finding that I had only dreamed this miracle. I did not go to bed; I sat near the window and looked on as the coming day spread over Geneva holding new signs of victory for the world and for my mission.

I counted every minute until I heard the voice of Ambassador Wilgress telling me that Dr. Evatt would see me at 11 A.M. Although he did not elaborate over the phone, he gave the impression that Evatt was interested. I had met Evatt for the first time in 1947 but never had had a long conversation with him; he always struck me as a man of action rather than words. In 1947, I was already impressed with his informality, warmth, and the feeling of helpfulness he tried to convey, which could be expressed more or less as follows: "Little man, don't be afraid, nobody is dangerous here. Just stop and think and we will work it out." This was my impression of Dr. Evatt before the crucial conversation I was now to have with him in Geneva. But there was another Evatt, much more meaningful to me, whom I found sitting in a big chair in his hotel room, with his sleeves rolled up over the bushy hair on his hands and arms. He said simply: "The ambassador told me about your troubles; it must have been hard on you all these years. We will work together; I promise to conspire with you and to get the thing through in Paris." The words "conspire with you" struck me with a tremendous warmth because, indeed, we had to conspire and plan and scheme to meet opposing schemes; the adversaries must be met on their ground. I was looking for this ground and I found it. I told Dr. Evatt that the Assembly in Paris would acquire a deeper meaning if under his leadership the Genocide Convention were adopted. The last case of genocide had happened in Europe; the answer to it should come from Paris, which "would act in this case not only as a capital of the world but also as a spokesman for the martyrdom of Europe."

Dr. Evatt understood fully: I sensed it and I did not have to say too much. Soon, in a very businesslike manner, he called his personal secretary and gave him instructions to be ready at all times for my proposals and to act as liaison officer between him and myself. He asked me if something could be done during the present session of the Economic and Social Council, on which he represented Australia.

"Of course," I said, "it will be good to have an endorsement by the council."

"Our delegate in the Economic and Social Council, Colonel Johnson, will support the convention," he answered, "but he must be briefed on the details."

In the afternoon I sat in a comfortable chair in the Australian delegation to the U.N., not as a poor relative and petitioner but as a full-fledged partner in the most beautiful adventure that a man could imagine, and I talked to friends who were closer to me than my own relatives. I had finally found a fighting statesman in the big arena of world affairs who could meet the opposition with the strength of his own conviction and with diplomatic skill.[13]

As the day of the discussion of the Genocide Convention at the Economic and Social Council approached, it was important to anticipate the opposition's arguments. The British delegation did not hide its hostility.[14] First they criticized the term "genocide" because it was formed of the Greek "genos" and the Latin "cide"; they talked about being allergic to hybrids, and in answer I cited other hybrids, such as "bicycle," which is composed of the Latin "bi" and the Greek "cyclone."

In vain I tried to convince them that the Greek "genos" was broader in meaning than the Latin "genus." I quoted in vain Plato's use of the term "genos" to describe spiritual or religious groups. It was of no avail. They answered that, formally, we already had the Nuremberg Judgment and that this could eventually be codified to cover the need. "But gentlemen," I answered, "the Nuremberg Judgment applies only to aggressive war and not to every kind of war, not to a defensive war. Aggression was not at all defined in Nuremberg."

"In this vein," I pleaded, "you cannot base the lives of nations on vague formulations. Crimes committed during a war are always pardoned after the war because war, a product of hatred, must naturally be forgotten since hate cannot endure forever. But the life of nations is too valuable to put it into an old boat with big holes floating on the stormy seas of world politics." Some members of the British delegation saw the validity of my reasoning. But they would not move an inch. This convinced me that they wanted a vague formulation so that it could be applied whenever convenient. I told all this to my new Australian friends while sitting in a comfortable chair on this memorable day in the Palais des Nations.

Finally the day arrived when the Genocide Convention was to be discussed. The British delegation reiterated its position that the convention was not necessary because the Nuremberg Judgment covered all needs. Colonel Johnson of Australia had a unique capacity to defeat an opponent. When his opponent reached the weakest point of his speech he would, with the most amiable smile, ask him to repeat this point so that the entire body of delegates would concentrate on it. "Pardon me, sir," he said, with his broad Australian drawl, "do you mean to say that the Nuremberg Judgment applies in times of peace as well as in times of war?" The British delegate paused for a moment and answered in a weak voice, which delighted me immensely, "yes." Colonel Johnson was the third speaker at this session. He dwelt at length on the British delegate's erroneous statement and kept repeating it in various versions. Of course, he also read the text of the Statutes of the Nuremberg Tribunal and the relevant part of the Tribunal's decision. Not only did the issue become clear to the listeners but, the entire background of this fight having been drawn so close to them, they made Colonel Johnson's thinking their own. It was a marvelous piece of educational work performed, outstanding among the many flat discussions that were so abundant at the sessions of the U.N. I felt next day that the entire atmosphere around the Genocide Convention had suddenly changed. Yet the council, having created this favorable climate, went no further. Many reasons were found simply to transmit the convention to the General Assembly at Paris. The easiest way was found, and this was not to prejudice the decision of the General Assembly. Still, I knew very well that a great breakthrough had been achieved and that the eighteen-member delegations of the council had been thoroughly educated.

Next day I called Hans Opprecht in Zurich, the great publisher and parliamentarian who served at the time as chairman of foreign affairs in the Swiss parliament, the Nationalrat. We had corresponded occasionally when I taught at Yale, and we were mutually sympathetic. He told me he was leaving the following day for Berne and asked me to meet him there and have lunch in the Schwitzer Hoi. I intimated that I would like to use my stay in Switzerland to arouse the interest of both the government and the press in the Genocide Convention. Opprecht agreed with this and proposed to work out a plan.

When I took the train to Berne I was in a lighthearted, almost playful mood. The narrow seats on the Swiss trains, with their faded brown plush cushions, did not seem as shabby as usual. I watched the changing landscape of the beautiful country again, this time with the eyes of a tourist. We passed Versoix on Lake Leman, a curious mixture of water and roses, sprinkled with hotels; and Lausanne, with dreamy Ouchy at its foot and an ocean of sunshine spreading over the fields and lakes through Neuchâtel to Berne.

Dr. Opprecht was late for his appointment. I waited half an hour and thought that I might have been mistaken about the restaurant. I walked several times through the narrow corridor between the tables, until entering guests mistook me for the headwaiter and asked me for a seat. This little episode amused me so much that I forgot about my problems.

Suddenly Dr. Opprecht appeared with his delightful wife. "Well," he said, "I thought about your phone call of yesterday and arranged for you to see the minister of foreign affairs, Max Petitpierre.[15] We might ask him what the position of Switzerland would be if and when the General Assembly adopts the Genocide Convention." And, he added, "because of the Swiss tradition in humanitarian matters he will probably be sympathetic."

I asked Dr. Opprecht to talk to his wife in the Swiss dialect while I continued to speak in German. I always enjoyed hearing the sound of Swiss "dytsch," which goes so well with the good, solid Swiss food. From my previous visits to this country I knew that the Swiss feel more at ease when they do not have to strain to express themselves in "hochdeutsch." So, each speaking his accustomed tongue, we felt a kind of easy happiness pervading all of us who were together again after many years of separation. Next morning Dr. Opprecht and I visited Max Petitpierre, the minister of foreign affairs, who is called "conseiller federal." Since in Switzerland every conseiller federal becomes president of the state for a one-year term, they enjoy great prestige. Petitpierre, a lawyer from Neuchâtel, received us with friendly if impersonal cordiality. His office was plain, with no symbols of power: a small room with austere chairs that in no way betrayed its occupant's influence. Switzerland, I explained to Mr. Petitpierre, was the birthplace of many humanitarian movements. Dunant started the International Red Cross there, and Switzerland had saved many prospective victims of genocide by giving them refuge.[16] If I could have your assurance that Switzerland will ratify the convention, this would be a great help in Paris. He did not commit himself, but he declared that his government would look with sympathy on my undertaking. Then Dr. Opprecht charged in. He asked whether it would be possible to have a press conference for me under governmental auspices. "Of course," said the minister. A few minutes later we were introduced to Mr. Key, an amiable and very efficient press officer. The next afternoon I was explaining to more than a hundred newspapermen the draft convention on genocide, at the main seat of the Swiss government. Many questions were asked, and I felt that I was speaking to a competent and highly trained group of people, and I was especially delighted when a question relating to history arose. The next day's press coverage was more than good; in some of the large papers the report was printed in headlines on the first page. Although I did not conquer Switzerland, I felt that the first trenches in the assault had been taken.

The Assembly in Paris was scheduled for September 15, and now it was the end of August. I decided to take a short vacation. I packed one suitcase and went to Glion above Montreux—actually, between Montreux and Caux. I stayed in a half-deserted hotel; the hostess kept complaining that the golden days were over for Swiss hotels. The quiet atmosphere soothed me and gave me the strength to meet the demands of the work awaiting me in Paris. After a day in Glion I began to enjoy the beauty of the place. It was especially healing to watch my surroundings from a huge terrace, which I occupied by myself. In some places one feels that the air is not ethereal but something of concrete substance. I tried to analyze this feeling. It comes from the sight of the hills and chalets, with the greeting extended before one's eye like a magic ladder stepping into the sky. Sometimes one feels like jumping into the air without fear of falling because the air and the chalet are one. I could better understand the reality of Chagall's visions from the terrace in Glion.

Next day I visited the castle of Chillon, which stands on the banks of the lake at Territet, below my terrace. Although I intended to forget about genocide for these few days, the basement of the castle, with all the implements of torture, reminded me of it. These chambers spoke to me of it in a strange language. It was the language of history, which is so powerful because it is so inescapable!

I broke my pledge to avoid thinking about the Genocide Convention. The hostess in my hotel told me that the Assembly of the Moral Rearmament Movement was meeting a little higher up, above Glion, in Caux. She emphasized that people of different countries were represented. I called up the headquarters of the Moral Rearmament Movement in Caux. The amiable voice of Professor Martin of Cambridge invited me for lunch. I was placed at a table together with some interesting people and listened to their conversation without talking myself. I thought it might be valuable to meet a Frenchman who could help me later in Paris.[17]

In the afternoon a French newspaperman, Scotta-Lavina, participating in a symposium, appeared to be the right person. We walked in the garden and I told him of the forthcoming discussions. All French intellectuals are interested in new ideas and he was no exception. I was under the impression that one could stop every second Frenchman in the street to ask what was going on in the theater, or the title of the most recent good book, and be certain of getting an intelligent answer. The French have an ever-present intellectual curiosity that never rests, even if the essentials of life such as potatoes or fuel are missing. This was the case in France at this time.

I was not mistaken; Mr. Scotta-Lavina warmed up more as we walked in the garden. *"C'est merveilleux,"* he said. Late in the evening, as I descended back to Glion, I felt that I had won a new friend in Paris.[18]

Every day I gained more strength, grew more rested, and saw more clearly the task ahead of me in Paris. Obviously, all the worries did not disappear. Would I find answers for all questions? Would I have the moral strength to sway the Assembly, even with the help of Dr. Evatt? Would I be able to mobilize French public opinion? Would I be able to bypass the opposition?

One evening, while sitting in the half-empty ballroom of the casino at Montreux, I invited a young lady to dance. She happened to be a professional dancer at the casino. A Spanish tango was played, and she danced with an exquisite slant, her eyes half closed. Her face intrigued me: blue eyes and a large nose. It seemed to me that I had seen this face many times in photographs of foreign lands. She told me that she was of Indian descent, born in Chile. Every word the girl said was very intelligent and meaningful. I invited her to join me at my table and we discussed a thousand different subjects. Inevitably, we approached my work. I told her that this should be of special interest to her since the Incas and the Aztecs had been destroyed in her hemisphere. In her strange French she said, "Do you really hope to stop this slaughter?" I was struck by the firmness of her challenge. I heard the same challenge in the voices of almost all people who had been subject to genocide. On the one hand, minority groups wished for a law that would stop or curb genocide; on the other hand, under the impact of their own shock they could not believe that such a law could really be created. At the end of the conversation she looked at me strangely, like someone who was reaching into the beyond, and said distinctly, "You will be a famous man after your death." The little dancer in Montreux with the innate vision of a great extinguished race saw, in her own way, the immortality of the law in which I so firmly believed.

Soon my ten days' vacation ended, and I returned to Geneva. The station at Geneva was full of delegates. The president of the Economic and Social Council, Ambassador Charles Malik (now minister of foreign affairs of Lebanon), greeted me with the words, "Good that I see you now; this very afternoon I signed a paper passing on the Genocide Convention to the General Assembly in Paris."[19] So we went to Paris, the Genocide Convention and I.

CHAPTER TEN

Paris, 1948

IT WAS DRIZZLING IN PARIS, but this did not destroy the feeling that everybody has when arriving in Paris, this peculiar feeling or lightheartedness and intriguing joy. One feels Paris in one's bones—rather in the hips, which make you walk lightly and carefree. I wondered sometimes how people feel when they come to Paris for a funeral. Did they have the same feeling? In my many visits to Paris, this feeling never left me. I always liked to stay in one of the small hotels on the Left Bank, but this time I could not. I had chosen one of the large hotels on the Champs Elysées, where most of the delegates stayed, to facilitate my contact with them. The Hotel Claridge was within walking distance of the Palais de Chaillot, where the Assembly was meeting.[1]

The opening of the Assembly was still several days off. I walked over to the Palais de Chaillot, where the carpenters were still busy preparing for the big event. But the U.N. offices were already active. The same day I visited the Australian delegation and paid my respects to Dr. Evatt. He asked me which of the delegates was sympathetic to the Genocide Convention so that he might be chosen as chairman of the Legal Committee, which would work on the convention. "Ricardo Alfaro," I said, "the former president of Panama who is now chairman of the Panamanian delegation." From this question I understood that Dr. Evatt meant business. Dr. Alfaro actually became the chairman of the Legal Committee.[2]

I spent the following days learning the composition of the delegations and lining up strategic forces. I had a bold plan. Usually, a draft law is sent first to a subcommittee, where a fight is waged for its passage; then the subcommittee's draft is submitted to the full Legal Committee, where another fight takes place over particular provisions. In the past the draft has emerged from a subcommittee at the end of the Assembly, so that there would be no time for the Legal Committee to discuss and eventually adopt it. Obviously, I thought, the opposition would use this double opportunity to delay action on the entire project. Such a procedure must by all means be avoided if we wanted to see the Genocide Convention adopted at this session. Why should we not try, I asked myself, to convert the entire Legal Committee into one big working group? Every delegation would express its opinion directly, and there would still be ample time to adopt the convention. Why not sidestep the subcommittee altogether? All that was needed was the decision to do this by the Legal Committee.

Once I had this thought, I proceeded to discuss it with Dr. Alfaro and a number of friendly delegates. They saw the validity of my argument, but they also saw the difficulty of adopting a new procedure. I then proposed that the Australian delegation suggest such a simplified procedure. I rushed over to the Australian delegation. They agreed to propose it. Now I had to find a delegation to second the Australian proposal. This was not too difficult, but I thought that the speakers supporting the idea should give weighty arguments. I submitted different memoranda to several delegations, all of them stressing the necessity of adopting the convention at this session and pointing out the impossibility of doing so under the double procedure. I thought that some European delegation should stress the martyrdom of Europe under genocide. I also wanted the decision to be unanimous.

We would have to win the Eastern bloc. That evening I was invited to dine with the delegate from the Philippines, Senator Quintin Paredes, and my very close friend Judge Ingles, his advisor.[3] I confided my strategy to them. "But do we have the voting strength for this procedure?"

they asked. "It can be done," I said. "If you as representatives of a nation that suffered so much in the last war would propose it, the Soviet Bloc might agree." "What do you have in mind?" "Make a speech to the effect that in this common work for humanity, the East contributes the memories of its suffering, which were especially great in Poland and Russia, and the West contributes its feelings of compassion—then you have the climate for unanimity."

So it actually happened. Many of my friends spoke for this plan, but the decision was carried by the speech of Paredes, who spoke with great feeling in fluent Spanish. An argument attains additional persuasive force for Latin American delegates whenever a foreigner presents it in their language. The most important hurdle was overcome. The unusual procedure was adopted. From now on, unusual efforts were required.

The Legal Committee proceeded with the actual work on the convention. Before the drafting of the articles, a general discussion was deemed necessary. Two previous drafts were available: one prepared by the secretariat in 1947, with my participation as an official expert, the other prepared by a Special Committee of the Economic and Social Council in May 1948, with my participation behind the scenes. At present, the main task was to keep the Legal Committee's interest constantly alive with stimulating new material. Little had been published on this subject. Some of my articles, which I had already distributed, had appeared in magazines. My book *Axis Rule in Occupied Europe* was made available to the delegates. But the Nazi experience was not a sufficient basis for a definition of genocide for international purposes. One cannot describe a crime by one example; one must rather draw on all available experiences of the past. A definition of a crime involving the participation of societies must fit all social structures. It is necessary to describe the division of the roles and to foresee all modalities, all possible techniques. The formulation must be made valid for all times, situations, and cultures.

From my previous work in the Polish Committee on Codification of Laws in Warsaw, particularly in the Penal Section, I knew that the legislator's imagination must be superior to that of the criminal. The definition of the crime must be as complete as possible, otherwise the criminal would escape through the loopholes of the law. I would have to start digesting historical cases of genocide and submitting them to delegates in the form of memoranda. My valise with records of past cases of genocide seemed to ask me: "You dragged us here from the peaceful shelves of Yale, you promised that we would invade the minds of the delegates. What are you going to do about us now when we are really needed?"

I had to organize myself for the big task. A bilingual secretary-assistant was found in the French radio to help me prepare and type short memoranda in English and French. She agreed to work with me for an hour and a half, several mornings a week, before sessions started. We produced a number of short memoranda for the general discussion. I carried them in my pocket and distributed them to delegates during the general debate. I also tried to see delegates socially at receptions, which took place almost every day. But this plan did not work. It was simply the wrong place and time for a specific discussion of this type. As soon as I started the conversation I would be interrupted by somebody barging in with light social talk. Although these parties were the main battlefields for political issues of the Assembly, they could not be used for discussing a serious legal and moral item. If this proved that legal and moral issues were of a higher caliber than political issues, it was little consolation.

A better system had to be found. I was aware that Paris, with its theaters and its accent on the gay and interesting aspects of life, would claim much of the delegates' free time. I used to call some delegates and ask them to come half an hour earlier to the session. With some I discussed it at lunch. As time went on and the interest grew stronger, the delegates were more eager to talk with me and to get my memoranda. I stopped worrying that my book on the history of genocide was not published yet, because by using the short memoranda to illustrate a point under discussion, I could make more progress. I did not miss even one meeting of the committee, although I arrived every morning with a heavy head, tired after a sleepless night of worries followed by early morning dictation.

And still I could not forget that I was in Paris. There was hardly time to go to the theater, to walk without particular purpose in the streets, and to mix with the most wonderful crowd of all cities. I could do this only on Sundays.

It was the beginning of fall. Yellow and reddish leaves were falling from the trees on the Champs Elysées. When passersby would step on them you could hear their complaining murmur. The terraces on the Champs Elysées were full of people sipping their coffee, wine, or aperitif. They were talking in such a way that you could not help but think that what they said really matters, even though nothing happened after their talks. The good reasoning of the French, like that of the ancient Greeks, came to light not only in the academies but also in the cafes. And these faces, even when they are silent, tell you that they have much to say. This takes away one's loneliness and the feeling that you are lost in an abyss of nothingness and indifference. Maybe Matthew Arnold was right in saying that because of the French Revolution, France is the country in Europe where *the people* is most alive.[4] Only in Paris can you cultivate friendship with an unknown crowd. Looking at the Parisian crowd on the Champs Elysées was comforting and noisily peaceful to me.

I went to visit my publisher Pédone, at 13 rue Soufflot on the Left Bank. Pére Pédone had built this firm into one of the most important enterprises among those dealing with international law. He was the publisher for the League of Nations. There is something pleasantly peculiar about French publishers. Although one comes to them originally for business, gradually they develop into personal friends. They add personal notes to their business letters, inquiring about your health and family, and are sincerely concerned if something wrong happens to you. Between the two European wars Pédone was a great clearinghouse for friendship and news about authors, jurists, and professors. This news concerned not only their books but also their wives, children, career advancement, and many other personal events. To Pédone, his authors were the extension of his own family.

The Pédones, now consisting only of a mother and daughter, meant a great deal to me. They helped me considerably in my campaign to outlaw genocide, and in the last war they had also helped me get back into intellectual life when I emerged with a long beard from many months of half-savage existence in the Polish forests, where I had taken refuge following the Nazis' conquest of Poland. When I escaped to Vilnius in then-neutral Lithuania in 1940, I sent a cable to the Pédones to inquire about the manuscript I had sent them a week or so before the outbreak of the war. A warm cable came from Paris, expressing joy at my survival. Many letters followed. The Pédones understood that my manuscript was my only possession saved from the burning house of my past and that, if published, it would be a bridge to the future.

The book was indeed published with great speed and sent by Pédone to my friends, and to universities in the countries where I intended to eventually establish myself. A copy was sent to Karl Schlyter, the former minister of justice in Sweden, with whom I had collaborated at various international juridical conferences. Another was sent to Duke University. At this university was my friend Professor Malcolm McDermott, who had visited me in Poland. Together we published a book on the Polish criminal code. A month later Schlyter arranged for me to come to Sweden, and McDermott started to work quietly but energetically for an invitation to me from Duke University. This was Pédone to me.

"Bonjour, bonjour!" Two smiling faces, mother and daughter, greeted me at their Left Bank office. I had last seen them in 1946, when I passed through Paris on my way to Nuremberg. The two ladies already knew much about the Genocide Convention. What they failed to see was how there could be any doubts or question about such a moral, plain, and sound idea. "The last war has shown that this convention is necessary," said daughter Pédone. "The Assembly will have to adopt it," said mother Pédone, "if not for other reasons then for a feeling of embarrassment and even shame before the entire world." She was right, but I did not want to worry her about the many sidelines and backgrounds, invisible to many good people but painful to those who come in touch with them. Then the two ladies adopted a resolution that the Assembly must act and the world must ratify the convention, especially since their bon ami was the author of and spokesman for *"cette idée si belle."*

The two Pédones quietly went to work among their many friends and authors, who, like me, adored them. They insisted that I see their friends in the Ministry of Foreign Affairs, in the university, and in the press. A new problem had been added to the lives of the Pédones: how to start moving Paris. It moved indeed, slowly but steadily. I published an article in the influential paper *Le Monde*; then I delivered a lecture at the Center of Foreign Affairs. Ambassador Amado, in a black tie, anticipating a dinner and pleasant company somewhere on the Left Bank, presided. The two Pédones sat in the front row, happy, confident, already anticipating victory on all fronts.

But there were clouds in the skies of Paris. They appeared that very evening, when two gentlemen asked the question, Why is a Genocide Convention necessary? Is not the Nuremberg Judgment sufficient? I explained that the Nuremberg Judgment applies only to times of war. But they kept denying it; they hoped to confuse the audience. They even tried to confuse the press. An answer to my article appeared in *Le Monde*, and my second article refuting these misstatements was not published. I called Scotta-Lavina, whom I had met in Caux during my vacation in Glion. He was only too happy to publish an interview with me in the paper *Le Combat*, which was widely read by French intellectuals. I explained again that the convention was necessary because the Nuremberg Judgment did not establish any legal precedent and left genocide not punishable in times of peace. This had its effect, because the interview was prominently displayed and appeared to be clear. There were also bad tidings in the Legal Committee. I watched the opposition. I knew them well by name, by acts, by innuendos. Small groups would form before and after the meetings. Since I was constantly in the room of the Legal Committee, they would smile with embarrassment when I spoke to them and turn their eyes away. I decided to fortify my position by directly approaching my friends in foreign offices, asking them to issue instructions to their delegations in Paris to support the Genocide Convention. Surely the opposition would not talk with the foreign offices. This new tactic proved useful. I received an encouraging letter from the foreign office of Sweden.

I also cabled Sigrid Undset, the Nobel Prize winner in literature, in Oslo, who in 1947 signed a common appeal on genocide in the U.N. and received a most encouraging reply.[5] I wrote to Clarence Pickett in Philadelphia asking the support of the Quakers. In several days a copy of his cable to the U.S. delegation was on my desk.[6]

I waited nervously for the first open attack. It came! The British delegate Sir Hartley Shawcross, the attorney general of his country, declared that his delegation could not support the Genocide Convention. "Nuremberg is enough! A Genocide Convention cannot be adopted," he said, "because of the problem of political groups. To include political groups in the definition would mean to enter the controversial issue of civil war. On the other hand, how can political groups be omitted?" There was an ominous silence among the delegates, who were always respectful of the rank of the speaker.

I sat with a sunken head at a luncheon table on the terrace of a small cafe near the Palais de Chaillot. It was Indian summer, caressingly warm. The sun was shining, but it could not reach my frozen inner self. I felt I was shrinking. At the next table was Dr. Karim Azkoul, the delegate of Lebanon. I asked him why he was not attending the Legal Committee. The answer was clear: he was assigned to another committee and was working on the Declaration of Human Rights. He asked me whether I could give an interview on genocide for a Lebanese magazine for which his wife was writing. "Gladly," I said. A moment later I strolled to the Palais de Chaillot and tried to think quietly. It would be good to have Azkoul back on the Legal Committee. He had been a forceful member of the special committee that prepared the second draft of the Genocide Convention.

It occurred to me that if I paid a visit to the chairman of the Lebanese delegation, the Prime Minister Riad el-Solh, to thank him for the contributions of the Lebanese delegation to the Genocide Convention, the conversation might get around to Dr. Azkoul.[7] Next morning I was sitting in the office of the Lebanese delegation facing the prime minister and the secretary general of the Ministry of Foreign Affairs, Fouad Ammoun. In this friendly atmosphere I could not but be direct.

I started: "This visit is both an honor for me and a cry for help. The Genocide Convention was always strongly supported by Lebanon. You were represented in the Special Committee on Genocide by Mr. Azkoul, who made such a great contribution. He is the man who knows so much about the issue. We have to build up good defenses against an opposition that is showing its teeth." I did not mention who was fighting the convention, but the prime minister smiled and said to Fouad Ammoun: "Why could we not send Dr. Azkoul to the Legal Committee, where he could help with his expert knowledge?" Mr. Ammoun nodded approvingly. This was all.

Another plan simmered in my mind. I rushed to my friend Mr. Sutch of New Zealand and asked for an appointment with the chairman of his delegation,[8] Prime Minister Peter Fraser.[9] I was afraid that New Zealand might follow Britain's lead. Fortunately the prime minister was on the political committee of the Assembly, and faced by the prospect of listening to a long discussion in which he was not interested he readily agreed to see me at once. In a moment the huge figure of Peter Fraser loomed over me. We sat in a corner of the lounge. Fraser's huge head was falling from his shoulders almost into my lap. It seemed to me that he was falling asleep, but in the midst of my profound discouragement at this obvious failure of my persuasive powers, he would throw at me a sharp question, which proved how intently he was listening and how quickly his mind worked. He gave me no commitment, but there was a broad smile on the lips and a look of deep friendly approval in the eyes of this strangest of all statesmen.[10]

Mr. Sutch told me I had made a good move, because there were difficulties over the genocide question in his delegation. He promised to watch over the situation and advised me to talk to another member of the delegation, Mrs. Newland. The next day we had luncheon in the press room and had a most rewarding meeting. Mrs. Newland had clear eyes and a face in which one could see her entire personality. "My husband is a carpenter and I work among laboring people. I will speak about genocide when I come home. I will educate them to support this good law. Nobody should be killed, tortured, maimed. It is so simple; why do people confuse simple things?" Mother Pédone had asked the same question. In recent years I have often asked myself this question, and always the clear eyes of Mrs. Newland of New Zealand and mother Pédone of Paris come to my mind.

Azkoul delivered his speech in the Legal Committee. "The Attorney General of England," he said, "did everything he could do to confuse us, but we refuse to be confused. The convention is essential for the protection of small nations. Big nations can protect themselves with arms, but our only protection is international law." His philosophical mind had a field day. He explained the meaning of the convention to an intently listening committee. "The majority of the nations want the convention, and we will not permit ourselves to be talked out of this important law by arguments in which we do not believe." His voice carried firmness and conviction.

Next day the situation improved even more. A young attractive lady dressed in a sari, Begum Ikramullah, started to speak. Before her was the sign of her country—Pakistan. Her words still resound in my ears. "Pakistan," she said, "is strongly in favor of the Genocide Convention, which is written with the blood and tears of more than one million Moslems who perished through genocide during the partition of India in 1947. We need this convention also to prevent other people from similar sufferings. Genocide was often committed through the ages," she continued. "While it has always shocked the conscience of mankind, nothing has been done to punish the crime. The discoveries of science put such weapons in the hands of men that genocide today can be swift and terrible indeed. Therefore such a convention becomes imperative and its acceptance should not be delayed."[11] I watched the faces of the delegates when she spoke. It was as if an angel had entered this drab room and touched them with its wings. I saw a sign of preoccupation on the face of Sir Hartley, but I was so elated that I even liked him at that moment. I thought how true was the saying of the ancient Greeks, that only a wounded physician can heal. Here was a delegate speaking for a wounded people, bringing these sufferings within the context of present history. After the meeting I rushed over to the Pakistan seat to thank Begum Ikramullah. This was the beginning of a long and lasting friendship which proved most fruitful at the Paris and other Assemblies. Begum Ikramullah introduced me to her advisor Agha Shahi, who defended the convention then and many times thereafter with great skill.[12]

When I left the room I met Sir Hartley in the corridor. He said, "The committee is becoming emotional, this is a bad sign, it might go in the wrong direction." "Why is it wrong to prevent slaughter?" I asked. "You yourself defended the resolution on genocide in the 1946 Assembly. Did you forget that Gladstone fought for the life of the Armenians in the British Parliament?"[13] Sir Hartley was worried, but this did not mean the end of my worries. I knew the opposition would try new avenues of attack. How could I foresee all of them? To think constantly in terms of troubles, attacks, and dangers is not healthy. It takes away one's feelings of inner security, strength, and hope, and the ability to inspire others. But to let it go and hide one's head in the sand like an ostrich might lead to defeat. A way must be found between these extremes. I felt that the work must be strengthened by the injection of popular support. I started with religious leaders. My first visit was to Pastor Boergner, the head of Protestant church in France. "The Huguenots, of course," he said. In France we think of the Huguenots and the Jews when we speak of genocide, but there are also many others. "I will try to help." I visited the cardinal of Paris. Several times I went to see the papal nuncio, Monsignor Roncalli, who was as learned as he was clever and understanding.[14] He promised to talk to some delegates from Latin America. The nuncio had an office full of sunshine, which blended with his smiling square face. We talked for hours. I used to emerge from conversations with him somehow healed from the wounds of ceaseless struggle. Jacques Herrissay, the president of the Association of Catholic Writers, invited Catholic personalities to dinner, at which I explained the convention. Then I invited Monsieur Herrissay with a list of his friends for a glass of wine at my hotel. Articles started to appear in *France Catholique* and other organs of the Church about the Genocide Convention. From among the Protestants the most interested proved to be Jean Nussbaum, a Swiss living in Paris who organized and is directing the Association de Liberté Religieuse.[15]

The Legal Committee took up the problem of including political groups in the definition of genocide. Some delegates desired to protect not only national, racial, religious, and ethnic groups but also political groups. I felt that this issue might divide the committee almost evenly and would be an obstacle to the adoption of the convention. Ambassador Gilberto Amado of Brazil argued: "We in Latin America make revolutions from time to time, which involves the destruction of political opponents. Then we reconcile and live in peace. Later the group in power is thrown out in another revolution. Why should this be classified as the crime of genocide? Genocide is ignominious and inhuman, because it is directed against innocent human beings, including children and aged persons." Said Ambassador Perez Perozo of Venezuela: "Political groups are nowhere defined. They are indefinable. They lack permanency and consistency. If genocide is to be an extraditable nonpolitical offense, how can it include the destruction of a political opposition? Let us first outlaw the destruction of national, racial, and religious groups— the basic groups of mankind against whom genocide was practiced through all ages."

Other delegates argued that the term "national" includes by implication the political leadership of a national group, and there is no need to mention specifically political groups. I thought the destruction of political opponents should be treated as the crime of political homicide, not as genocide. Every revolutionary regime comes to power by destroying some of its opponents. Later this regime is recognized by other nations, sometimes the whole world. Should political groups be included in the definition of genocide, recognition of a revolutionary regime would imply acceptance of genocide as legal. This would kill the Genocide Convention before it took root in world society.

My apprehensions were justified. A vote was taken and, by a small majority, political groups were accepted. I considered it a blow to the convention. I discussed with friends this new obstacle to the acceptance of the convention in Paris. Organizations wrote letters to their delegations. I felt that unless the vote was reconsidered, there would be no convention. With this in mind I rushed to Dr. Evatt, the president of the Assembly. He had a gift for analyzing situations. "What is the position of the British delegation on this point?" he asked. "Sir Hartley Shawcross," I said, "argued at the beginning of the general discussion that a Genocide Convention that included political groups would enter into the controversial issue of civil war, and this would make the convention unacceptable. On the other hand, he argued that the omission of political groups was impossible."

"You have here the answer to the hurdle," said Evatt. It became clear that the British delegation intended to destroy the convention through the inclusion of political groups. Evatt continued: "I am having luncheon today with Mr. Dulles.[16] I am afraid I am late. Could you drive with me to Hotel de Crillon and we will talk in my car."

When Dr. Evatt left his car he told me, "I will ask Dulles for new instructions to the American delegation. The vote must be reconsidered, otherwise the convention is lost."

So it happened. Next day a move for reconsideration of the vote started in the Legal Committee. A two-thirds majority of the votes was necessary, and the U.S. delegation was helpful in obtaining it. On the third day the vote took place, and political groups were omitted. This hurdle was out of the way. I could hardly stand on my feet when I emerged from the Legal Committee. I took a cup of tea instead of dinner and went immediately to bed. Then I suddenly realized that I had not thanked Evatt for his help. I phoned his hotel, left a message, and fell asleep as if I had just completed a long, tiresome journey.

The next day I waited quietly for the next hurdle. I realized that if my work were to have any effect and if I should outlast all storms, I would have to preserve my nervous energy. There would be more obstacles, and some smaller ones should be left alone. I would fight only the big battles, those of real importance to the convention. I decided also to participate more fully in the social life of the Assembly. The delegates had shown me their friendship and appreciation for my ideas and work. I was, however, somewhat embarrassed by the fact that some of them started to talk to me on an exceedingly high plane, as if I were not interested in normal conversation. There are two ways to dehumanize a human being: one is pushing downward, as was done in the concentration camps, and the other is by elevating upward or by treating somebody as an individual dedicated exclusively to high ideals. I was afraid that I was becoming a minor domesticated saint for the consumption of the U.N. Assembly. I did not want to lose the intimacy of some of the delegates, whom I had learned to love dearly. So I went to receptions, drank cocktails and danced, joked and refused to speak about genocide. When somebody would start a conversation about the convention, I would simply ask, "Genocide, what's that?" They laughed, and I laughed too. Still I was condemned to loneliness. This was an essential condition of my life. For I felt that only lonely persons can reach the borders of the unconscious and achieve the state of intuition which were so necessary for appraising situations at once and acting quickly. This intuition was a most valuable part of my equipment for many years.

Through my new friend Agha Shahi of Pakistan I received an invitation to lunch from the chairman of the Pakistan delegation, Sir Zafarullah Khan, the minister of foreign affairs.[17] I sat with both of them in the delegates' dining room, opposite the great glass wall through which one could see the life of Paris and the Eiffel Tower. It was again a sunny day and I felt cheerful. Sir Zafarullah was one of the most colorful personalities in the U.N. A great jurist who had been a member of the cabinet before the partition of India, he was a progressive man and at the same time a very religious Moslem. He belonged to a small sect which believed that Mohammed was not the only or the last prophet. His religious beliefs brought him strong opposition in his own country. He was then faced with two struggles: one for Pakistan and the other against a fervent religious majority in his own country. On his expressive scholarly face one could easily notice the traces of this struggle. But he had a dry sense of humor, which he used as a defense against his problems. He told me that he stayed in a hotel near the Assembly so that he could go to his room to pray several times a day. "After the prayer I have a feeling of peace and of inner direction. Then I know where I am going."

The conversation naturally reached the Genocide Convention. "In a larger sense," I said, "the convention will strengthen the moral sense of the community of nations. In some countries, especially in the disillusioned West, materialism is rampant. Society falls more and more under the spell of sensory values. The number of these values is limited and a struggle for their control and possession has already set in. Force and violence will be used more and more for securing their possession. This is especially true of nations which still abide by the principle 'right or wrong —my country.' The convention cannot be a panacea for all ills, but certainly it can serve as a rallying point for idealism, human sympathy, and even solidarity." The conversation with the minister was rewarding. He talked so humbly and simply about the most important things in life.

This man became my friend, guide, and philosopher in all the difficult situations I faced in later years in the U.N. He was later elected as judge of the International Court of Justice in The Hague. In many situations where I verged on anger, fear, or pride, I thought about Sir Zafarullah's formulation of the problem of inner direction. There are meetings with people that make you feel something of value has entered into you. This luncheon was one of them. I was not conscious of its "spirituality" because it was so simple and sincere and left me with a much-needed feeling of peace.

There was still some time before the beginning of the meeting. I went to the terrace of the Palais to enjoy the sunshine. Several delegates did the same. A young lady from the New Zealand delegation said with a warm voice, "This is your great Assembly. I am curious to know how you take it." "Sometimes I see only troubles splintered with resurging hope and underlying obstinacy," I replied. "Come on," she said. "Don't be ungrateful. Did it ever occur to you that your fight would never be so meaningful to yourself without these troubles and opposition?" This was a refreshing lesson from a representative of the younger generation. It was also a sign that the young lady of New Zealand thinks about the convention as already a fact, which I failed to see myself.

We are again sitting in the long drab chamber of the Legal Committee. The article saying that genocide is a crime in times of both war and peace seemed self-evident and was adopted. Then the delegates seemed to get lost in an endless discussion of the motives for genocide. The Soviet delegate wanted to make genocide a crime only when it was committed out of Nazi or Fascist motivations. Most of the delegates were opposed because this would restrict the concept of genocide only to the past. What about the future? Moreover, they argued, motivations do not usually belong in the definition of a crime. They can be used only as a guide to the judge in administering the penalty. Motivations can serve only as an aggravating or extenuating circumstance in the actual application of the law, but not in the making of the law. For example, a man kills his partner in order to take over his business. Killing is the crime, but the motive of gain is taken into consideration during the trial as a matter of judicial appreciation. This was so clear in law schools and textbooks. Why should it become controversial here in a committee that was supposed to be the least political of all committees of the Assembly? Dr. Perozo came out with a proposal to add the words "as such" after the words "Genocide means the destruction of a national, racial, religious or ethnic group." The words "as such" would strengthen the element of intent, he said, "and would lay emphasis on the significance of the groups as basic elements of world society which must be preserved." All agreed readily and proceeded with the other point.

Erling Wikborg, of the Norwegian delegation, proposed to include in the definition the partial destruction of a group. He argued that when intellectual leaders, who provide the forces of cohesion to the group, are destroyed, then the group is destroyed as such, or as a group. I thought of the prophetic saying of Carlyle that "ten men can make a national culture."[18]

The Chinese delegation complained that during the last war more than 200 million of their citizens suffered under the occupation of the Japanese, who built a huge factory for narcotic drugs in occupied China; drugs were distributed to the population in order to destroy their minds and make them forget their national aspirations and their craving for national freedom. The speaker demanded that the administration of narcotic drugs under such conditions be included in the definition of genocide. Said the Polish delegate: "The Nazis paid our workers with alcohol with the same intent. Could we not find a formula which would indicate the area of damage rather than the means of action?" Quietly I passed on a little note, that as a result of tortures and fear of impending death, former inmates of concentration camps were losing their minds. It was difficult to cure the concentration camp psychosis after liberation. The Armenians in their death marches had also lost their minds before succumbing to death. Then the delegate of India proposed a formula, "serious mental harm." He insisted on the word "serious" to indicate that there must be grave injury to mental capacity. I thought the delegate of India formulated it well, because the qualification "serious" is used analogously in much legislation to indicate the grave nature of bodily harm. I also thought that this formula fits well in the concept of genocide. When minds are destroyed, the cohesive force of the group, which is essentially a mental quality, cannot be maintained. Was it not the Frenchman Focillon who said that nations are families of minds?[19]

The next point in the definition was the problem of life in a concentration camp or similar conditions. The authors of the draft produced by the Special Committee on Genocide felt that the formula should be as flexible as possible, to permit the inclusion of all eventual criminal plans and techniques. Death marches, deportations, work in mines, and other means of destroying the health cannot be mentioned all by name, because another important means of genocide might be left out. Also, the idea had to be conveyed that people condemned to such a condition are basically "living corpses." Life is not yet extinguished in them, but their bodies are so weakened that they can die at any time. This idea was conveyed through the words "physical destruction" instead of "death" or "killing," which was included elsewhere in the definition. Finally the following formula emerged from the discussion: "deliberately inflicting on the group conditions of life calculated to bring about its physical destruction in whole or in part." In order to avoid misapplication of this article in cases when people objectively suffer from bad conditions such as extreme poverty, unsanitary conditions, and the like that are generally prevalent in a country or locality, the committee required that the intent to destroy the group should be strengthened by two additional expressions of intent, such as "*deliberately* inflicting conditions of life *calculated* to bring about" destruction. To achieve proper judicial guarantees, three expressions of intent altogether were inscribed in this important provision.

The next point in the definition dealt with the problem of reproduction within the group. The continuation of the group beyond the life span of its individual members is a basic condition of the group's life. In the present, the life of the group coincides with the life of the individual members of the group. However, the group is endowed with a historical existence, while its members enjoy only physical existence. This historical existence is achieved through reproduction within the group. The delegates remembered the problem of sterilizations and castrations, but not all of them were aware that in many past cases of genocide measures were undertaken to prevent births within the group through prohibition or mass restriction of marriage.

In the latter case one must have clearly in mind that the overriding intent must be to extinguish the group in whole or in part. For example, if in a country marriage licenses are issued to persons over twenty years of age with the exception of a certain minority, where they are issued only to persons of thirty years of age, then the intent to destroy this minority becomes clear. The Polish delegation complained that during the German occupation, the Germans imposed restrictions on marriage licenses.

Concern over the continuity of the group also made itself felt in another proposal. The problem of forceful transfer of children from one group to another raised considerable interest. In my work at Yale on the history of genocide, I discovered that this technique was quite common. I also described it in my article on genocide that was published in *Le Monde*. When religious intolerance ruled Europe, children were taken from their parents. During four hundred years of control over the Christian countries in the Balkans by the Ottoman Empire, the Turks used to take away a certain number of teenage boys from Christian communities every year. They were brought up in Turkey as Moslems and were trained as future policemen, to be assigned to their home countries. Being bilingual now, they could render valuable service to the Turkish government. They were called Janissaries and proved to be very cruel to their own people. My Greek friends told me that Greece, now a nation of seven million, would have a population of sixteen million if not for the Greek children who were taken away for four hundred years. Such were the frightful consequences of this genocidal technique.

Another example was provided by a practice under the Russian tsar of enlisting Jewish boys into military service for twenty-five years. They were sometimes converted to the Orthodox Russian faith and later married Russian wives. These boys were called in Russian "Kantouraty." I remember a story about them which I read many years ago, by the Russian writer Gertsen.[20]

The Greek delegation now formally proposed to include in the definition of genocide the practice of taking away children. The Greeks had a new reason for this preoccupation. Some thirty thousand children were kidnapped in the civil war of 1947 and transferred to countries in the Eastern bloc. This type of genocidal practice appeared to be one of the cruelest. It tended to interrupt the cultural continuity of a group. It destroyed the spirit while it kept the body alive. It created irreparable pain for the parents and sharp suffering among the kidnapped children.

Parents in the Christian Balkans frequently hid their children when the Turkish police came to pick up their prey. One mother hid her son for fourteen years in a stable. He forgot how to walk, and when she took him out of the stable he crawled on his hands and feet like an animal. Some parents used to marry off their teenage boys to young girls to avoid the ordeal of separation. The law did not permit the taking of married persons. Soon even this device ceased to provide protection.

Thus a tragic experience of deep human significance was added to the definition of genocide.

Of considerable interest to the committee was scope of persons liable to punishment for genocide. In a previous chapter I reported how the attempts to limit responsibility for genocide to unidentifiable culprits in government had failed. The Legal Committee had now before itself two drafts. In both, responsibility for genocide was placed on heads of states, public officials, and private individuals. The problem of responsibility of heads of states raised certain doubts. The delegate of Sweden, Sture Petrén, argued that kings must be treated differently from presidents of republics.[21] He was joined by the delegates of England and the Netherlands, all countries having kings as heads of state. "The king reigns, but does not rule," they said. The problem appeared to be clear. A new proposal was introduced to change the phrase "heads of state" to "constitutional rulers." In this way the responsibility of kings, whose power is only symbolic and who do not participate in actual government, was excluded. It was replaced by the responsibility of those who hold actual power and can by their acts influence the commission of the crime of genocide. I was glad that the Legal Committee did not substantially change the provisions on responsibility. I still remember the fight we had in the Special Committee on Genocide in May 1948, when a formula was proposed that would basically exclude private individuals or groups of individuals such as members of political parties or members of hate groups from criminal responsibility for genocide.

One afternoon Count d'Oultremont of the U.N. information office made arrangements for me to give a talk on genocide to the many representatives of organizations who were present in Paris. He chose a big room in the Palais de Chaillot which, to my amazement, was filled to capacity. Among my listeners I noticed a Catholic priest with a big black beard and piercing eyes that I felt were almost physically touching my face. I recognized the member of the French parliament, Abbe Pierre, who later became famous for his one-man crusade against misery and rooflessness in Paris.[22] I felt strengthened by the presence of this man. I felt that the Genocide Convention means now a great deal more to people.

Every action generates a reaction. Through one lady I found out that a letter had been sent out by several representatives of pressure groups, including herself, to all the different organizations present in Paris. The letter claimed to show that it would be impossible to draft a Genocide Convention and asked for the reader's endorsement of this view. This lady later became aware that her signature had been misused. From the names of the other signers I understood their intentions. They worked for the Human Rights program of the U.N. and were afraid that adoption of the Genocide Convention would take away some of the area of application from their projects. The U.N. was working at the time on a Declaration of Human Rights, and some people hoped also to create a Covenant on Human Rights. I saw that the letter must be counteracted immediately.

I was in a relatively good position, because the lady had the right to withdraw her signature and to explain that she misunderstood the intentions of the other signers of the unfriendly declaration. I was afraid that if some organizations endorsed this statement, it would mean a setback to the convention. There was not one minute to lose. We borrowed a type-writer, prepared and mimeographed a letter repudiating and denouncing the first letter as a nonconstructive approach to an important humanitarian issue, and sent it out the same evening. This was quick work, but there was a casualty. We left the typewriter in the Palais de Chaillot, and when I came in the morning to pick it up and return it to the owner, I discovered that it had been stolen.

As if to heighten my discouragement, James Plimsoll, assistant to Dr. Evatt, told me that the beginning of the Assembly had seen another unsuccessful attempt to sidetrack the Genocide Convention.[23] An effort was then made to send the Genocide Convention for drafting to the Humanitarian, Social, and Cultural Committee, which was charged with the drafting of the Declaration on Human Rights. Since this declaration took up all of this committee's time, the Genocide Convention, the proponents hoped, would be automatically postponed at least for one year. And then, they hoped, forever.

I went to Dr. Evatt's press officer and asked him whether he thought it would be possible to issue a public statement by the president of the Assembly on the importance of the Genocide Convention. He was willing to prepare a statement and let Dr. Evatt see it. The statement appeared several days later and made a strong impression.

I felt that the Genocide Convention and the Declaration on Human Rights projects must be kept separate, and each must be treated on its own merits. The differences appeared obvious to me. The Declaration on Human Rights is only an enunciation of general principles. It has no binding force as international law. It contains no provisions for enforcement, and being a declaration it cannot be enforced as law. It cannot be signed by representatives of governments or ratified by parliaments, because it is not a treaty of nations.

On the other hand, the Genocide Convention *is* an international treaty. It can be enforced both as an international law and as a domestic law. It deals with international crime and carries with itself penalties and the higher degree of legal and moral condemnation. The Genocide Convention is a definite and precise commitment before the world not to murder peoples and races. Therefore it must be signed by representatives of governments and then ratified by the parliaments.

The Declaration on Human Rights is only a date, but the Genocide Convention is a marriage.

I also thought that in the present age, with the world trembling under convulsions of change, impatience, fear, and anxiety, genocide is a real danger. It has already claimed the lives of so many millions, and many more millions might die.

When Dr. Evatt's statement on the Genocide Convention appeared, some spokesmen for the human rights project came to congratulate me as if nothing had happened. But I knew quite well that they would not give up. They represented organizations that were well equipped with staffs, funds, and even social prestige. It never occurred to them that their membership would not approve their fight against the Genocide Convention. I told the story to a Swiss friend. He raised his shoulders with a smile: "This is natural. You have to deal not only with human enthusiasm but also with human frailties. Do you know that nice people fought Henri Dunant, the founder of the Red Cross?" "Anthony said that honorable men killed Caesar," I replied. This all was known to me, but it did not diminish my worries. I knew that I would have to fight on a new front.

We proceeded faster with the drafting of the convention. Then we reached the article on cultural genocide. This idea was very dear to me. I defended it successfully through two drafts. It meant the destruction of the cultural pattern of a group, such as the language, the traditions, monuments, archives, libraries, and churches. In brief: the shrines of a nation's soul. When Janet Flanner (Genêt) of the *New Yorker* came to interview me on the Genocide Convention, I told her how important cultural genocide was. She reported in her letter from Paris my saying, "First they burn books and then they start burning bodies."[24] But there was not enough support for this idea in the committee. We would have to spend considerable time making a good draft of this complicated matter. The chairman of the Legal Committee, Dr. Alfaro, who gave me the original support on the Genocide Convention during the 1946 Assembly, did not support the inclusion of cultural genocide. Many delegations fell silent when I endeavored to explain the importance of this matter. On this issue the wind was not blowing in my direction. After having overcome so many hurdles and with the end of the Assembly in sight, I questioned the wisdom of engaging in still another battle. Would it endanger the passage of the convention? Dr. Evatt was also against inclusion of cultural genocide. So with a heavy heart I decided not to press for it.

The night after the negative vote on cultural genocide, I talked things over with myself in the following way: Some elements of cultural genocide were included, such as kidnapping of children. Moreover, the destruction of a group entails the annihilation of its cultural heritage or the interruption of the cultural contributions coming from the group. Finally, if the convention were adopted and ratified, it would always be possible later to adopt an additional protocol on cultural genocide. On the whole my calculations proved to be sound, if one considers that the drafting of the convention took up all the time available to the Legal Committee and the convention was ready just in time to be adopted one day before the end of the Assembly. A long discussion on cultural genocide would undoubtedly have prevented the committee from finishing the drafting of the convention at the Paris Assembly. I wanted to get the convention through the Paris Assembly at any cost, because I could never hope to have the president of the Assembly and the president of the Drafting Committee on my side at another Assembly. Indeed, the Paris Assembly was the end of the golden age for humanitarian treaties at the U.N.

Now we reached the implementation stage in the drafting. Everybody saw that in this aspect one should look for the middle of the road. We had to seek blending and cooperation between the national and international elements. It was clear that genocide must be punished, first of all, by national courts, and penalties must be provided by national laws. But if a nation did not enforce these laws, then international action should be sought, either through the U.N. or through the International Court of Justice in The Hague, a familiar institution to all civilized nations of the world. The French delegation wanted to have an international criminal tribunal, but there was not enough support for this idea. I remembered that the League of Nations, after having adopted the idea of such a criminal tribunal in relation to acts of terrorism after the murder of Barthou in 1934, failed to see it established.[25] Moreover, more than half of the world's nations require that their permission be obtained before any dispute between them and another power can be examined by the International Court of Justice. It would be enough, I thought, to make all nations accept the principle that in cases of genocide they should drop the requirement that their permission was necessary for a proceeding before the International Court of Justice. The French delegation pressed for an International Criminal Court and even declared that France would not sign or ratify the convention should their demand not be met.

A compromise was found. Mention of the International Criminal Tribunal was included in the convention, but a provision was also included that should such a tribunal be created, it would be binding only on those nations that accept its jurisdiction. Naturally, such acceptance would eventually require a special convention. The French delegation accepted this solution and pledged to sign the Genocide Convention in Paris. This was politically important, because France was the host country.[26]

The Legal Committee continued its daily work. I tried to communicate as much as possible with the delegates, asking them to make proposals and to second useful amendments. The basic task now was to reconcile differences and avoid long discussions. Time was suddenly of great importance. It was necessary to accelerate the drafting. I talked about it with Dr. Evatt, and he promised to discuss it with his friends in the Legal Committee. The article on extradition was adopted. It was self-evident that those who have committed genocide should not enjoy asylum in other countries. The moral and legal standards of mankind with respect to this crime should be equalized so that we can really speak about a unified ethos. But a snag occurred on an important article dealing with the action of the U.N. (now Article VIII).[27] The committee did not discuss it at length but put it to a vote and decided to delete it. This article was important, because it was endeavoring to establish an international control over acts of genocide by the U.N. One of the delegates declared that this was unnecessary, since the U.N. can always take action against genocide. I did not agree. A convention must spell out the rights and duties of the parties; these cannot be left to interpretation. Moreover, Article VIII stipulated expressly that cases of genocide could be brought up in all organs of the U.N. This meant that the Security Council, with its veto, could be avoided. How can one veto the protection of life, which would mean a veto on life itself? I decided to work for the restoration of Article VIII. When I called the delegates during the evening, they were as usual at a reception. These were their last weeks in Paris and social life became more and more intense. This evening I hated these receptions more than ever. Finally, at midnight, I reached John Maktos, the U.S. delegate.[28] He saw the point and volunteered to call some of his friends in the delegations. "Please call them now," I pleaded. "Yes, I will call tonight." I also called some of the delegates. They promised sympathetic consideration, and I was particularly happy that they did not bawl me out for calling them so late. Dr. Alfaro saw the point immediately. I explained: "If we have two basic international controls, the International Court of Justice (Article IX) and the action of the U.N. (Article VIII), we must pressure both of them.[29] The convention will be dead otherwise, particularly if some nation would later make a reservation to Article IX. Then there will be no international control whatsoever. For practical reasons, however, to influence a nation quickly, action by the U.N. is more important than action by the International Court of Justice, where it sometimes takes one year before a case is heard. The persons against whom an act of genocide is directed would be all dead by that time." "You are right," said Dr. Alfaro. That morning a vote was taken and Article VIII was reintroduced in the draft of the convention. I felt like the pilot of an airliner who had managed to restart a couple of dead motors.

With the adoption of Article IX on the International Court of Justice, all substantive articles of the convention were finished. The committee then suspended its activities and elected a subcommittee to draft the final clauses. At last the files on the cases could rest for a while. I sighed with relief. I was so tired that I could hardly stand. Later I found out that

I had no right to be tired at that time. The opposition used this occasion to put a few Trojan horses in the text of the convention.

I saw them, if only dimly, but I could not rally myself for more understanding and vigorous counteraction. There was a psychological truth in all this. While one is running after a goal, one acts under the impetus of the constant movement and gathers force from the movement itself. But should one sit down, even for a moment during the running, it would be impossible to regain force and speed immediately. That is exactly what happened to me.

What were the Trojan horses? In Article XIV, a provision was adopted that limited the basic duration of the convention to ten years from the time of its coming into force. A practical example can elucidate this point. The convention came into force on January 12, 1951. The term of expiration is formally January 1961. However, in order to put Article XIV into effect, parties to the convention must renounce it at least six months before the term of its expiration. This means by July 1960. Should the number of parties, as a result of these renunciations, fall to fewer than sixteen, then the convention ceases to exist.[30]

The other Trojan horse was Article XVI, which permits revision of the convention at any time. This is unusual for this type of convention. Normally, revisions take place after a certain number of years have elapsed.

There is no reason to defend myself on this score. I should never have permitted the inclusion of these articles, but this would have required a new fight. I felt like a babysitter who takes a nap at the wrong time. I later made up for my weakness by turning this partial defeat into a victory. With all the forces at my command I worked at the next stage to obtain a great many ratifications, to make the Genocide Convention the best ratified of all treaties. I always remembered the fatal number "sixteen." I also fought off all later attempts to revise the convention. I will take up this matter in other chapters of my narrative report.

The Legal Committee finally approved the text of the convention and submitted it to the General Assembly for final action. I was glad, to put it mildly, that we had reached this stage, but I was so exhausted that my mind failed to fully grasp the significance of this event. I walked and talked automatically, as in a dream. I noticed everything around me but did not react as I should have. I awoke from my "dream" for an hour or so when the Assembly started to discuss the Genocide Convention on December 9.

There were many lights in the large hall. The galleries were full, and the delegates appeared to have a solemn radiating look. Most of them had a good smile for me. John Foster Dulles told me in a somewhat businesslike manner that I had made a great contribution to international law. The minister of foreign affairs of France, Robert Schuman, thanked me for my work and said he was glad that this great event took place in France.[31] Sir Zafarullah Khan said this new law should be called the Lemkin Convention, and then Dr. Evatt put the resolution on the Genocide Convention to a vote. Somebody requested a roll call. The first to vote was India. After her "yes," there was an endless number of "yeses." Nobody voted against. South Africa was absent. Basically, the vote was unanimous. A storm of applause followed. I felt on my face the flashlight of cameras. Delegates of Latin America, many of them close friends, rushed to give me an *abrazo*. Dr. Evatt strolled from the podium with a radiant face, and with his hand around my arm took a picture with me. The world was smiling and approving, and I had only one word in answer to all that: "Thanks." It was short word for acknowledging this new partnership between two worlds: my own world of long, frustrating efforts, hopes, and agonizing fears, and this new official world which now made a solemn pledge to preserve the life of the peoples and races of mankind.

John Hohenberg of the *New York Post*, a most level-headed gentleman, said: "Stay where you are. Don't move. They will come to you."[32] So it happened, and so I understood finally, almost physically, the power and significance of the Genocide Convention.

The jubilant mood of the Assembly communicated itself to the gallery. Many strangers came to congratulate me. Among them was an elderly man with long white hair who kept my hand a long time, while looking at me with sad eyes. Then he left, saying nothing. But those who say nothing sometimes carry off with them part of our souls.

Later, the press came to interview me. In my campaign I had worked closely with the press and developed deep friendships with many correspondents. They were genuinely interested in my campaign. We had to educate world opinion on a difficult problem that, although moral, had a legal form. Basically the press does not like to report on legal matters. But the correspondents made this exception because together we found the human kernel on which it was built. They reported on all the difficulties and victories in Paris, as they had done from Lake Success. Now we shared in a common victory and we were all happy.

Two days later, the representatives of twenty-two nations signed the convention.[33] Signature means the intention to ratify by the parliament. It is an act of government, but it must be followed up by an act of parliament, if a nation decides to ratify a treaty.

Sir Zafarullah came to this ceremony in his national clothes, which he seldom wore in the Assembly. The lights flashed again. The U.N. correspondent, Mike Hayworth, grabbed me during the ceremony to his recording booth and asked me to improvise a message. I obliged: "The U.N., acting as Santa Claus, is giving the world a beautiful Christmas gift. The Genocide Convention is being signed by the first twenty-two nations. Congratulations!"

And then the lights in Palais de Chaillot went out. The Assembly was over. Delegates shook hands hastily with one another and disappeared into the winter mists of Paris.

The same night I went to bed with fever. In his broadcast from Paris, Lowell Thomas called me the "happiest man in Paris." But I was aware of only one thing: I was sick and bewildered.

Next day the French radio asked me to make a recording. I could not refuse, although I felt sick. The radio people promised to make the recording in my room. I tried to assemble my thoughts, but nothing sensible came out of my throat when I started to talk into the recording machine. The following day I went to the hospital in Paris, where I was sick for longer than three weeks. Nobody had established my diagnosis. I defined it myself and I called it genociditis: exhaustion from the work on the Genocide Convention.

A month later I was returning by boat to New York. I made new friends and had long walks with them on the upper deck. The salty sea air was invigorating. Staring for hours at the futile struggle of the waves was both relaxing and absorbing. The waves seemed to be angry without reason. I did not dare to make comparisons, to avoid reminding myself of my past experiences.

I could engage only in small talk and avoided anything that would draw me into a serious conversation. Instinctively, I was defending myself against something which, I thought, almost destroyed me in Paris.

CHAPTER ELEVEN

Climbing a Mountain Again[1]

I WAS BACK WITH MY YALE students but could not regain my health completely until May of 1949. Then new life started on the campus and also in me. I always liked spring on the campus. The challenge of youth moving noisily with fast and sure steps matches the vigorous bursting of life into the trees, grass, and flowers. It matters little that the students themselves are not aware of this. Their minds are on examinations and graduation. They are as unconscious of their real contributions to campus life as the trees and the flowers, because they are life itself in its most truthful and expressive manifestation.

My classes were small and I was able to know my students intimately and have many searching conversations with them. The mind of the student is critical. He likes to disbelieve, to ask questions and to control the answers. He is a philosopher without philosophy. At the same time, he tries to be practical. He knows he is living in a competitive society.

I gave a course on genocide. In directing the frequent discussions I tried to keep the students within the scope of the problem and then would drop a thought almost casually, which they would grab avidly, like a ball in a baseball game. They understood and approved of the humanitarian aspects of the Genocide Convention, but could not see immediately and readily the implications of genocide in terms of cultural losses. Their minds more easily grasped the procedural issues than the substantive ones. Although my class was for law students, I took an interdisciplinary approach and introduced concepts from psychology, sociology, anthropology, and even economics.

We even discussed word formation. I explained the importance of the term "genocide," which conveys the idea of the basic social unit (the genos) through which man grew and developed in his social and cultural dimensions. The Roman "genos," the Greek "genos," and the Sanskrit "genos" are basically the same social unit, originally conceived as an enlarged family unit having the conscience of a common ancestor—first real, later imagined. It is in the "genos" that the peculiar spirit of the group grew and where a peculiar way of life developed, whether in Greek, Roman, or Arian societies. Other ancient societies—the Aztecs, the Iroquois, Indians, and others—had similar social units. "Can you form a word half Greek and half Latin?" I was asked. "Why not? Our language is full of hybrids. In this case we used a word that would also convey the religious connotation. Since in some cultures philosophy and religion are the same, the Greek 'genos' is more appropriate than the Latin since it appears in Pseudo Plato-epistola 7 in the expression 'genos philosofumtion'—those who study philosophy, the group of the thinkers. Thus 'genocide' conveys the meaning not only of a nation, race, tribe, but also of a religious group."

"Moreover," I continued, "the broad 'O' in the middle of the word 'genocide' is always used in words to convey the meaning of a large object, and this is very appropriate in this case. Genocide conveys the concept of destroying great masses of peoples of a nation. The 'genos' is thus a primary and universal institution of mankind, whatever its actual evolution may be, and it is clear that mankind spent most of its history within the framework of this social unit. It was here that the original esprit de corps, the way of life, the traditions, the forces of cohesion and solidarity were born. It was also here that the spirit of exclusiveness, suspicion, and hatred of other groups was bred. At the same time, the genos became the residue of racial memories and the transmitter of idiosyncrasies and prejudices. It became the nursery of group pride and group hatred. This spirit of the 'genos' is deeply entrenched in the psychology of mankind. It finds expression in the pervasive feeling of superiority of one group over all others. This is sometimes subconscious, sometimes conscious, but always dangerous, because it creates a pragmatism that justifies cold destruction of the other group when it appears necessary or useful. The cult of common ancestors was pursued in the genos.

"Thus the genos is both the unit against which the crime is directed and the unit from which it originates. Genocide is a crime perpetrated by one genos against another. That the checks and balances of a criminal nature find place in relations between one genos and another is easily seen from the fact that if a member of one genos kills a member of another genos, the duty of the perpetrator is incumbent upon the genos that was injured. Here we are dealing not with casual events but with deeply entrenched anthropological and sociological patterns. Until now, we have done very little to eradicate these patterns. We are only at the beginning of this great work."

"Can you really achieve results against such a disease?" I was asked.

"Yes, you can, if you do not look at the watch while you are asking this question. It will take a long time before results are noticeable. The Genocide Convention is only a framework for this task, a rallying point for thinking and acting. A starting point for a new conscience! Not only lawyers but also representatives of other disciplines will have to help. The Genocide Convention is predestined not only to punish but also to prevent genocide. The work of the anthropologist, social psychologist, historian, and even the economist could help in planning prevention. Only a combination of punishment and prevention can bring results. Through repeated invocation of court action over a long time, through repeated condemnation of genocide in public opinion, conscience in the form of the integrity of the other group will grow. Conscience operates mostly with the feeling of shame. Once this feeling envelopes an act of genocide, half of the work will be done. The moral condemnation will become easier because genocide was made a crime. It must be condemned by national society.

"It was made an international crime. This means the condemnation by world society must also follow. The peculiar moral degradation that accompanies this crime against innocent people will help to articulate this condemnation and to mold world conscience."

"What are the economic implications of genocide?" I was asked.

"These can be seen in both the consequences and the origins of the crime. Please look up the U.S.A. consular reports to the Commerce Department for 1932. From these reports it will be easy to see that even sixteen years after the genocide of the Armenians, the volume of foreign trade dropped considerably (32 percent by 1932). The economic deterioration in Spain after the expulsion of the Jews and Moors in the fourteenth century was very great.

"There is also a very characteristic economic consequence of genocide, which works like a vicious circle. The religious, moral, or national groups were not admitted to government service because of prejudice. They had no other choice but to engage in trades and commerce. This kind of occupation brought them income and pushed them upward into the richer classes. When they became too rich, they would inevitably invite the animosity of the majority of the population. This led to genocidal actions against them."

Of course, I was continuing to write the history of genocide and continued to bring this history into the classes, all in moderation, in order not to do more harm than good by confusing the students. The result proved to be rewarding. By the middle of the course they saw the problem of genocide very clearly. It was like making a picture, except that after the last brushstrokes, the painting comes to life.

Late in the evenings I used to walk in the quadrangle before the library on the Yale campus. It was one of the most beautiful and quiet corners. In the moonlight one could read a book there. There was so much steady caressing and inspiring light. Sometimes some of my students would come to join me, occasionally bringing their friends, even their girlfriends. The light would last late into the night. It was like a meeting of the minds of the ancient Druids. In this quadrangle one felt very close to the cosmos itself. Everything one said seemed to be more important than if it had been said in the class. Does the mere absence of classroom walls free our souls? Do we need the help of natural beauty to increase our intellectual perception? Or maybe it is the voice of the night: "Listen to the voice of the night! The voice of the night is true."

After every discussion on the quadrangle I could better understand why Socrates had such a great influence on the youth of ancient Athens. Through his creative dialogues he used his powerful mind to stimulate wisdom in his pupils' minds, in the natural settings of the seashore and the fields. Every one of his young friends would become both a pupil and a teacher. To teach is to instill a teaching ability in one's student, even if temporarily. Footnotes are not absolutely necessary to the perception of truth, or to the love of truth. Teaching creates a new world in the soul and mind of the student. Footnotes should be used later to strengthen this world, as bricks are used to carry on the design of a building. Why did the teachings of Socrates survive only in the form of tutorships in England? On one of these evenings we began to talk about Edmund Burke, the famous English historian of the seventeenth century. Burke said that in every society a controlling power is necessary to curtail tyrannical wills and cruelty. Without such a controlling power society cannot exist. Moreover, one society can infect another, and whole civilizations may suffer. In brief, morality must be made a common good of most of the world.

"What is more dangerous," a student said, "[is] that evil statesmen are so blinded that they do not see the evil they are producing and the bad reaction they are creating in others." I quoted the diary of Henry Morgenthau, Sr., the American ambassador to Turkey who tried to save the Armenians in 1915 when they were engulfed by genocide of some 1.2 million persons. While Morgenthau was talking to the minister of the interior, Talaat Pasha, endeavoring to prevent deportations of the Armenians to the death camps, Talaat Pasha interrupted him with an "innocent" question: "By the way, Mr. Ambassador, on some of the Armenians we found insurance policies, and even reassurance policies from companies in the American city of Hartford, Connecticut. Since they are Turkish citizens, could you help the Turkish government to cash these policies?"

Another example of the moral isolation of the genocidist can be found in the case of genocide of the Hereos in 1896. This African tribe was driven by the German colonists into a forest together with their cattle. Deep trenches were built around a section of the forest so that the people and the cattle could not escape. Then kerosene was sprinkled on the trees in this section and it was set afire. The people and the cattle perished together. In his report to the German Ministry of Foreign Affairs, the German consul of the area complained that only the cattle were destroyed.

My quadrangle audience unanimously agreed that genocide creates a subliminal mentality that becomes natural. On this night we were all thinking of the prophetic words of Edmund Burke in relation to the Genocide Convention.

I was sure of the stability of their knowledge and to some degree of their moral integrity, because I did not impose my knowledge upon them. They arrived at their ideas by themselves under my direction. Soon I had proof of this.

A church in Hartford, Connecticut, invited me to give a talk on genocide. I answered that I was busy that day, but I recommended one of my students. He went and enchanted the audience with his masterful and scholarly presentation. In addition, he was presented with a check for ten dollars, which he proudly displayed to the class.

I once took my students to the United Nations and introduced them to some of my friends in the delegation. They stood dignified and self-assured in the Delegates' Lounge and discussed genocide with the delegates with a superior knowledge, while sipping orange juice.

The universities and colleges in the U.S. are the only place where you can express feeling without fear of being sentimental.

Lake Success

I felt that I should resume my U.N. activities. The Assembly was meeting that spring in Lake Success as a continuation of the Assembly in Paris. It had to deal with the problem of Korea, which was left over by the Assembly of 1948. I went to Lake Success. When I entered the Assembly Hall, Dr. Evatt, who was presiding, sent an Assembly usher to ask me to join him on the podium. I told him that I had been ill after the Paris Assembly but was now ready for the ratification campaign. It would be good to start, symbolically, with one ratification for every continent and then use this intercontinental symbol of humanitarian solidarity in approaching other governments. Dr. Evatt saw the validity of this approach and promised to arrange speedy ratification by Australia. Indeed, he introduced the bill of ratification in his parliament on May 19, 1949. The speech in parliament of his prime minister, Mr. Chifley, was sent to me at Yale.[2]

I saw Stuart Spencer, the American advisor to the Ethiopian government, and asked him to send a cable to his government about ratification. On May 1, 1949, Ethiopia became the first country to ratify. I also sent letters to Terje Wold, the chairman of the committee on foreign affairs of the Norwegian parliament, with whom I had stayed in Paris, and to Judge Paal Berg, the heroic leader of the resistance in Norway in the last war.[3] Their answers were most reassuring. I thought also that ratification by Iceland would have a symbolic significance. I cited Iceland so often in my conversations with the delegates, as an example of how genocide can not only destroy a small people but also extirpate an original culture carried by some 168,000 persons. All these initiatives soon bore fruit. I went to the Icelandic delegation in Washington and got a good reception for my suggestion. All four nations ratified and thus a new stage of my work began.[4]

My plan was to obtain at least twenty ratifications so that the General Assembly of 1950 could draw up the protocol to bring the convention into force. There were already signatures from three continents: two from Europe (Iceland and Norway), one from Australia, one from Africa. But there still were none from Latin America or Asia. I confided my concern to Dr. Jose Correa, of the delegation of Ecuador. He had an answer. "Jorge Villagómez Yépez, a professor of philosophy of law and a member in the Chamber of Deputies, will be soon in New York," he said. "Talk to him. I will let you know when he comes."[5] I invited Professor Villagómez Yépez to Yale, where we had an entire day to ourselves. He promised to do his utmost, and Ecuador became the first Latin American nation to ratify the convention. We made also a lasting and rewarding friendship.

To reach my goal for 1950 I thought I should concentrate on Latin America, because small nations need the protection of international law more than big nations. Latin America has an abundance of small nations; some with populations under one million (Panama, Honduras, Costa Rica); some with two or three million (El Salvador, Guatemala, Cuba, the Dominican Republic, Uruguay). These populations, two or three times as small as the number of Jews murdered by Hitler, could easily see the reality of the genocide threat. Latin American nations faced the leadership of a new humanitarianism, while Asia and Africa were preoccupied with the formation of new states and Europe was healing the wounds received in two wars. In fighting for a new concept I could also lean more heavily on the philosophical undercurrent and on the conceptualism of Latin intellectuals.

(Of course I could not neglect Europe, where the memories of genocide were still fresh. The approach to every nation must be made by stressing values peculiar to it. The correspondence must be in the language of the nation approached and in appealing to the traditions of her people. A bridge of sympathetic understanding and "at home" feeling must be established. I understood that from now on I would have to do more working than talking.)

I found at Yale a graduate law student from Colombia, Jaime Angel, who was idealistic and skillful. Then I engaged a Spanish secretary of Cuban origin. Angel told me that, in general, people in Latin America are slow in answering letters. Letters must be short and strong. First we wrote to all ministers of foreign affairs, then to the presidents of republics. The Catholic church wields great influence in Latin America, so we sent letters to archbishops and bishops in all twenty republics.

Angel's apprehensions were not fully justified. He did not realize that the U.N. correspondents had done a great job in bringing the Genocide Convention to the attention of the people. My letters fell on prepared ground. Slowly but surely, the Latin American nations started to work on ratification.

In the spring Assembly of 1949 I met Amalia de Castillo Ledón, a member of the delegation of Mexico and the president of the Inter-American Commission of Women.[6] She was idealistic and clever, and among all the Latin American ladies I knew, the only blonde. She had a sense of humor and could meet every adversity with genuine laughter. (We talked about the most serious matters in the form of jokes. This was the form to which she reacted best. Once I wanted her to sign an important document for action on genocide. My conversation with her secretary, Consuelo Rodriquez of Guatemala, was as follows: "Tell Mrs. Ledón that if she does not do that, I will marry her mother [who was a widow] and thus will become her stepfather and then I will spank her legitimately.") Born and raised in Mexico among intellectuals, Amalia Ledón had a deep conscience and a profound sense of compassion. She could talk about human misery and the bitter struggle against it with a long, grim face. When she heard about the Genocide Convention she offered the help of her organization. She was about to visit Central America on behalf of her organization. I told her that I had already written to the ministers of foreign affairs, as well as to the presidents of the republics. "I will refer to your letters and will support your request in the name of my organization," she replied. "Moreover, our branches will work for ratification."

This promise was followed by action. For several years I worked with her organization. Once I phoned Mrs. Ledón from Yale to San Jose in Costa Rica and she told me triumphantly that the minister of foreign affairs had just sent the convention to the parliament for ratification.

I also wrote to other organizations in Latin America. Some did not reply, but most sent delegations to the ministers of foreign affairs of their countries and talked with members of parliament. The issue was growing in importance in the eyes of the people. This was what I really wanted.

I used to spend my weekends in Saybrook, half an hour from New Haven, at the Castlebroom Inn, with a terrace over the water. One Sunday morning, while lounging lazily on the terrace and reading the Sunday paper, I found a report from Guatemala City. A congress of Latin American universities was meeting there. Among the organizers was Méndez Pereira, president of the University of Panama, with whom I had remained friends since the Assembly of 1946.[7] He was always enthusiastic about the endorsement of the convention by Panama. I immediately sent a cable asking the congress to endorse the Genocide Convention. I was not mistaken.

Later, the congress adopted a resolution and submitted it to all ministers of foreign affairs of Latin America. As a result, many presidents of universities (or rectors, as they are called) became interested and worked individually in their countries for ratification. The president of the congress was the rector of the university in Guatemala, Señor Carlos Duvan. He became enthusiastic about the issue and proved to be a great source of ideas and initiatives. Later, when he was appointed minister to Rome, he offered to continue his help from his new post.

I felt that I was not working in a vacuum. The universities meant not only the presidents, but the professors and students as well. From that time on I received numerous letters containing questions about genocide and asking for information to support doctoral dissertations. Work on genocide started in many universities.

One day at the United Nations I was introduced to the ambassador of Haiti, who was also a famous novelist. He was called the Black Maurois. Tall, with a handsome ferocity in his meaningful face, he was one of those men who could captivate one's mind with every word he said and with the pulsations of his intense personality. Black Maurois lived with the knowledge of countless cases of genocide against his own race.

When the Assembly of 1949 started, I began to travel from Yale to Lake Success more often. I began to think about a resolution, working with new member states, to ratify the convention. This possibility was foreseen in the convention. At that time the U.N. had only sixty members. Many nations, kept out by the big powers, were frustrated in their international feelings and eager to prove their faith in the U.N. They could give no finer proof than by ratifying the convention, if given a chance.

I confided my plans to the delegates of Australia, Cuba, and the Philippines. Promptly, they introduced such a resolution, and it was adopted. Accordingly, in January 1950 the secretary general of the U.N. sent invitations to ratify the convention to the following nonmember nations: Korea, the Federal Republic of Germany, Italy, Laos, Ceylon, Jordan, Monaco, Bulgaria, Romania, and Hungary. (Although they were not U.N. members, their ratifications would count among the twenty necessary to bring the convention into force.)

At this Assembly I met two parliamentarians from the French delegation who were of decisive importance for France's ratification: Marcel Plaisant, chairman of the Commission on Foreign Affairs of the Council de la Republique, and Pierre Montel.[8] I talked with both of them at length. Plaisant, a leading intellectual in France, listened attentively, stopping to sip his orange juice for long intervals. His round face was serene and concentrated. I sensed immediately that I had a powerful ally in this man. "This issue corresponds to my own ideals and to those of France," he said. "I will work for ratification. Rest assured France will be on the list of nations whose ratification will bring the Genocide Convention into force." I sensed in his voice the self-assurance, serenity, and revolutionary zeal of those wonderful generations of French philosophers and intellectuals who for centuries have embraced progress as a self-evident truth and as a new religion for modern man.

Pierre Montel was different. A businessman from Lyon, he was preoccupied with difficulties—those faced by France and Frenchmen in the last war, and those of the future, which he did not appear to find very bright. We had several long conversations. His face was tense and pale: "My son was tortured to death by the occupier in the last war." He said this with such a voice that I could almost see a young man hanging from a tree: "When the treaty is submitted to our Parliament, I will alert all commissions of the Assembly. It should be ratified without one word of discussion. This is a matter of national honor. Please keep me informed and write to me as often as you wish."

I felt that these were very significant conversations and reiterated them to my students the next day. Among them was a young Frenchman whose father was the famous economic historian, Black, who was shot in the last war. He said nothing during the class. His face became paler than ever. After class he stayed on and asked whether he could show me a picture of his father. It was a worn picture, which he carried constantly in his wallet. It seemed tired from the languishing eyes of the young man, who looked so often at this piece of paper, which was all that was left to him from a full and once happy life.

I dispatched letters to Édouard Herriot, the president of the French National Assembly, to Plaisant and Montel, and to the former prime minister of France, Leon Blum, whom I knew.[9] Blum had spent several years in a concentration camp in Germany. They all replied to my letters and actually gave help. Then I entered into correspondence with the rapporteur on genocide of the French National Assembly, Minjoz, who did everything he could to accelerate ratification.[10]

While my correspondence with France continued, Miss Zahir Hossovan was checking on the ratification process in Paris and informed me of every step. In July 1950 the French law on ratification was published in the official gazette of the French government. As Montel had promised, it was ratified without debate by the plenary session of the Assembly. The need for ratification was considered self-evident.

I met the minister of foreign affairs of Canada, Lester B. Pearson, at the Assembly in 1949.[11] There was something solidly impressive about this man, who carried his deep concern about his country and the world with such natural simplicity and grace. Although an intellectual (he started out as a history instructor at Yale), one could really see not only that he relied on the findings of the brain and on intelligence reports, but that he also kept in touch with reality through the avenues of intuition. Statesmen do not like the word "intuition." They are afraid that intuition is too much an attribute of women and prefer to call it "horse sense." But horse sense also helps them to easily detect a moral problem. Lester Pearson saw the value of the Genocide Convention, but he saw it first as a human being and only second as a master of external affairs. When presiding over an Assembly he sat on the podium of the world with the same easy and natural manner as a storekeeper at his counter. And yet in the U.N., this man made momentous decisions affecting the peace of the world. In 1956 he was responsible for setting up a U.N. police force in the Near East. One could feel his intellectual independence, which he was only too eager to put into action. One could also recognize what is so appealing about all Canadians: they basically reject the theory that international feeling must necessarily be devious. "Let us first try it straight," they imply by all their behavior, and they remain at that point. Such was all of Lester B. Pearson.

I told him what a great contribution his countrymen and his fellow diplomats had made to the Genocide Convention. He took it as a matter of course and promised to get his department to work on ratification. I was in constant contact with his department and continually received information on the state of affairs from his associates. I also organized support for the convention by approaching many organizations throughout Canada. They responded most avidly. Of particular help was the Canadian vice president of the International Council of Women, Mrs. Hardy, who lived in Ottawa and had good social contacts with people in government. All women's organizations, many church groups, national groups such as the Ukrainians, the Lithuanians, and the Poles, as well as the Jewish groups, also wrote to the Canadian Department on External Affairs.[12] However, the Canadian ratification was not ready before 1950, and Canada became only the fortieth country to ratify the convention.[13]

I was always in friendly relations with the delegation of the Philippines, especially with Ambassador Carlos and his deputy, Judge Joye.[14] In Paris I worked closely with Senator Quintin Paredes. It was not diffi- cult to convince the Philippine delegation that their country should be among the first twenty to ratify the Genocide Convention. (I submitted a memorandum and stressed especially the importance of ratification be- fore the Assembly of 1950. It is always easier to get results when one has an agenda. Governments also like to work this way.)

The Filipinos were so interested in this convention that Senator Jesus Queuco submitted a draft of a domestic law against genocide in 1947, a year before the Assembly in Paris adopted the Genocide Convention. This interest can be explained by the fact that the Philippines suffered a great deal under Spanish colonial rule and also in the last war under Japanese occupation. Many attempts were made to destroy the national character of the Philippine people. Their national pride suffered many injuries. Their vivid imagination, intellectual generosity, and innate sense of drama found expression and release in this convention. They promised to ratify quickly, and they kept their word.[15]

After the secretary general of the U.N. dispatched invitations to non- member nations to sign the convention, I started to work with these nations as well. I sent out letters to Korea, to the president and to the minister of foreign affairs.[16]

But somehow the document of ratification was late to arrive. I found out about Korea's ratification by accident only at the beginning of the 1950 Assembly. At that time, every ratification was very important. In the Delegates' Lounge at Lake Success I met a man who was introduced to me as the Korean minister of foreign affairs. I told him that we were in correspondence, and he replied that Korea had already ratified, and that the document was now circulating somewhere in Seoul between the prime minister's and the president's offices for completion of the neces- sary formalities. Since we needed twenty ratifications for bringing the convention into force, the minister was ready to sign a letter to the Sec- retary General to the effect that Korea had ratified. The next day the consulate general of Korea brought the letter and deposited it in the secretary general's office. We had another ratification among the minimum of twenty that were needed.

Ratification by France would influence ratification by several non-member nations, as Laos, Cambodia, and Vietnam were at that time French protectorates. Their ratification was easily arranged and completed almost automatically by France. Several conversations with their representatives at the U.N. and with their ambassadors convinced me that these ratifications were completely in accord with their feelings.

My friend Jean Nussbaum visited me at Yale and delivered a lecture to my class on the problem of the reform of the calendar, a problem that was on the agenda of the council.[17] I consulted with him about Monaco and he offered to stop there on one of his trips to his home in Switzerland.

A conference of ministers of foreign affairs of Latin America and the U.S.A. was taking place in Washington, D.C., in April 1950. I decided to go to this conference and talk to some of the ministers personally. The meetings took place in the Pan American Union, in a beautiful stone building on Constitution Avenue. The day I arrived, a blending of white clouds wandering on a blue firmament of a summer day was brought to a standstill through its own laziness. I walked into the conference during a recess. The delegates were engaged in conversing among themselves and their visiting friends. Lively, not loud, friendly but not too familiar, the Latin always instinctively know the right tone for their social gatherings. Although Latin American diplomats are conscious of their official position, there is no stiffness about them. They do not carry defense mechanisms like Roman shields around their personality. Their inner self is always open to human touch. From a small group in the middle of the crowd Amalia de Castillo Ledón nodded to me. She introduced me to the minister of foreign affairs of El Salvador, Dr. Rafael Urquia, who later became representative to the U.N. A friendly conversation followed. The minister knew about the Genocide Convention from Mrs. Ledón and from my letters. "El Salvador has been working on the ratification—it will be ready for the 1950 Assembly," he assured me. I also met Minister of Foreign Affairs Carressa, who introduced me to his assistant.

I called the Embassy of Haiti in Washington and asked for an appointment with the minister of foreign affairs, Monsieur Leger. "Your ancestors, Excellency, were brought as slaves to this hemisphere," I said to him. "They were tortured and beaten; now you are a free people. Please translate your own experiences into an act for the good of all humanity. Your government should be in the forefront of this action. Otherwise, what is the meaning of the death of those who perished in the past?" I pleaded. "This man will certainly do it," I thought when I looked closer at the face of the minister, who was now sitting with me on the sofa. I felt that I was no longer speaking in general terms about the much-abused word "humanity," which was like the inaccessible idea of good. Instead, I approached the substance of concrete people, their wounds, their sweat, their fears and longings. They appeared in my imagination in long lines on the shores of sunny Africa loaded on boats with their wives and children crying goodbye. When they turned their eyes to look for the last time at the place of their vanishing happiness, a slash of a whip would descend upon their brown bodies. Then, crowded on the decks of ships, they would suffocate from stench, tremble from fever, and look with stupor at the bodies of their countrymen as they were flung into the sea.

"What happened to these people?" Did he not want to be reminded about his ancestors, since he was now a man in power, or was he unaware?

"Give me more details about the convention," he said with a voice that came from afar. The afternoon sun spread a bright design on the walls of this quiet room. It trembled on the rug, the chairs, and the little statue on the desk. Then it occurred to me that I was pounding at an open door. This man next to me feels this thing in me as vividly as I do. It is his "thing" now. This was already in him long ago, but it was covered with dust, as it was in many other statesmen. A jewel regains its shine when the dust is removed. He accompanied me to the door, warmly gripped my hand, and said, *"Nous allons le faire."* (We will do it.)

While in Washington on another occasion I visited several embassies. Sir Carl Berendsen of New Zealand received me graciously and promised to convey my request of ratification to Wellington.[18] Then I went to the Embassy of Ceylon. The ambassador was away and I was received by the charge d'affaires, Gunewardene, a man with an ascetic face half covered by large eyeglasses. But the eyes were penetrating, and while I talked, I felt them burning on my face. "You people are predominantly snobbish. The sanctity of life is a basic tenet of the religion of the majority of your people. Buddhism has removed through its teachings many incitements to genocide: greed, anger, illusion. Buddhism has already stopped genocide in the past. The Mongolians slaughtered many millions of people. When they came to China and their Kublai Khan adopted Buddhism, he stopped slaughter. Should not the practical workings of your religion cause your government to ratify the Genocide Convention now so that your government may be considered among those who brought the convention in force? Ceylon would become a founding nation of the convention."

My interlocutor was a learned man who liked to talk history and philosophy. When I said goodbye to him, I received a promise that he would urge upon his government ratification before the Assembly of 1950. All this appeared to me quite natural, when I talked to the right people, at the right time, and in the right place. I also sensed that my arguments were well founded and presented with enough sincerity to make an impression.

While in Washington I was asked to call Angela de Chacon, who was representing Costa Rica for the plight of women. She was a lawyer, a fighter for the rights of women, a person with a highly developed conscience and imagination. She wrote a feature story for a legal magazine in her country and for the Colombian magazine *El Lumbre*. One day she advised me to see her ambassador in Washington: "Your idea about concentrating first on the small nations is good. The ambassador is young, idealistic, and a lawyer who likes new concepts," she said. I saw the ambassador. He asked me to write to him as soon as I returned to Yale. In reply, I received the following letter:

June 9, 1950

Embassy of Costa Rica
Washington 8, D.C.
N. 1988
Professor Raphael Lemkin
School of Law
Yale University
New Haven, Conn.

Distinguished Professor Lemkin,

For your information I have the pleasure to transcribe the note Number 7185/e dated the 3rd of the current month received today from the Ministry of External Affairs of my country, which verbally says:

"Dear Ambassador: I have the pleasure to acknowledge the receipt of your note Number 1943 dated the 29 of the last May in which you enclose a copy of a letter of Prof. Raphael Lemkin of Yale University, which he sent to you and in which he explains extensively the convention on the crime of genocide, which was presented at the U.N. some time ago. The contents of Professor Lemkin's note is highly interesting and I am taking the liberty of preparing several copies of it in order to present them to members of the Cabinet as well as to the Directional of the Legislative Assembly in view of considering the possibility of ratifying the convention by our country. I am using this opportunity to sign attentively as your friend (—) Ricardo Toledo, Undersecretary in charge of External Affairs." Since there is nothing else in particular to report at this time, I am pleased to send to you my warm esteem.

Mario Echandi[19]
Ambassador

Ambassador Echandi followed up his action in his country. He understood the convention and contributed greatly to its ratification.

In the spring of 1958, Echandi became president-elect of Costa Rica. On his visit to the U.S.A. I called his secretary at the Waldorf-Astoria, and he expressed interest in seeing me. He was glad that the convention had already fifty-eight ratifications and promised to cooperate fully in furthering this cause.

When I was in Washington I went also to the delegation of Liberia, in a modest house on Sixteenth Avenue, and met the charge d'affaires, Mr. Bright. "Mr. Charge d'affaires," I started out, "I am specializing in a sad subject: genocide. There is drama in it and a promise to end slaughter in the future. The races that were persecuted should be especially interested in this law. There were attempts in the Assembly to prevent its adoption. Since it is adopted now, let us concentrate on bringing it in force," I pleaded.

I told him about the target date. He fully understood and approved. There was a soothing quiet in this room, with its green plush sofas. He looked pensively through the window and said, "We have to move fast, and not allow this movement to halt before it obtains real force." He looked young, but there was a great maturity and force in his thinking and feelings.

What made all these people talk to me in terms of common concern and serious planning? Maybe I had been doing an injustice to others, and to myself, by thinking that I am a lonely fighter for this cause. The truth was that after the impact of a few kind reactions I could not formulate an opinion about the rest of the world. After a case of genocide the feelings are widely aroused, but then people again become indifferent. I was at a stage when the ebbing had not set in. Moreover, I had been talking to those who suffered and to those who were free from the power complexes of large states. But how long could I draw on their support and sympathy?

Clouds had been gathering on my horizon, but I was too busy to notice. I did not desire to be sidetracked from my plans by surrendering to doubts and fears.

Meanwhile, the ratification by Ecuador was being planned at the

U.N. This was to be a big event. I asked Trygve Lie to attend the ratification ceremony and phoned the *New York Times* to say that it would be helpful if a portion of the ceremony were recorded.[20] This actually happened, and the necessary effect was produced.

In the U.N. I had a luncheon with the delegate of Guatemala, Dr. Garcia Bauer, presently minister of foreign affairs of his country.[21] He was one of those blond and youthful-looking Latin American diplomats who could be taken for a native of more than one European nation. There are people who do not easily betray their inner selves. But a heart-to-heart talk makes them natural friends, dedicated and reliable. Then you start wondering why you did not talk to them much earlier: life would have been simpler. I confided to him my plan of twenty ratifications before the 1950 Assembly. We surveyed those that were already deposited: "I know that Guatemala with its humanitarian traditions will ratify this convention. But now is necessary. These first twenty nations will have to, in a larger sense, be the spokesmen before the world for this cause. They will be the founding nations of a new humanity. Quick action is necessary. All red tape must be cut." "It can be done, but you must write a letter to the president of Guatemala. My brother, who is now in New York, will deliver your letter directly to the president. This is the only chance to accelerate action. I will also work on it through regular procedures." Thus was speaking Ambassador Bauer of Guatemala.

After luncheon I wrote the letter and was introduced by the ambassador to his younger brother. To him this plan appeared so simple, so direct, that I could not but believe I was complicating the issue through unnecessary doubts. The letter was indeed delivered to the president, as Ambassador Bauer informed me in 1950.

However, I did not let the case rest on that. I asked several organizations with whom I had been in touch in that country since the Assembly of 1948 to request ratification. I also wrote to the rector of the University of Guatemala. On my next trip to Washington I also saw the minister of foreign affairs of Guatemala, who was visiting the U.S.A. at that time. It was always my contention that acts of government cannot and should not emanate exclusively from one high official but should be carried by the collective will of the people. Then and only then can the government reach the social and communal depth of the act. I thought that there would be more stability and continuity in my work if I proceeded that way.

Several weeks later the hearty smile of Ambassador Bauer greeted me at the Delegates' Lounge. "I received the notice of ratification and am presenting it any day now." Thus the ratification by Guatemala was achieved.[22]

I knew that I could count on two additional ratifications from Latin America: from Cuba and Panama. In view of Dr. Alfaro's dedication to this idea, and the pride the Panamanian people took in endorsing the genocide cause, ratification by Panama was a natural thing. I informed Dr. Alfaro about the plan and left it there. Indeed, the Panamanian document of ratification was deposited. But things appeared to be slower in Cuba. I wrote to the president by letter via the minister of foreign affairs, but the dates appeared not too well timed, and Cuba's ratification came after the Assembly of 1950.[23]

A bold plan was formulated in my mind: I would obtain ratification by Turkey among the first twenty founding nations. This would be atonement for genocide of the Armenians. But how could it be achieved? A longer conversation was required. I called the counselor Adnan Kural, with whom I was on friendly terms, and asked for an appointment. The previous night I kept thinking and planning how I would address the matter with him. I could not reach any decision but this: let me rely on intuition, which would guide me during the discussion. A few ideas simmered vaguely in my mind. The Turks are proud of their republican form of government and their progressive ideas, which distinguish their government from the rule of the Ottoman Empire. The Genocide Convention might well put this within the framework of social and international progress. I knew, however, that in this conversation both sides would have to avoid speaking about the other, although it would be constantly in their minds: the Armenians.

In the morning I started planning. I would like to see the name of Turkey among the first twenty nations, which would bring the Genocide Convention into force and open the way for the U.N. to proclaim social progress and advancement of international law. Modernized nations should help bring forward modern ideas. "Your country has achieved great reforms: the modern transformation of your alphabet, the liberation of your women, and the introduction of modern methods in education. The world has been watching you. The Genocide Convention is the best logical step. But this progress must be dramatized during the next General Assembly. Otherwise, your ratification, in which I believe, would be lost in later ratifications. Why not be a teacher instead of a pupil?" And then I added: "In the light of your present progress I see you are breaking radically with the past." Adnan Kural was a man made of one piece, like many Turkish diplomats whom I knew. So was the ambassador to the U.N., Selim Sarper.[24] The Turks never learned to speak with both sides of their mouth like their present Western friends. They have been either more outspoken in the U.N. than the others or completely silent. Kural promised to relay our conversation literally. He hoped for the best. The next day I saw Ambassador Selim and repeated my plea. He even promised to send a cable.

Things were really moving. I saw Sir Zafarullah Khan, of Pakistan, who told me that he talked in Washington with the ambassador of Saudi Arabia and convinced him to suggest ratification by Saudi Arabia. The ambassador was sympathetic, he reported. "However," he added, "things on ratification do not look too promising in my own country for the present." I was so grateful to this man for his help and sincerity. Jordan informed me in the meantime that it had also ratified. Things were moving indeed. Twenty ratifications by the Assembly of 1950 suddenly ceased to be an obstacle. I started to see with all my heart how the mirage in the desert was gradually transforming itself: on approaching the oasis, I saw flowers and water.

I was spending the end of the summer in Washington, D.C. On June 24, North Korean troops marched into South Korea.[25] The U.N. took steps to protect Korea. At the beginning of July the Korean ambassador addressed an urgent note to many U.N. representatives, in which he drew their attention to the fact that the threat of genocide was looming over Korea. He urged the governments to speed up ratification of the Genocide Convention so that an international law would exist to protect his own people in South Korea. This note was even discussed in certain parliaments. Through the American ambassador at the U.N., the Korean note also reached President Truman, who asked the chairman of the Senate Foreign Relations Committee, Tom Connally, to accelerate ratification by the U.S.A.[26]

From Washington I again sent several cables to Costa Rica and El Salvador. I saw Ambassador Héctor David Castro of El Salvador several times in Washington.

I firmly believed that during the Assembly, the convention would obtain the ratifications necessary for its coming into force. Before leaving for New York and Lake Success I received from the Cuban ambassador in Washington the news that the government of Cuba, in recognition of my work for the Genocide Convention, had awarded me the Grand Cross of the Order of Carlos Manuel de Céspedes of Cuba, the human rights medal of Cuba.[27]

The Cuban delegation had been one of three original sponsors of the Genocide Convention in 1946. I invited my friends for the ceremony at the Cuban Embassy. At the last moment I realized that I could not appear at the ceremony in brown sporty shoes, the only ones I possessed in Washington. I bought black shoes to match my dark blue suit, got a haircut, and appeared at six o'clock at the reception room of the Cuban Embassy on Sixteenth Street. I was calm and collected and tried to hide my pride as best as I could. But my friends, especially those from Latin America, became so conscious of the great honor bestowed upon me and showed it so profusely that I could not maintain the appearance of angelic modesty any longer and succumbed to human frailty with grace.

Of course I made a speech and thanked the government of Cuba. I used the occasion to stress the importance of the Genocide Convention at this hour of human history. Again there was a flash of cameras, a barrage of questions by the newspapermen, and off I went to Lake Success for the opening of the crucial U.N. Assembly of 1950.

This Assembly was crucial indeed. It was a mixture of innocent joy, great success, distress, deceit, and danger to my life and health. I did not at first see the blows and knives put in the body of the newborn baby, the Genocide Convention, which was permitted to be brought into force for the purpose of bringing it to its death a little later. Thus, at least, hoped the opposition at that time.

The drama before my eyes unrolled gradually. I was so focused on bringing the convention into force that I did not realize the opposition had been working quietly and astutely all the time, with superior techniques, on destroying the very building I was erecting. My intuition told me something was wrong, but at first it was very vague, like anticipating the sickness and death of somebody very dear.

One day in the overcrowded Delegates' Lounge I noticed consultants of organizations talking to each other. They were my main opponents and did not see me. I distinctly heard that they were discussing the Genocide Convention. One of them mentioned my name and said, "It is over his head." He was wrong; it was not over my head, it did not even reach my head yet. It was only in my skin. But I decided to find out. That afternoon I was consulting the U.N. documents officer on the new documents that were issued before the Assembly. Three were of interest to me. A memorandum issued by the British delegation on the problem of reservations to the Genocide Convention, the preparatory draft of the Draft Code of Crimes Against the Peace and Security of Mankind, and the Report of the International Law Commission. A cursory perusal of them filled me with dread. I never like to read U.N. legal documents. They are always written in a way that hides their real meaning. Their intent emerges only gradually, when one watches the interested delegate discussing them. Then one can see how from behind the corner of every ambiguity crawls a snake, first slowly, then faster and faster . . .

The U.K. memorandum was addressed to the secretary general of the

U.N. Attention was drawn to the fact that the Soviet Bloc delegations signed the convention with reservations to Article IX. The general meaning of these reservations was that if a case of genocide should ever be brought before the International Court of Justice, the agreement of these governments would have to be obtained before such a case could be heard.[28]

I was not happy about these reservations, as I was not happy about any limitation put on the obligations of governments in relation to genocide. But upon consideration I decided that these reservations had little practical significance. The Soviet Bloc nations were still bound by Article VIII (which was first thrown out in Paris but restored next day by my efforts), which permits the U.N. to exercise control over cases of genocide in all its organs. Counteraction to genocide must be exercised with all speed, before the victims are dead, and that could not be achieved by the International Court of Justice, where it takes around a year before a case is heard. Further, the U.K. memorandum pointed out that the Convention on Genocide did not contain any provisions as to the handling of reservations, and means would have to be sought on how to handle this problem. In brief, this memorandum endeavored to create a new difficulty, throwing a monkey wrench into the Genocide Convention. Normally, reservations to the treaties were treated as a matter of courtesy between governments. Mutual agreement was sought and mutual accommodation was the end of such negotiations.

The British, who were in principle against the Genocide Convention, had grasped this opportunity. Later I read that Sir Anthony Eden, the minister of foreign affairs, when asked in the House of Commons when the U.K. would ratify the Genocide Convention, declared in July 1950 that the matter was now different because of the Soviet Bloc reservations.[29] In short, this meant trouble of the kind at which the U.K. delegation had excelled these last years.[30] This time, I thought, the troubles may be real, because Dr. Evatt did not come to the Assembly during elections, which he ultimately lost. This meant for me another lonely battle, and an unexpected one.

The second document that I studied on a soft sofa in the Lake Success Delegates' Lounge was a preparatory draft of the Code of Offenses Against the Peace and Security of Mankind. This ambitious project was the result of efforts to introduce the principles of the statute and judgment in international law. In 1946 the General Assembly had adopted a resolution affirming the principles of the judgment, and of the Tribunal.

Since the 1946 resolution was without legal meaning (because a resolution of the Assembly is nonbinding), it was decided in another resolution of the Assembly of 1947 to ask the International Law Commission to formulate these principles and to submit them to the Assembly for confirmation, in order to incorporate them in the draft of the Code of Offenses. I had these two documents before my eyes. It was clear that no vote on the Draft Code of Offenses could be taken until the Assembly confirmed the principles of the Nuremberg Judgment. The Legal Committee would then have to use those principles in preparing its draft of the Code of Offenses at the 1950 Assembly. However, the draft code offered a good clue to what might happen to the Genocide Convention if and when the Nuremberg principles were confirmed. The draft code contained proposed offenses that did not yet exist in international law, such as strife, annexations, and maintaining military forces in excess of contingents established in advance. These were and remain highly important issues.

One small paragraph contained a definition of genocide (the term "genocide" was omitted). For the first time a new type of responsibility was introduced in this draft: that of authorities of a state. But authorities of a state are corporate bodies, and corporate bodies cannot be held responsible in criminal law. A definition was offered to replace the reality of the Genocide Convention. In addition, all formulated offenses from the Nuremberg Judgment—such as aggression or even threat of aggression, war crimes, and, last but not least, crimes against humanity, or inhuman acts—were included. These last were to be offenses only when committed in execution of a war of aggression. Since aggression was not and shall not be defined, the entire concept of crimes against humanity was not defined either. We were once again in 1950 where we had started in 1946: the life of nations was to be kept in jeopardy, and enforcement was to depend on opportunity's consideration. The entire British plan was here, but I was more than curious how they would put it into effect. My problem now was not to lose my head. The opposition must be daring and far reaching, because the convention was becoming a reality. This was natural, and there is even a principle of Buddhist philosophy to confirm it: "Every action generates a reaction." But what should I do with the plan of bringing the convention into force during the present Assembly? What about the honor test of the twenty nations, founders of the convention? I promised it. Not all ratifications had arrived yet. Should I continue to press for the first twenty ratifications, or delay action? Surely I did not have all the information.

I must find out more. But from whom? Let me think it over.

The next day I spent all day in the Delegates' Lounge doing nothing, just thinking and observing. Dr. Ivan Kerno, the assistant secretary general in charge of legal affairs, was having a drink with some delegates at the bar.[31] I waited until they had left him. Dr. Kerno knew about the plan with all the details, but he would not tell me. I would stop talking about the Genocide Convention and discuss the draft code or the Nuremberg Judgment. As a lawyer, he would be unable to resist the temptation to talk about law and to express ideas that appeared new and original to him. With this idea in mind, I headed to the bar.

"Would you have a drink with me, Dr. Kerno?"

"Gladly."

It appeared to me that he really was glad to see me, although he seemed depressed at that moment.

"Dr. Kerno," I said, "the Nuremberg principles are on the agenda, and some delegates told me they are not quite sure how these could be actual international law."

"This is simple. These principles must be made part of customary international law."

"But there is the principle of legality in criminal law, which means that a crime must be defined in a law that was enacted in advance of the commission of the crime."

"The Assembly, with its resolutions confirming the Nuremberg Judgment, certainly creates customary law," said Dr. Kerno.

It dawned on me that I had heard this argument in 1948 in Paris when I paid a visit to the soft-spoken Monsieur Boissane, the attorney general of the Court of Appeals. I had answered at that time that customary law cannot be made by repeating resolutions but only by actually rendering judgments in courts. Moreover, I pointed out that this type of customary law would destroy all judiciary guaranties for the individual introduced by the French Revolution, of which France is so proud. I repeated my argument to Dr. Kerno, and only added a question: How many resolutions, which are nonbinding recommendations, would the U.N. Assembly have to adopt before one could say that customary law had been established?

Dr. Kerno remained pensive. He was finishing his drink and was about to reach for the cherry at the bottom of his glass, but he forgot about the cherry. I proposed another drink. His glass was refilled and there were two cherries in it, and many grave legal doubts in the head of the legal officer of the U.N.

I tried to adjust to the new draft code as best as I could. It was hard, especially at night, when I was alone with my thoughts. It was like standing over an abyss. Gradually I decided to go on with my original plan for bringing the convention into force. I figured it this way: the opposition will not give up, so I am sentenced to constant struggle, until the end of my days. In this struggle I must keep building positions for victory, one after another. Some might be destroyed, but I hope not completely. Those damaged may be repairable, with patience and endurance. Let me proceed with my original plan for 1950 and make the most of it. The convention will become a positive international law, and the opposition will have more difficulty destroying it. At least they will have a hard time explaining why they are opposed to a positive law so much needed in this turbulent world. I could also invoke the sanctity of treaties. And last but not least, since I am again alone, because Dr. Evatt is not returning for the time being, let me have positive law on my side: not just an idea, but a law duly enacted and sanctioned by the peoples through their parliaments. There will be new dangers, new battles. Let us cross the bridges when we approach them. With this in mind I resumed my activities with the delegations from whom I was expecting the deposit of instruments of ratification. I met with Ambassador King, who served at the Liberian Embassy in Washington, D.C. He had a long gray moustache that covered an engaging smile of friendship and encouragement. "We expect a great deal from the Genocide Convention. Especially we in Africa," he said. Later I discovered that this man had a great heart. I developed a friendship not only with him but also with his two sons, who served with the Liberian delegation to the U.N.

I was invited to luncheon by Ambassador Price-Mars, chairman of the delegation of Haiti. He was president (rector) of the University of Port-au-Prince and a good sociologist. I told him of my conversation with his minister of foreign affairs in Washington. He promised to get in touch with Port-au-Prince. I knew he would do it. After this luncheon he would stop every time he saw me to say that he had not received the document yet, but that I should be optimistic and patient. I regained my self-assurance because I was working for a concrete and positive step and did not have to worry while waiting for the next blow. Occasionally one gets the impression from this kind of statement that it's a personal battle rather than an ideological one.[32]

The ambassador from El Salvador told me that his country's ratification document had arrived. I quickly arranged for a deposit of the instrument, this time with a young lady from the Protocol Division of the U.N., because the legal officers were busy in the Legal Committee and I wanted to speed the formalities.

Then one day, Ambassador Price-Mars waved to me from afar in the long corridor of the U.N. From his radiating face I knew immediately what had happened. "It came, it came," he repeated with sincere joy, and then he stretched out his hand to me as he added with a coquettish confidence, "I must say, the document is very, very beautiful." *"C'est tres, tres joli,"* he kept repeating. All of Africa was in these words. It is an appreciation of beauty as part of life in all its manifestations, and not only a single compartment into which Western man has relegated beauty.

Also in this concept was a wholesome, ancient pagan vision. Were not the concepts of the gods of the ancient Greeks based on the same elements? Did not these concepts once penetrate into Africa and spread over Asia? How curious and wonderful that they should survive in Haiti and speak to me through this great intellectual with a mysterious language of the unconscious, which braved all barriers of diplomacy and has been superimposed by a new archive. I felt sincerely in tune with the ambassador and gave full expression to my joy. We celebrated the event with a glass of wine we took at luncheon together. I was as happy as a child who had refused to delay a game for fear of being spanked later. I would not have seen the deep meaning of the joy of the ambassador of Haiti, who knew that his country is proclaiming a law together with other nations to avenge the cruel past inflicted on his people, had fear of opposition to the Genocide Convention led me to delay its coming into force. His joy gave me a new influx of strength, whose memory and moral impact has outlasted the following trying years.

The same afternoon I spoke with a member of the French delegation. There were too many private conversations between some members of the Legal Committee. These were not good signs. They were always a prelude to action, in which every party had a price to offer and a consideration to obtain. My interlocutor did not know that the French wanted a decision to establish an International Criminal Court, which was mentioned in the Genocide Convention barely as a possibility. Now they took concrete steps toward its establishment. They desired that a committee be set up to work on a statute. For this price they would not mind bargaining away the Genocide Convention so that it might be replaced by crimes against humanity from the Nuremberg Judgment. In this respect they were approaching the point of view of the U.K., with one difference. The U.K. was opposed to an international criminal tribunal. The American delegation worked as an intermediary between the French and the British.

These three delegations were already dividing the skin of the bear before the animal was killed. I checked with other delegations. The Australians, in the absence of Dr. Evatt, were ready to accept this plan. The South Africans were happy. The Latin Americans seemed confused. The details of the plan were withheld from them. Dr. Alfaro did not attend the Assembly. My friends in other delegations were busy with their own problems. Moreover, the entire plan of the opposition sounded so fantastic that the serious delegates would not believe me if I started explaining it. They believe too much in international law, and in the sanctity of treaties, to accept such a plan as a reality. Still I was not sure how the opposition would deal with this: how to switch from the formula of genocide as an international crime based on intent to crimes against humanity, which were crimes of a different legal structure.

As I see all this confusion from the vantage point of the present day, I realize that I did well in not inquiring too much into the details of these plans. It might have turned me away from the plan of making the convention positive international law. I was living with law too much. As a teacher and as a man who worked so many years on international law, and as a man who administered law as a public prosecutor, I refused to believe that law could be handled in any way other than by open and legitimate processes. If there is due process of law in the treatment of individuals, why should the same not apply in the handling of law itself? In these dark days I felt intuitively that I was right, but as I am writing this now I have come to this conclusion after long and bitter experience. Anyway, I decided to counteract even a temporary success by my opponents. In the Assembly of the U.N. I met Ambassador Garrand of the French delegation, with whom I was on good terms.[33] I told him about the plan of bringing the convention into force and expressed my concern that the French document of ratification was not deposited yet. "The treaty was adopted in Paris; it may bear the proud name 'The Fact of Paris.'" Why shouldn't France, by depositing its ratification document now, earn credit for bringing the treaty into force as the twentieth ratifying nation? In this way France would go down in history as the nation that actually brought the convention into force. Garrand promised to talk about it with the minister of foreign affairs, Monsieur Schuman, who was expected in Lake Success any day. When Schuman appeared several days later in the Delegates' Lounge, we greeted each other like old acquaintances from the Paris Assembly. He told me that Ambassador Garrand had spoken with him, and he liked this idea. I really do not know how much good my conversation with Garrand and Schuman actually did, but France did deposit the document several days later.

By the middle of October, twenty-four delegations had deposited their documents of ratification, four more than were needed to bring the convention into force. I mentioned this to the president of the Assembly, the ambassador of Iran, who was glad that the convention would come into force during his presidency.[34] Several days later President Truman was scheduled to address the Assembly. The president of the Assembly gave me the good news that he would speak about the convention coming into force in front of President Truman. I was particularly glad because Truman was well endeared to the convention.[35]

According to Article XIII of the convention, a special protocol had to be drawn up about the deposit of the number of ratifications necessary to bring the convention into force.[36] The convention would actually come into force ninety days after the deposit of the necessary ratifications. But the protocol had to be signed now. This was the historic date. Secretary General Trygve Lie had promised to be present at the ceremony. On October 16, 1950, we met in his office with the ambassadors of France, Korea, Haiti, and Costa Rica, the assistant secretary general of the U.N., and myself, and celebrated this important event by taking a group photo. It was published in the *New York Times*.[37]

Thus the plan for which I had worked so many years was finally materializing. I could hardly believe it. Looking around the table with blurred eyes at the concentrated faces of my companions in the secretary general's office, I asked myself: Is this the moment for which I was hoping and working so many years? It was raining outside, the room was gloomy. My joy was mixed with anxiety and fear. I could not even reproach myself for being a habitual pessimist, unable to enjoy joy. I knew that this moment of ratification was only a formality before the convention would be shelved according to a plan whose details I did not know at the time. I knew that my enemies were treating the ratification as a temporary permission to accept it, a permission that would be revoked when the time for administering the death blows arrived. I would gain more insight from a conversation I had with Lord Willis, of London, in the summer of 1951 at the convention of the Young Men's Christian Associations in Cleveland, Ohio.[38] When I asked him when England would ratify the convention, he answered with a mysterious monologue, based on particular knowledge, asserting that the convention had not really come into force. On that rainy day on October 16, 1950, in Lake Success, and later during my conversation with the very proud English lord in Cleveland, and now as I write these lines, something in me was saying: This law cannot and shall not die, because so many human beings died to make it live.

After the ceremony I issued a statement for the press. I did not like it. It was heavy with my worries, depression, and fears, and not jubilant enough for the occasion. I could not lie. But it served the purpose. The next day the entire world read that the U.N. had signed a protocol bringing the Genocide Convention into force. People in all corners of the globe believed in what they read: that the U.N. was bringing into force an actual law for the outlaw of slaughter of the innocent. I hoped they rejoiced. This was enough. For the time being, my purpose was achieved, even if I had to pay a heavy price for it later. The press coverage was excellent. Many people congratulated me, those who knew the truth turned their eyes away from me when we met.

The *New York Herald Tribune* wrote an editorial, and apparently this editorial alarmed the opposition. They were always aware of the support the Genocide Convention enjoyed in the press. A certain diplomat approached me several days later and said, with a face that did not betray any embarrassment, "You will be ill advised if you would stop what we are trying to do on the Genocide Convention." "You are putting a needle in my heart and you want me to smile," I replied, and walked away. I have not spoken to this man since that day, for, more than violence, I detest threats. Violence is directed against the body, but threats are meant to paralyze the will of a man who might remain by force. When I met this man I looked at him as if there was an empty space before me. I considered my inability to smile and greet brutality as a shortcoming in my dealings in the modern market of human affairs. But one cannot fight an incompatibility within oneself, as this requires a biological quality.

I must report here on an important detail of my personal life that had some bearing upon my mood, behavior, and health. In August 1950, as my plans for bringing the convention into force crystallized, it became clear to me that I would have to spend all my time at the Assembly. Consequently, I would be unable to give my course at the school in the fall semester. I phoned the dean of the school. When I returned to New York I stayed with a friend whom I knew closely from Europe and whose family I considered my own. The relationship was close indeed. When his daughter reached college age I arranged for her to be accepted at the university where I had taught in 1941. His family and I joked and laughed together; we knew all our secrets, worries, and joys. We had common acquaintances, who, as I understood later, were connected with the U.N. consultants who worked for other projects and were opposed to the Genocide Convention. One morning, as I was about to leave for the U.N., my friend told me unexpectedly that he needed the room I occupied in his house. He talked to me like a stranger, so much so that I almost failed to recognize him. I spent that day looking for a room. In the evening I found myself in new surroundings, which added to my feeling of being lost in solitude and strangeness. I felt wanted neither by the world nor by my friends. What I failed to see was that this was proof not of my weakness but of the strength of the things I had accomplished. I did not realize in my dismay that this type of retribution was always natural for those who dared to believe and to act. But the problem was not only philosophical. I had to borrow money to buy food. When I could not do it, I went hungry. I had been living on a diet because of bad health, and now I found myself suddenly exposed to the food of cheap restaurants. My health was deteriorating from one day to the next. At the U.N. I could hardly stand on my feet and often had to look for the support of a wall or a sofa.[39]

In such physical condition I sat in the chamber of the Legal Committee while it took up the problem of the liquidation of the Genocide Convention. Formally, of course, members were discussing the U.K. memorandum on reservations. Of course not all the delegates were aware of all the consequences and implications of this discussion. This was still the age when several delegates could continue to debate U.N. decisions without being challenged.

There were several treaties or conventions that did not contain provisions as to the treatment of reservations. Logically, all these treaties should have been accorded the same treatment. But the plan called for the liquidation of the Genocide Convention while all the other treaties were to be preserved. The following plan emerged from the discussion: The Genocide Convention would be sent to the International Court of Justice, which would have to answer the following questions: 1) Can a government that has signed a treaty but not ratified it oppose a reservation made by a government that has ratified the treaty? 2) What effect on the treaty has an objection by a ratifying government upon a reservation made by another government?

All other treaties were sent to the International Law Commission for an agreement as to the treatment of reservations. Thus a double standard was established, for the Genocide Convention on the one hand, and for other treaties on the other hand. When I asked how such a strange procedure was possible, my interlocutors nodded their heads with an ambiguous smile of embarrassment. Then the Legal Committee reached the point of the principles of the Nuremberg Judgment as formulated by the International Law Commission. On this point there was a deflection for the opposition. The Legal Committee refused to approve them. I talked to the press about the blow delivered to the Genocide Convention. I was so sick at that time that possibly I did not make much sense. However, the *New York Times* carried the following story on my protest.[40]

That night I felt a strong pain in my stomach. The doctor seemed bewildered and advised immediate hospitalization. I found myself in Bellevue Hospital before the Assembly acted on the resolution of the Legal Committee. From my hospital bed I could not possibly propose an opposition to this resolution, as I had in 1947. But I tried. Defying the doctor's orders, I sent out telegrams in the night to my friends in the delegations. It was, however, like a cry in the wilderness. The resolution of the Legal Committee was adopted and the Genocide Convention was submitted to the International Court of Justice for an opinion on reservations.

My health was deteriorating rapidly. The pain in the abdomen did not let me sleep. With praying eyes, I used to look at the nurse, waiting for the calming needle. Then for a while the drugs would start singing melodies in me and building enchanting worlds, which would disintegrate as I fell asleep. One afternoon, several days later, I suffered such a severe attack of agonizing pain that I could hardly breathe. I was put under an oxygen tent. Drugs were administered constantly. Then my doctor took me in his confidence. "I think an operation is necessary, and if you agree, it should be done at once." Of course I agreed, or rather I nodded my approval.

While I was being prepared for the operation and asked to sign papers that hinted ominously at the possibility of death, a great calm enveloped me. I knew that I would not die. I could not die for the simple reason that I was convinced my work would have died with me. I had not had the good sense to prepare enough disciples to continue my work. I was constantly under strain and did not have time to organize any.

The strong feeling that my mission depends so much on this harassed body made my inner will issue orders to it: do not cease to exist! This order filled all my consciousness, or what was left of it at that moment. Then I was taken away as a thing on leave of absence from life.

After the operation I regained consciousness in the quiet of my room.

Return to life was slow. I felt like leaving sleep and entering it again. It is strange that I should remember these feelings now in all their physical scope and subtle sensations. Then my tongue felt a warm greeting of recurring life. The nurse put a spoonful of tea in my mouth. I opened my eyes and saw a woman in white with a responsible smile on her face. Responsibility for life. She must do the same thing as I, but her job is much more concrete. Only I call it with a bigger name and the newspapers write more about my work than about hers.

To be born again was both joy and pain. There was the joy of touching the world again, though weakly, but still vaguely through the senses. There was also the joy of seeing again a ray of sun playfully trembling on a wall. There was the smell of soup invading my nose and throat. And there was the perfume of roses that brought greetings from a distant garden and somebody who had sent a message of closeness. Pain. Where was it? This time only in the body. I could not turn freely. It would be Christmas soon and I was wrapped up like a Christmas gift. I was even sealed, tied with a string around the chest and abdomen.

The days in the hospital were reminders that I was a human being again, that I was wanted and cared for, that my progress meant something. I thought that all persecutees, even those self-appointed, should be permitted to enter a hospital to undress, lie in a bed, and be asked how they feel. Only after that could they be tormented again.

Since this was my first real vacation in years, I rested comfortably and finally had a chance to have a heart-to-heart talk with myself. "Listen, Raphael Lemkin," I said, "they fixed you up, finally, all right. This happened because you wanted to fight the whole world." "Not really," I answered. "I am not fighting the whole world but only a small part of the world, which arrogates to itself the right to speak for the entire world. What you call the whole world is really on my side." "How do you know? Who determines the right to speak for the world?" "Conscience. Sincerity. If they could have this right, they would say so openly. They would even openly declare that they decided to kill the Genocide Convention."

"But be practical. These things cannot be done openly."

"This is exactly it. Civilization depends to a great extent on a feeling of shame. They know it is shameful to destroy a law that protects life, a law for which humanity has been working for thousands of years."

"Maybe they would replace the Genocide Convention with a better law."

"Better laws are made by people with greater hearts. They want non-enforceable laws with many loopholes in them, so that they can manage life like currency in a bank. Life is absolute and so must be the law for its protection."

"But this fight will finally destroy you, yourself."

"So what? Whoever fights for an ideal must risk his life. You have not said anything new. What was fighting for an ideal without sacrifice? Ideals, like ancient gods, demand constant sacrifices."

It was warm in the room, the conversation was heart searching, and I felt like a hero who was fighting in a battle for a country called "the whole world."

As my health returned, so did my problems and worries. It was impossible to keep serene all the time when I knew what had happened. But I knew also that I needed my health soon for the new phase of the fight.

A good remedy in this situation was laughter. I always liked a good joke, an amusing story, and I felt intoxicated when the faces of my interlocutors would start jumping with many convulsive rays of a sudden sunshine. Soon my hospital room became a center where people hungry for warmth and laughter would congregate. Many came out of simple curiosity. I felt my fame spreading over all the floors when one morning a new doctor from England paid me a visit and said outright that he came on account of my stories. I advised him to entertain his fellow doctors by memorizing jokes, numbering them, and then inviting laughter by calling the number of the joke. All this made me think that laughter is not practiced enough as a therapy.

Several weeks later I traveled to a rest home in Lakewood and found myself under the control of two ladies, owners of this abode for the restoration of health. They wrapped me up, this time in blankets, and I sat drinking tea on the terrace for hours, feeling the winter sun and smelling the air of pines. Every day brought progress. Already I was feeling my muscles and looking for noses to punch. I knew to whom these noses belonged, but they were not yet within my reach.

CHAPTER TWELVE

Nearing the End

EDITOR'S NOTE: A FEW TYPED pages of notes for this chapter—titled Chapter Thirteen by Lemkin—exist.

The Korean ambassador, Dr. Chang, appeals to the U.N. to accelerate ratification of the Genocide Convention in order to protect his people in the Korean War. Truman sends a letter to the U.S. Senate, urging them to ratify. The Senate opposes the Genocide Convention and me. Arthur Spingarn, new man, takes his place, a very nice person.[1] Because of numerous handicaps to his work in New York, R. Lemkin decides to go to the "grass roots" of America with the problem of genocide. Trips to the Middle West, meeting with church groups, national groups, et al. Help from the editor of *America*. (Name?[2]) I organize the Lithuanians in Chicago. Extreme poverty. My friends came to my aid, installing me at the Edgewater Beach Hotel, where they hope I will recuperate from my operation and find strength to go on fighting. A brief vacation, warmth of the sun plus warmth of my friends, somewhat restores me. Numerous conventions held at the Edgewater Beach Hotel. I take advantage of their presence to preach the evils of genocide and the need for the U.S. to ratify the Genocide Convention. Polish and Greek groups in Chicago are alerted. Archbishop Michael. In 1947, fifty thousand Greek children had been kidnapped during the Greek civil war. Use this as a basis to interest Queen Frederica in the Genocide Convention. As a result, a new crime is included in the convention: "forcible transfer of children of one group to another group." Talks with Henry Grady, U.S. ambassador to Greece. My work with the Greek Orthodox Youth Groups (AHAPA).[3] Reminders of Turkish genocide in Asia Minor. My work with Armenian groups (Armenian Convention in N.Y.). I go to South Bend, and work with the Hungarians there. German groups in Chicago become interested in the problem. The Draft Code of Offenses partisans are very active, thus I "play down" the ratification of the convention by the U.S.A. at that time. "No compromise on a principle of irresponsibility." Upon rereading the draft code, I become aware of the place to attack it. Article V, which prohibits American help to nations behind the Iron Curtain. I emphasize this line of thinking in my talks with the Eastern and Central European groups in Chicago and the Middle West, and work with them on a draft of a letter that they send to the State Dept., saying, "The Draft Code will not permit us to save our people behind the Iron Curtain." In Sept., I return to N.Y. The *Herald Tribune* and the N.Y. *Times* correspondents urge me to release this story; my reply that the Lithuanians should release it. They do, whereupon thirty Republican congressmen send a telegram to Dean Acheson in Paris, saying, "Don't sell these national groups down the river."[4] The State Dept. turns its back on the draft code. Congressman Kirsten sponsors a bill in the House to get $100 million to help the underground behind the Iron Curtain, then sends a letter to Warren Austin at the U.N., asking: "Am I guilty under Article V of the Draft Code?" Austin's answer.[5] Thereupon Cong. Kirsten puts his letter and Austin's answer into the *Cong. Record*. Gromyko protests this to the American ambassador. It becomes a big issue. As a result, the draft code is virtually a dead issue for ten years. A so-called friend tells me my moves are "deadly." My reply: "I am an old, sick man. How can I be deadly?" Friend: "I am not at all sure you're a dead duck." This encourages me. I am virtually without funds by now. I borrow money from friends in N.Y. to travel to Washington, then borrow money from Wash. friends to repay the people in N.Y. My hotel bill in N.Y. goes unpaid for some weeks. The calculated insults of the elevator boy. Finally, my clothes are confiscated, and I am locked out of my room. I arrange to pay off my bill, giving a few dollars each week or month, and finally redeem my things, only to find that they have served as banquet for the hotel's moths. Thus, I find myself pleading a holy cause at the U.N. while wearing holey clothes. My friends at the U.N. "plot" to see that I eat at least one meal a day. I am ashamed and try to limit myself to a bowl of soup when I am their guest. I move into a furnished room in an apt. on the West Side. For a time, I manage to borrow out enough money to pay my rent promptly, but eventually my "lend lease" arrangements fail, and I fall behind. My landlord takes to coming into my room at midnight each night and pouring abuse at me for not paying my rent. I pretend to sleep, although soon even my snoring cannot drown out his shouts. He disconnects my heat and takes my blankets away. He fixes the lock so I cannot lock him out at night, so I shove the dresser against the door each night, leaving him to shout at me.

In the midst of all my personal trials I learn that two Latin American countries have ratified the Genocide Convention, but they are pressured into not sending the ratifications to the U.N. I thank them publicly for having ratified, send letters to the newspapers congratulating them on their ratification, and express the hope that they will send the official ratifications to the U.N. soon. I also make a speech before the U.N., thanking them for their help in this fight. I contact their embassies in Washington and am told that the documents of ratification have been "lost in transit." Expressing surprise, I ask if a duplicate cannot be sent. I am then told that the papers are locked in a desk of one of their representatives, and he is in Paris. I suggest that a cable be sent to Paris. Meanwhile, I locate the official proceedings of ratification in the Official Gazettes of these two countries. I inquire if the parliaments of these two republics cannot pass this ratification again. After two months of such maneuverings, the ratifications are sent in to the U.N.

I start working on those nations that are on the verge of ratifying. I collect all pertinent documents and go to the *New York Times* with the story that twenty-eight nations have already ratified and six are on the way. The next day, at a party given by the minister of foreign affairs of

Indonesia, I notice that I seem to be the center of attention as far as the diplomats are concerned. People crowd around me, due no doubt to the story in the *Times*. Sensing that they have been encouraged by the growing strength of the Genocide Convention, I feel instinctively that the six ratifications will soon come in.

Back in N.Y. I work with members of the U.N. Commission on the Rights of Women. A friend, Mrs. Pendleton Goldman of Urbana, Illinois, a member of the commission, gives the Genocide Convention several good "boosts" in her speeches and in conversations with other delegates. I meet Miss Helga Pederaen, a member of one of the Scandinavian countries and a member of the commission.[6] I borrow $5 and invite her to lunch. She and I talk about genocide and the Genocide Convention, and she says, "I will ratify the Genocide Convention." And she did. One by one I work on the nonratifying countries through these dedicated women, all of whom are devoted to social justice. I have correspondence with Lester Pearson—Canada ratifies. With friends in Sweden—Sweden ratifies.[7]

From now on my work consists more of perspiration than of inspiration. The work is increasingly an uphill fight, especially since I have to borrow money for postage to write to influential and interested people about ratifying. My opposition, aware of my extreme poverty, uses it to humiliate and undercut me. I concentrate on Burma, which has had a recent civil war and knows of genocide firsthand because of the Karens' fight for independence. One day U Nu comes to the U.N. During a press conference, Joseph Lash of the N.Y. *Post* asks him why Burma hasn't ratified the Genocide Convention. After a consultation with his advisors standing nearby, U Nu answers, "We are working on it." Six months later Burma ratifies.[8]

Outline for Chapter One

1. Introduction—Day on the Farm
2. Image of Entirety (tree climbing)
3. The Forest
4. The Lake
5. The Birch
6. Riding Horses
7. Stealing
8. Riabczyk[1]
9. Ceremony of the Harvest
10. Children of Farm Hands
11. Buying the Right to Live
12. Mother's Songs and Fables; Evenings in the Winter
13. Owl and Vegetarianism
14. First Love and Early Education (the Prophets)

Summary of Activities and Chapter Outline

A. Summary of Activities
   Biography in Who's Who[1]
   Summaries of activities
   Definition of genocide (included in above [sentence illegible or unfinished]
   Article for Chicago Jewish Forum (?) [illegible] missing[2]

B. Autobiography
   Chapter I. Early Childhood 29 pages
   Chapter II. The Flight 16 pages
   Chapter III. Flight from the Russians. 26–27 [pages]—1939–40
   Chapter IV. Interlude in Lithuania. [40–60 pages] 1940–41
   Chapter V. Travel to America via Russia and Japan. 1941 pp. 70–90
   Chapter VI. A Pole discovers America. [illegible] and at Duke University and collecting violence [illegible] genocide. 1941–42. 91–105
   Chapter VII. Work in Washington as an advisor on foreign affairs to the U.S. War Dept. and other agencies. My work in reparations for the Nuremberg trials. 1942–45. pp. 1–3
   Chapter VIII. Birth of the Convention. 1946 pp. 1–21
   Chapter IX. Introducing a resolution before in [illegible—UK?] call-

ing for a Genocide Convention. Lining up friends in Geneva. 1948 pp. 1–20

Chapter X. Adoption of the Genocide Paris 1948 pp. 1–39 [crossed out and replaced with handwritten note: "24–62"]

Chapter X. Years of Trial. Convention comes into force. Opposition increases. [illegible]

Chapter XI. Missing. Working in isolation. Further successes. Ratifications 59. [illegible] (see summary)

Outline

Chapter 1: War breaks out. Flight from Warsaw through the Polish Forests with other refugees, [illegible] (1939) Recollection of peacetime years.

Chapter 2: Flight from the Russians. Interrogation by Russians. My last visit with my parents. Escape to Lithuania. (1939–40)

Chapter 3: Interlude in Lithuania and Sweden. My efforts to collect documentary evidence of genocide. (1940–41)

Chapter 4: Travel to U.S. via Russia and Japan (1941)

Chapter 5: A Pole discovers America. Teaching at Duke U. and collecting further evidence on Genocide. (1941–42)

Chapter 6: My work in Washington as an advisor on Foreign Affairs to the U.S. War Department and other agencies. My work in the preparation of the Nuremberg trials. (1942–45)

Chapter 7: The Nürnberg trials. Genocide strikes home. My discovery that my parents had perished in a concentration camp. (1946)

Chapter 8: Introducing a Resolution before the U.N. at Lake Success for a calling for a Genocide Convention. (1946)

Chapter 9: Preparatory work in Geneva—lining up friends for the Genocide Convention. (1946)

Chapter 10: Adoption of the Genocide Convention at Paris. (1948)

Chapter 11: Years of trial. The Convention comes into force. The opposition increases. I am beset by sickness & poverty.

Chapter 12: Working in isolation. Further successes in the face of increased opposition. New ratifications from 58 countries.

The challenge of the future.

Outline for "Totally Unofficial"

EDITOR'S NOTE: ABOVE the proposed title for his book, Lemkin hand-wrote "The Unofficial Man," perhaps thinking about a more descriptive and specific name for his autobiography.

Chap 1

2 Chapter 2 [crossed out, replaced with "2–3"]: War breaks out. Flight from Warsaw through the Polish forests, with other refugees. Bombings and death (1939). Recollections of peacetime years. Flashback to my first proposal to outlaw the destruction of peoples (Madrid 1933).

3 Chapter 2 [crossed out, replaced with "4"]: Flight from the Russians. I am captured, interrogated and released. My last visit with my parents. Escape to Lithuania (1939–40).

4 Chapter 3 [crossed out, replaced with "5"]: Interlude in Lithuania and Sweden. My efforts to collect documentary evidence of genocide (1940–41).

5 Chapter 4 [crossed out, replaced with "6"]: Travel to America via Russia and Japan (1941).

6 Chapter 5 [crossed out, replaced with "7"]: A Pole discovers America. Teaching at Duke University and collecting additional evidence on genocide (1941–42).

7 Chapter 6 [crossed out, replaced with "8"]: Work in Washington as an

advisor on Foreign Affairs to the U.S. War Dept. and other agencies. My work in the preparation of the Nuremberg Trials (1942–45).

8 Chapter 7 [crossed out, replaced with "9"]: The Nuremberg Trials. Genocide strikes home (my discovery that my parents perished in a concentration camp (1946).

Chapter 8 [crossed out, replaced with "10"]: Introducing a resolution before the United Nations, calling for a Genocide Convention (1948). [Here Lemkin has indicated that he may combine this chapter with the following chapter issuing a cautious handwritten "maybe."]

9 Chapter [crossed out, replaced with "11"]: Lining up friends for the Genocide Convention. Work in Geneva.

10 Chapter 10 [crossed out, replaced with "12"]: Adoption of the Genocide Convention at Paris (1946).

11 Chapter 11 [crossed out, replaced with "13"]: Years of trial. I am beset by illness and poverty. The convention comes into force. The opposition increases.

Chapter 12 [crossed out, replaced with "14"]: Working in isolation. Further successes in the face of increased opposition. New ratifications (now 59 countries). The challenge of the future.

Outline for "Totally Unofficial"

12 Chapters—roughly 450 pages

Chapter 1. War breaks out. Flight from Warsaw through the Polish forests with other refugees. Bombardment and death (1939). Recollection of peacetime years.

Chapter 2. Flight from the Russians. I am captured, interrogated, and released. My last visit with my parents. Escape to Lithuania (1939).

Chapter 3. Interlude in Lithuania and Sweden. My effort to collect documentary evidence of genocide (1940–41).

Chapter 4. Travel to the U.S. via Russia and Japan (1941).

Chapter 5. A Pole discovers America. Teaching at Duke University and collecting further evidence on Genocide (1941–42).

Chapter 6. My work in Washington as an advisor on Foreign Affairs to the U.S. War Department and other agencies. My work in the preparation of the Nuremberg Trials (1942–45).

Chapter 7. The Nuremberg Trials. Genocide strikes home—my discovery that my parents perished in a concentration camp (1946).

Chapter 8. Introducing a resolution before the U.N. at Lake Success calling for a Genocide Convention (1948).

Chapter 9. Preparatory work in Geneva—lining up friends for the Genocide Convention.

Chapter 10. Adoption of the Genocide Convention at Paris (1948).

Chapter 11. Years of trial. I am beset by sickness and poverty. The convention comes into force. The opposition increases.

Chapter 12. Working in isolation. Further successes in the face of increased opposition. New ratifications. The challenge of the future.

Summary and Outline

Summary

This is a book concerned with the Genocide Convention and the part I played in making this convention possible.

It starts in September 1939, when I was forced to flee Poland. The opening chapters deal with my desperate and starving flight through the forest of Poland to safety in then neutral Baltic states and Sweden.

During the course of the flight I flashed back to my childhood, studies, and professional life as a public prosecutor in Warsaw. I also described my wartime journey through Sweden, Russia, Japan, and eventually to Duke University and Washington, D.C., where I was an advisor on foreign affairs to U.S.A. War Department.

I first formulated the concept of genocide at an international conference of legal experts meeting in Madrid in 1933, but my proposal for a convention was tabled. Since that time I have continued to unceasingly struggle for this idea. I later coined the word "genocide" (which is now in all recognized dictionaries) in my book *Axis Rule in Occupied Europe*.

My efforts began to bear fruit when I was sent after the war by the U.S.A. government to London and Nuremberg to help prepare the indictment against the Nazi war criminals. I included the charge of genocide in this indictment. This event will cover one chapter. In 1946, I caused three delegations to introduce a resolution in the General Assembly at the United Nations which called for the preparation of the Genocide Convention.

The chapters submitted now deal with intermediate stages with my work on genocide in Geneva and Paris. Later chapters not only will explain cases of genocide in antiquity, the middle ages, and modern times but also will describe my individual efforts to obtain approval of the convention by the parliaments of most of the sixty-eight nations which have already ratified the convention.

The closing chapters of the book will deal with my continuing effort to obtain approval by new states. I will also describe how I dealt with individual statesmen of different countries, such as Jan Masaryk, the emperor of Ethiopia, the prime ministers of Ireland, Pakistan, New Zealand, and Ghana, and the foreign ministers of many countries, including Robert Schuman of France, John Foster Dulles of the United States, Lester Pearson of Canada, Herbert Evatt of Australia, and many others.

My efforts have been recognized by many governments in the form of highest decorations, including one from Cuba in 1950 and one from Western Germany in 1955. I have also been currently nominated as candidate for the Nobel Peace Prize.

This book will be interesting because it shows how a private individual almost single-handedly can succeed in imposing a moral law on the world and how he can stir world conscience to this end.

Outline for "Totally Unofficial"

12 chapters—roughly 450 pages

Chapter 1 [crossed out "1"]. War breaks out. Flight from Warsaw in a train which is bombed. Witnessing death. Starvation and the fight for survival. My first contact with genocide in action. Sudden contact with the suffering of the people of Poland; guilt at not having been aware of this before. Flashbacks to childhood and periods of professional life as public prosecutor and lawyer in Warsaw. Flashback to period when the writer initiated the Genocide Convention in Madrid, in 1933.

Chapter 2 [crossed out, replaced with "4."]. The Russians invade Polish territory, to which I have escaped. I am captured, interrogated, and released. I hide with a Jewish family in a small village in eastern Poland. Description of the cultural and religious concepts of the prospective victims of genocide, in particular, their relation to God and to death. My last visit with my parents.

Chapter 3 [crossed out, replaced with "5."]. Escape to then-neutral Lithuania. Description of this precarious neutrality. Demoralization of the escapees from Nazi genocide. The sufferings of the intellectuals. Betrayed hopes of the Lithuanians, who were later occupied by the Russians. My last conversation with the great Jewish historian Dubnow, who was later killed by the Nazis. I move to Sweden while the Nazis occupy Western Europe. I study the genocidal techniques of the Nazis in Poland while preparing my campaign against genocide, which I hope to start in the U.S.

Chapter 4 [crossed out, replaced with "6."]. Comparisons between present-day methods of genocide as practiced by the Nazis and the Mongolian genocide against Poland and other Central European countries seven hundred years before. Travel through Russia and Japan. My impressions of the Russian people. Arrival in Japan. I am struck by the beauty of that country. Two facets of Japanese psychology: the tea ceremony as an example of harmony, and the "singing bridge" in Kyoto as an example of the tradition of suspicion and the atrocious samurai struggle. Reflections on the impact of this suspicious period on a case of genocide against fifty thousand Japanese Catholics in the seventeenth century. I leave Japan for the U.S. The American spirit is typified by the behavior of the immigration and customs officials.

Chapter 5 [crossed out, replaced by "7."]. A Pole discovers America: Parallels and contrasts. The atmosphere of the campus of Duke University. I appeal to American tradition in protection of minorities in foreign lands. First attempts at introducing the U.S. War Department to the problem of genocide. Lectures on genocide at the School of Military Government in Charlottesville, Virginia. Appearances before the M.C. Bar Association and the American Bar Association in Indianapolis. Germany invades Russia and overruns the town in eastern Poland where my parents live. Agonizing hours in the American paradise. I discover my uncle and aunt, and cousins in Chicago, New York, and Hartford, Connecticut. My aunt, symbol of my past. Pearl Harbor: America goes to war.

Chapter 6 [crossed out "6."]. In summer of 1942, I move to Washington to join the Board of Economic Warfare as chief consultant. My impressions of Washington. Atmosphere of improvisation in fighting the war and knowing the enemy. My friends disbelieve my talks of genocide. My approaches to the White House. Efforts to win over American officials and members of Congress to save the peoples of Europe from genocide. Difficulties and disappointments at their lack of understanding of the problem. Shiploads of refugees nobody wanted. I coin the word "genocide" and publish *Axis Rule in Occupied Europe* with documented evidence that shocks America. The book is reviewed on the first page of the *New York Times.* I win the support of Eugene Meyer of the *Washington Post.* My realization that my efforts to prevent Nazi genocide came too late. President Roosevelt declines my proposal to outlaw genocide by treaty, as a warning to the Nazis. My conversations with the Vice President Henry Wallace and with Allied diplomats in Washington.

Chapter 7. In 1945 I am appointed advisor on foreign affairs to the U.S. War Department. I am sent to London as advisor to Associate Justice Robert Jackson to assist in the preparation of the Nuremberg Trials. I include genocide as a charge in the indictment. My negotiation with the British, Russians, and French. My impressions of London. I meet former friends from Poland and am shocked by their stories of their own experiences under the Nazis. I return to Washington to help prepare the War Crimes Trials in Tokyo. I return to Europe for an inspection tour of all military tribunals in occupied Germany. I visit camps and see survivors. My hopeless search for remnants of my family. Realization of the consequences of genocide. Perpetuation of hatred among survivors. Contacts with judges and prosecutors of the Nuremberg Tribunal. Discovery that the personnel of the Tribunal is engaging in illegal trade. Heartbreak about the lack of ethical integration. I fly to England to address a conference of three hundred lawyers from England and the Continent, to win support for the concept of genocide as an international crime. It's a cool reception. I fly to Paris to introduce the concept of genocide into the peace treaties between the Allies and the Axis powers. I fail. I am confined to a military hospital in Paris. After my release I return to Nuremberg and discover that my brother and his family, the only survivors of my forty-nine-member family, are in Berlin. I bring them to Munich and settle them in a refugee camp. The verdict of the Nuremberg Tribunal proves disappointing. It fails to establish a clear precedent to outlaw genocide. I am again confined to the hospital, where I arrive at the decision to ask the U.N. to prepare a treaty against genocide. Upon returning to America I arrange for a leave without pay from the War Department. I go to Lake Success to line up support for a resolution to make genocide an international crime. Cuba, India, and Panama agree to sponsor my resolution. I enlist the support of the American delegation, including Ambassador Warren Austin, Adlai Stevenson, and others. Contact with leading newspapermen, churches, and civic groups in support of my idea. The resolution on genocide is unanimously adopted by the U.N. I am appointed by the secretary-general of the U.N. as an expert consultant to help prepare the Genocide Convention. At Lake Success I emphasize in talks with various delegates that genocide has occurred throughout history. The argument of the irreparability of the resulting loss to the world carries the day. Upon completion of the draft I return to Washington, where I continue my work with the War Department. The first opposition to the convention is felt.

Chapter 8. I resign from the War Department and come to live in a small furnished room in New York. As I am devoting all my time to the Genocide Convention, I have no time to take a paying job, and consequently suffer fierce privations. My premonition of strong battles to come at the 1947 General Assembly. Pearl Buck and I organize an appeal by leading intellectuals of the world to the 1947 Assembly, calling for adoption of the Genocide Convention. Presidents of many parliaments, including Herriot of France, and several Nobel Prize winners join in the appeal. The first open attacks delivered against the convention. The convention is defeated in the Legal Committee of the Assembly. I appeal to the president of the Assembly to organize a fight for the convention in the plenary session of the Assembly. We defeat the opposition, and a resolution to continue work on the convention is adopted. A special committee of the Economic and Social Council prepares a new draft of the convention. Unexpected help comes from the minister of foreign affairs of Pakistan, Sir Zafarullah Khan, who accuses India of having slaughtered one million Muslims during the partition of India. He brings out details of this most recent case of genocide. He appeals to the Economic and Social Council to accelerate the adoption of the Genocide Convention. Gandhi's efforts to prevent genocide. His assassination by a member of an organization actively engaged in genocide. I commemorate Gandhi's death on a national radio network, together with delegates of Pakistan and India.

Chapter 9 ["9" crossed out, replaced with "10.". In March 1948, I join the faculty of Yale University. I prepare to submit historical cases of genocide to the coming General Assembly, which will prepare the final draft of the convention. My flight to Geneva in the summer of 1948. The mood of the Swiss people. I obtain the endorsement of the Economic and Social Council for the Genocide Convention. International gathering of Protestant leaders also gives an endorsement. I see the Swiss minister of foreign affairs and give a press conference to Swiss newspapermen. The miracle on the bridge; a chance meeting with the ambassador of Canada, who later introduces me to the future president of the U.N. General Assembly, where help came from Australia. The Economic and Social Council transmits the Genocide Convention for action by the forthcoming General Assembly in Paris. Chapter 10 ["10" crossed out, replaced by "11."]. Arrival in Paris. Maneuvers of the opposition to place the Genocide Convention at the bottom of the agenda. My countermoves to transform the entire Sixth Committee into a drafting committee wins the day. I work with all the delegations and submit memoranda on past cases of genocide to illustrate points in the drafting of the convention. The opposition is beaten in the general debate and goes underground. They propose controversial and unenforceable formulae. I relax in Paris, seeing old friends and making new ones. The mood of the French people. I collect new material on genocide against the Huguenots. My conversations with French Protestant leaders and writers about the Genocide Convention. I meet and work closely with the papal nuncio in Paris, Monsieur Roncalli, the present pope. I strengthen my position by meeting with statesmen, including prime ministers. Avoiding newly discovered pitfalls in the drafting of the convention. I appeal to John Foster Dulles and receive his help in removing some of these difficulties. The archbishop of Canterbury and Sigrid Undset, Norwegian Nobel Prize winner in literature, give the Genocide Convention their help. Unanimous adoption of the convention. The French minister of foreign affairs, R. Schuman, the president of the General Assembly, Herbert Evatt, and many others congratulate me. The attitude of the press. Lowell Thomas broadcasts that I am "the happiest man in Paris." Illness and the return to America.

Chap. 12. I resume my duties at Yale. My close friendships with the students. Their growing interest in the problem of genocide. My plan to bring the convention into force by securing a minimum of ratifications by 1950. Correspondence with the ministers of foreign affairs, presidents of republics, and personal visits with prime ministers, heads of governments, and members of Parliament. The Conference of Ministers of Foreign Affairs of Latin America, in Washington. I organize support for the General Convention by women's organizations, church groups, and universities in many countries. Difficulties with ratification by the U.S. and England. During the 1950 General Assembly the required number of twenty ratifications is obtained. On October 16, 1950, a protocol is signed in the U.N. to this effect. The opposition succeeds in creating a hurdle based on reservations, and sends the convention to the International Court of Justice. I am prevented from attending to my duties at Yale, go hungry while working [illegible], and fall ill. I am taken to the hospital for an operation, and am released in January 1951.

Chap. 12 ["12" crossed out, replaced with "13."]. Changing strategy in my work after the heavy blows received from the opposition. My work with national groups in the Middle West. Breaking the withholding policy of ratifications. Poverty and starvation. My health deteriorates. Living in hotels and furnished rooms. Destruction of my clothes. Increased number of ratifications. I move ahead consciously. (The bridge in Poland.)

Chap. 13. Moving into new areas of the world for ratifications (Africa and Asia). New arguments. One year spent on ratification by Germany (1953–54). I attend the Ecumenical Conference in Evanston. Creation of new nations by the U.N. strategy of the backers of the Draft Code of Offenses, and differences between the two documents. Difficulty with Article VI of the Covenant on Civil and Political Rights. Saving clause included in 1957. Ratification by Pakistan (the *New York Times* editorial) and by new members of the U.N. I attend every Assembly and organize support. Increased research on the history of genocide. More understanding of the reasons for ideology. I find expression in poetry as the circle of my friends decreases. I become conscious of aging and try to adjust myself. The problem of diminished energy. The problem of ratification by Ireland. Conversations with Costello and the emperor of Ethiopia. My four years of work with Helen Steiger. The convention saves five nations. I attend a Conference in San Francisco in 1955. Support by the *San Francisco Chronicle*. Impressions of the West Coast, and of the continent on my trip by train back to New York. Cases of genocide in Algeria and other African nations. The Hungarians. Academic interlude in Rutgers and Princeton. My impression of Robert Oppenheimer. Sporadic support of the press in terms of reminders that the Genocide Convention exists. Protests by U.N. Delegates in general debate at attempts to undermine the Genocide Convention. The labors of Sisyphus. I work in isolation, which protects me.

Chapter 14—to be written after the book is completed—To include:

1.) General conclusions

2.) Personal outlook

3.) Hope for the future

The world becomes conscious of the concept of genocide, and of the law against it. This consciousness is not reflected [in] domestic legislation.

Notes

◼

1. In 1933, while describing acts of vandalism, Lemkin argued that an "attack targeting a collectivity can also take the form of systematic and organized destruction of the art and cultural heritage in which the unique genius and achievement of a collectivity are revealed in fields of science, arts, and literature. The contribution of any particular collectivity to world culture as a whole forms the wealth of all of humanity, even while exhibiting unique characteristics." Ten years later Lemkin explained that his new word "genocide" was intended "to signify a coordinated plan of different actions aiming at the destruction of the essential foundations of the life of national groups."

2. The Democratic Senator William Proxmire of Wisconsin pleaded for the United States to ratify the Genocide Convention in over three thousand speeches to the Senate between 1957 and 1989.

PREFACE

1. *Quo Vadis* by Henryk Sienkiewicz (1846–1916). He won the Nobel Prize in Literature in 1905.

2. If Lemkin is referring to ratifications rather than signatures, then this preface was written between December 16, 1954 (when Ukraine became the forty-first nation-state to ratify), and May 12, 1955 (when Albania became the forty-second).

CHAPTER ONE. Early Years

1. For a history of the town of Wolkowysk (now in Belarus), and its variant spellings, see the *Yizkor Volkovysk Memorial Book*.

2. A *Yizkor* book on Wolkowysk tells a similar tale: "There was a very thick forest in the place where Volkovysk is now located, where two gangs of bandits had their hideouts. The leader of one gang was named Volko, the leader of the second gang was called—Visek. These gangs used to attack and rob riders. . . . A man named Zavieka apprehended these bandits, hung them, and ordered that their hideouts where they concealed themselves in houses be built over. He named this new settlement Volkovisk. . . . On the spot where the bandits lived a large memorial was erected. Later, the memorial was cut up and used as a foundation for a church."

3. The black-and-white lithograph by Honoré Daumier (1808–1879) is titled *Buvant pour se désennuyer—Ayant réellement soif* (Drinking to kill time— Being really thirsty).

4. "Indeed Johnson was very sensible much he owed to Mr. Hunter. Mr. Langton one day asked him how he acquired so accurate a knowledge of Latin, in which, I believe, he was exceeded by no man of his time; he said, 'My master whipt me very well. Without that, Sir, I should have done nothing.' He told Mr. Langton, that while Hunter was flogging his boys unmercifully, he used to say, 'And this I do to save from the gallows.'"

5. Some anonymous poems were given to Lemkin's friend Nancy Steinson Ehrlich, possibly written by Lemkin. The following poem, along with some on genocide, suggests they most likely were written by Lemkin.

The Birch

Since I was walking on my knees,
I remember from all the trees,
A Birch proud and white
That stood in the countryside.
Daydreaming in September,
Weeping in November,
She became dear to me
And to one bee.
To drink her juicy milk
I pierced her trunk's silk.
Soon there was a bee,
A competitor to me.
Oh, you mother tree,
We both drank life from thee.

6. According to the *Yizkor* book, in 1891, nine years before Lemkin's birth, the merchants in Wolkowysk and its vicinity were predominately Jews, "because they were not permitted to engage in other occupations. Jews were forbidden to own land, and they were excluded from holding government positions."

7. Semen Yakovlevich Nadson (1862–1887).

8. The Bialystok pogrom occurred in June 1906 when Lemkin was nearly six. Chayim Nachman Bialik (1873–1934) was a Jewish Russian poet.

9. Ivan Andreevich Krylov (1769–1844) was a Russian fabulist, and Jean de la Fontaine was a French fabulist.

10. Menahem Mendel Beïlis (1874–1934), a Ukrainian Jew, was accused in 1911 of the murder of the twelve-year-old boy Andrey Yustschinsky. Beïlis' apparent motivation was a blood libel in order to perform rituals for the Jewish Passover, which sparked an anti-Jewish hysteria. Beïlis was jailed for two years before his trial in fall 1913.

11. Now called the Ivan Franko National University of L'viv, in Ukraine.

12. Shalom Schwarzbard (1886–1938) was born in Bessarabia in the Russian Empire.

13. Symon Vasylyovych Petliura (1879–1926).

14. Fifth Conference for the Unification of Penal Law in Madrid, October 1933.

15. "Les Actes Constituant un Danger General (Ineretatique) Consideres Commedits Delits de Droit des Gens Rapport," spécial présenté à la V-me Conférence pour l'Unification du Droit Pénal à Madrid (14–20.X.1933) (explications additionnelles) par Raphaël Lemkin.

CHAPTER TWO. The Flight, 1939

1. Karl Schlyter (1879–1959) was later instrumental in Sweden's obtaining signature to the Genocide Convention. On December 31, 1949, Lemkin wrote to Schlyter thanking him for his support and encouraging other Scandinavian countries to sign the convention. Lemkin also asked Schlyter to secure the ratifications of Sweden and Denmark, "and accession by Finland."

2. According to the Jewish Virtual Library, the Germans entered Siedlce on September 11, 1939.

3. The Maginot Line, built in France as a defense against the Germans, was made up of fortifications and other border defenses. It was named after the French minister for defense, André Maginot (1877–1932).

4. Now Lviv in Ukraine.

5. Ignacy Jan Paderewski (1860–1941) was a famous pianist and composer and prime minister; Józef Klemens Piłsudski (1867–1935) was first marshal and

chief of state; and Edward Śmigły-Rydz (1886–1941) was field marshal of Poland.

6. The author of *Grypa szaleje w Naprawie* is Jalu Kurek (1904–1983).

CHAPTER THREE. The Flight, 1939–1940

1. Stefan Starzyñski (1893–1939). A *Time* magazine article reported a week after Starzyñski's death that he was the "very marrow of the very bone of Warsaw's hopeless 20-day defense. Like a captain who goes down with his ship, like a wild animal which perishes defending its nest, Mayor Starzynski meant what he said when he cried over Warsaw's radio: 'We are fighting to death.'"

2. The "I-Thou" relationship became the prominent philosophical thesis of the Jewish philosopher Martin Buber (1878–1965). The philosophy was founded in Hassidic religious tradition.

3. Since Lemkin's death, decades of Holocaust scholarship, along with witnesses' video and audio testimony, have challenged the "lambs to the slaughter" myth. The concept of "resistance" too has been redefined to include temporary conversions and hiding. It is also possible to argue that Lemkin contradicts his own theory with the description of Jewish "councils of self-defense" later in this chapter.

4. *Tscholent*, or *cholent*, is the Yiddish name for the slow-cooked stew prepared and eaten on the Sabbath. The Heine poem to which Lemkin refers is "Princess Sabbath."

5. These descriptions of the Sabbath were etched in Lemkin's memory and formed part of his cultural heritage. A similar description appears in the *Yizkor* book about Wolkowysk: "Volkovysk on Thursday-to-Friday, comprised of so much harmony and beauty, etching itself into the memory and soul of each and every Jew from Volkovysk forever. The symphony of Erev Shabbat (eve of the Sabbath) began as early as Thursday morning. . . . Already before dawn, meats and cuts were brought from the slaughterhouse and the butchers . . . today is Thursday, and tomorrow is Friday—Erev Shabbat! The tumult in the street is the tumult of Erev Shabbat, the noises are those of Erev Shabbat, the entire racket is rooted in the preparations for the Sabbath."

6. Jizchok Lejbusch Perez or Isaac Leib Peretz (1852–1915) wrote many Yiddish fables and stories. The story that Lemkin refers to, "Ojb Nischt Noch Hechler," translates more accurately as "If Not Higher"; the literal translation is "If Not Even Higher."

7. Understandably, Lemkin may have confused the dates. According to Graebe's

testimony, he is describing massacres that took place on October 5, 1942. Regardless, Lemkin's subsequent translation/memory/transcription of the testimony is almost word-perfect to Graebe's affidavit.

8. Lemkin may have had the following lines in mind:

> Can he be bless'd who has no friend, or wife;
> No dear companion of the heart, to share
> His pleasures, and his pains? (lines 100–102) . . .
> A bride to this lone chamber thou wouldst lead?
> That, Hermann, is thy wish: to make the night
> The sweetest half of life; the comforter
> Of careful day? And is not this the wish
> Nearest thy parents' heart? (lines 210–14)

CHAPTER FOUR. A Refugee in Lithuania, Latvia, and Sweden

1. This would have been in October 1939. Lithuania took control of Vilnius (Vilna) on October 30.

2. Rudnicka Street eventually became the main thoroughfare of ghetto one in Vilnius.

3. Karl Schlyter (1879–1959) was later instrumental in Sweden's signature to the Genocide Convention. On December 31, 1949, Lemkin wrote to Schlyter thanking him for his support and encouraging other Scandinavian countries to sign the convention. Lemkin also asked Schlyter to secure the ratifications of Sweden and Denmark, "and accession by Finland."

   Henri Carton de Wiart (1869–1951) was pivotal in obtaining Belgium's signature to the Genocide Convention.

4. Lemkin is referring to Dante's *Divine Comedy*:

> Thou shalt leave each thing
> Beloved most dearly: this is the first shaft
> Shot from the bow of exile. Thou shalt prove
> How salt the savour is of other's bread;
> How hard the passage, to descend and climb
> By other's stairs. But that shall gall thee most,
> Will be the worthless and vile company,
> With whom thou must be thrown into these straits.
> For all ungrateful, impious all, and mad,
> Shall turn 'gainst thee: but in a little while,

Theirs, and not thine, shall be the crimson'd brow.
Their course shall so evince their brutishness,
To have ta'en thy stand apart shall well become thee.

5. Simon Dubnow (1860–1941). Regarding his murder in the genocide, and his last words, Koppel Pinson offers the following: "We have several versions by refugees from Riga about Dubnow's last days. They vary in details. But the main course of events was apparently along the following lines. When the Nazis entered Riga they evicted Dubnow from his home and seized his entire library. They summoned him for questioning at Gestapo headquarters and then placed him in a home for the aged. After a short period of ghetto organization the Nazis liquidated the ghetto at the end of October 1941 and at the end of October and a month later they carried out their first 'action' against the Riga Jews. Dubnow was seriously ill, but friends managed to conceal him for a while. On the night of December 7–8 the Nazis carried out their second 'action.' All the old and sick as well as the women in advanced pregnancy were herded together in buses. Dubnow was also taken outside to be squeezed into one of these overloaded buses. He was in high fever at the time and was hardly able to move his feebled legs. A Latvian militiaman then advanced and fired a bullet in Dubnow's back and the sainted martyr fell dead on the spot. The next day several friends buried him in the old cemetery in the Riga ghetto. A story went round that the last words that Dubnow muttered as he was being led out to the bus were: 'Brothers, don't forget! Recount what you hear and see! Brothers, make a record of it all!' His sense of history and the spirit of *Nahpesa v'nahkora* [the Hebrew title of one of Dubnow's essays] did not forsake him even to his bitter end."

6. A copy of this book is available at the American Jewish Historical Society.

CHAPTER FIVE. From Sweden to the United States

1. Leszek the Black died in 1288.
2. John III Doukas Vatatzes (1222–1254).
3. Birobidjan or Birobidzhan. This Jewish Autonomous Republic exists to this day with a thriving cultural presence.
4. Today the newspaper is titled *Newspaper Obschina*.
5. Bodidharma, the founder of Zen Buddhism.
6. Emperor Shōwa (1901–1989).
7. On this trip to the United States with Lemkin, Toyohiko Kagawa (1888–1960) was on a mission to promote peace between Japan and America.

8. This conversation took place ten months before the Japanese bombing of Darwin on February 19, 1942, which was ten weeks after the bombing of Pearl Harbor on December 7, 1941. Lemkin arrived in Seattle on the passenger ship *Heian Maru* on April 18, 1941. On the passenger records list his occupation is noted as "teacher" and his race as "Hebrew."

CHAPTER SIX. First Impressions of America

1. Lemkin lived in dormitory GG.
2. Robert Lee Flowers (1870–1951) was president of Duke University from 1941 until 1948.
3. The U.S. had a military presence in Nicaragua for over twenty years, from 1912 until 1933.
4. Judge Thaddeus Dillard Bryson (1873–1950).
5. Andrzej Tadeusz Bonawentura Kościuszko (1746–1817).
6. It is possible but unlikely that, in 1942, the judge would have used the word "holocaust" in relation to the genocide of the Jews. As Lemkin has typed the word with a lowercase "h," he may be referring to the genocide as "a" holocaust, rather than "the" Holocaust. According to the United States Holocaust Memorial Museum, "By the late 1940s . . . 'Holocaust' (with either a lowercase or capital H) became a more specific term due to its use in Israeli translations of the word 'sho'ah.' This Hebrew word had been used throughout Jewish history to refer to assaults upon Jews, but by the 1940s it was frequently being applied to the Nazis' murder of the Jews of Europe. (Yiddish-speaking Jews used the term 'churbn,' a Yiddish translation of 'sho'ah.') The equation of 'holocaust' with 'sho'ah' was seen most prominently in the official English translation of the Israeli Declaration of Independence in 1948, in the translated publications of Yad Vashem throughout the 1950s, and in the journalistic coverage of the Adolf Eichmann trial in Israel in 1961." In a 1949 memo from the Jewish Federation and Community Council that was in Lemkin's possession, it is stated: "Such a Convention [that is, the Genocide Convention] we hope might prevent the recurrence of the Hitler holocaust." Lemkin was using the lowercase "holocaust" in the 1950s. See Chapter Eight.
7. The Second International Congress of Comparative Law held at The Hague in 1937.
8. John Thomas Vance (1884–1943).
9. Colonel Archibald King (1882–1971) was a colonel in the judge advocate general's department, U.S. Army.

10. Alfred Rosenberg (1883–1946) was Reich minister for the Eastern Occupied Territories for the National Socialist German Workers Party.

11. One of the last letters from his parents is translated here from the Yiddish. From his father: "Dear Rafael, With great joy did we read your long awaited letter. We plead that you will continue giving us joy with your letters. Thank G-d I am feeling well, and in the future not any worse. Now I am [illegible] because the potatoes ended. In the meanwhile we are not missing anything. Elijah with Lizzy and the dear children send you their loving regards. They are all healthy. I am sending you addresses. If you will have time you should meet them. I send you my heartfelt regards. P." From his mother: "Dear Rafael, With great joy did we read your letter. We are all healthy, and we have what we need for our existence. Be calm about us! If it is possible write often. Elijah has work. He earns for his needs. Your father is in the house today. In the summer there is no work. Be healthy and fortunate. Your M." Thanks to Yeshaya Metal from YIVO at the Center for Jewish History, New York, for the translation.

12. Germany invaded the Soviet Union on June 22, 1941. June 24, however, is particularly poignant for Lemkin, as he would have most likely otherwise celebrated his forty-first birthday. The Nazis bombed Lemkin's hometown of Wolkowysk on June 23.

13. Jews from Wolkowysk were transported to Treblinka on November 6 and December 8, 1942, and then to Auschwitz on January 26, 1943. According to the *Yizkor Volkovysk Memorial Book*, Lemkin's parents died at Treblinka. The entry reads: "Joseph Lemkin. He and his wife were both killed in Treblinka. Their son, Dr. Raphael Lemkin, lives in America. Their second son, Eliyahu, and his wife (from Vinogradsky) and their children, traveled for a visit to Moscow during the time of the Russian occupation, and remained there. Today [that is, 1945 or 1946] they find themselves in Germany."

CHAPTER SEVEN. Alerting the World to Genocide

1. Henry A. Wallace (1888–1965).

2. The federal government's economic initiative the Tennessee Valley Authority Project was begun in May 1933. It was to provide a "unified program of resource conservation, development, and use in the Tennessee River Valley."

3. Lemkin's paper was tentatively titled "Legal Framework of German Control of Foreign Economies." It was for the 64th meeting of the American Bar Association, held September 29–October 3, 1941.

4. George A. Finch (1884–1957). Finch, like Lemkin, was a cosmopolitan

thinker. According to Lester Woolsey, Finch "believed vigorously in the sanctity and binding character of treaties." Finch is believed to have said that the "time has long since passed when the nations having a sense of honorable obligation should consider withdrawal of recognition of any nation which persistently refuses to comply with fundamental international obligations."

5. Lemkin is referring to Jan Karski's heroic efforts to inform the Polish government in exile in London of the genocide of Jews. Like Lemkin, Karski tried to convey the truth to President Roosevelt.

CHAPTER EIGHT. The Birth of the Convention

1. The Agreement for the Prosecution and Punishment of the Major War Criminals of the European Axis, and Charter of the International Military Tribunal in London, was signed on August 8, 1945: "Charter II: Jurisdiction and general principles, Article 6 lists war crimes as namely, violations of the laws or customs of war. Such violations shall include, but not be limited to, murder, ill-treatment or deportation to Wave labour or for any other purpose of civilian population of or in occupied territory, murder or ill-treatment of prisoners of war or persons on the seas, killing of hostages, plunder of public or private property, wanton destruction of cities, towns or villages, or devastation not justified by military necessity."

2. Otto David Tolischus (1890–1967) was arrested and tortured by the Japanese in 1941. He is the author of three books and the winner of the Pulitzer Prize in the category of correspondence for 1940.

3. Eugene Isaac Meyer (1875–1959) and Alan Barth (1906–1979).

4. The date is a typing error by Lemkin and should be December 3, 1944.

5. Frede Castberg (1893–1977) was a Norwegian professor of law.

6. Ricardo Joaquín Alfaro Jované (1882–1971). As Alfaro was the chairman of the U.N. Legal Committee for the Genocide Convention, Lemkin and Alfaro corresponded and met often. Despite Alfaro's support for the exclusion of cultural destruction in the Genocide Convention, he nevertheless supported the convention's ratification, as demonstrated in this January 18, 1950, letter to Lemkin:

"My dear Dr. Lemkins [sic] You happened to write to me on December 17th, which was the date on which the Foreign Office sent to our Permanent Delegate to the United Nations the Panama ratification instrument of the Genocide Convention. I am informed the ratification was deposited on the 10th instant, whereby Panama became the sixth state to ratify the noble pact. With hearty congratulations and the reiterated expression of my will to continue in behalf of the great cause which is so dear to you and to me, I am yours very sincerely, Ricardo J. Alfaro."

7. Guillermo Belt (1906–1989).

8. Margery Corbett Ashby (1882–1981).

9. Vijaya Lakshmi Pandit (1900–1990). Pandit was one of three delegates to sponsor a resolution outlawing genocide.

10. It is possible that Lemkin has confused Gray with John Milton Hay (1838–1905), who served as secretary of state under Presidents McKinley and Roosevelt (1898–1905).

11. William Howard Taft (1857–1930) was the twenty-seventh president of the United States, serving from 1910 to 1913.

12. Adlai Ewing Stevenson (1900–1965).

13. Ambassador Warren R. Austin (1877–1962).

14. Helen Gahagan Douglas (1900–1980).

15. Tolischus also wrote an erudite review of Lemkin's *Axis Rule in Occupied Europe*.

16. Frances Perkins (1880–1965).

17. Hanna Rydh (1891–1964).

18. Jan Garrigue Masaryk (1886–1948). In 1948, a California newspaper reported that "in early U.N. sessions at Lake Success, N.Y., [Lemkin] persuaded . . . Jan Masaryk, Czechoslovak foreign minister, to do spade-work for him with the Soviet bloc."

19. Tomáš Garrigue Masaryk (1850–1937).

20. Andrei Januaryevich Vyshinsky (1883–1954). Lemkin would have been acutely aware that Vyshinsky was Stalin's puppet for the Moscow "show trials" of 1936–38.

21. Paul-Henri Spaak (1899–1972).

22. Alexandre Parodi (1901–1979). The Institute for Advanced Studies on the United Nations has an Alexandre Parodi Scholarship Program in honor of Parodi's contribution to the U.N. and French intellectual life.

23. Sir Hartley Shawcross (1902–2003) was Great Britain's attorney general and the chief prosecutor for Britain at the Nuremberg trials.

24. Ernesto Dihigo (1896–1991). In a letter written to Maynard Gertler from New York on December 7, 1946, Lemkin wrote: "In the course of the discussion on Genocide in the Legal Committee of the United Nations Assembly many remarkable statements were made which have shown a warm interest and understanding for this problem by all the distinguished jurists representing their countries in the discussion on Genocide. Two statements should be

quoted specifically: that of professor Dihigo of Cuba stressing the restrained character of the resolution and that of Sir Hartley Shawcross, the Attorney General of the United Kingdom, calling energetically for immediate action. Both speakers seemed to represent the real necessities of our turbulent times: wisdom and intellectual force of a generous conviction."

25. Charles Fahy (1892–1979).

26. Avicenna (Abu Ali Sina) (980–1037).

CHAPTER NINE. Geneva, 1948

1. Víctor Manuel Pérez Perozo (1898–1969). Lemkin cabled Perozo immediately: "Dear Dr. Perozo, Thanks most cordially for your cable. I am prepared to take off by plane this Monday and will be in Geneva the next day. We both believe that the genocide convention is one of the most important issues of our times and you have proven to be a great and noble champion for this cause. In connection with the forthcoming discussion I take the liberty of sending you a short memorandum on genocide, which I have prepared exclusively for you. Please make use of it as you see fit. With my renewed appreciation and the anticipated pleasure of seeing you soon, I am sincerely yours."

2. Augustin Alfred Joseph Paul-Boncour (1873–1972) served as France's permanent delegate to the League of Nations between 1932 and 1936; Éamon de Valera (1882–1975) was president of the council at the League of Nations in 1932; Nicolas Politis (1872–1942); Eleftherios Venizelos (1864–1936); Lord Robert Cecil (1864–1958); Nicolae Titulescu (1882–1941); and Maxim Maximovich Litvinov (1876–1951).

3. Major John A. F. Ennals was the first secretary-general of the World Federation of United Nations Associations, founded on August 2, 1946.

4. Gilberto de Lima Azevedo Souza Ferreira Amado de Faria (1887–1969).

5. Pearl S. Buck (1892–1973) was a very active supporter of the Genocide Convention. The following letter is from Buck to Lemkin: "Dear Dr. Lemkin; I enclose herewith the proposed manifesto, as I have written it today. Having no secretary on Sunday, I have typed it myself, and your secretary can perhaps copy it. I do not wish to delay, and will mail it tonight, for I am leaving early in the morning. Please feel free to change this writing of mine. I have tried to incorporate all the points, also to make it simple and readable. I seem not to be able to make it shorter. My New York office will always know where I am. I shall be travelling part of the time, but except for two nights, can always be reached in the evening, or early morning. Yours sincerely Pearl S. Buck."

6. Mahmoud Azmi (1889–1954).

7. Morocco ratified the Genocide Convention on January 24, 1958.

8. Egypt signed the Genocide Convention on January 12, 1951, and ratified on February 8, 1952.

9. See Chapter Five for more details on the genocide of the Catholics in Japan.

10. Leolyn Dana Wilgress (1892–1969).

11. Canada signed the Genocide Convention on January 12, 1951, and ratified on September 3, 1952.

12. Herbert Vere "Doc" Evatt (1894–1965). Evatt is one of the few important ambassadors and memoirists to pay tribute to Lemkin: "Genocide was one of the crimes with which the leaders of the Hitler regime were charged at Nuremberg. The word itself was coined by Dr. Raphael Lemkin, a professor of law at Yale University, many of whose own family had suffered grievously from this crime. After the war he devoted himself with a single-minded purpose to securing international action to outlaw genocide and provide effective measures to punish it if it ever occurred again. He showed indomitable faith and energy both spurring on other people and in making concrete suggestions of a practical nature, and the final adoption of the convention is a great tribute to him."

13. Australia ratified the Genocide Convention on January 12, 1951.

14. The United Kingdom did not ratify the Genocide Convention until January 30, 1970.

15. Max Petitpierre (1899–1994). He was head of the political department from 1945 to 1961.

16. Jean Henri Dunant (1828–1910).

17. The Moral Rearmament Movement was a spiritual movement founded by Frank Buchman (1878–1961) in 1938. About the headquarters Lemkin visited, Leon Garth writes: "'True to their thought the previous summer Philippe Mottu and Robert Hahnloser, with their colleague Erich Peyer and others, had been looking for a place where people from the divided countries of Europe could meet in an atmosphere similar to Mackinac. After a prolonged search, they came upon the near-derelict Caux Palace Hotel, 3,000 feet above Montreux, which Buchman had visited during his trip to Europe forty years before. Now it was no longer an economic proposition and was due for demolition . . . a hundred Swiss backed by international volunteers set to work to refurbish the building . . . Buchman stood in the door looking from face to face in the ring of welcome, deeply moved. Then he said, 'Where are the Germans? You will never rebuild Europe without the Germans.'" The professor that Lemkin mentions may be Buchman's secretary, Dr. Morris H. Martin.

18. France ratified the Genocide Convention on January 12, 1951.
19. Charles Habib Malik (1906–1987).

CHAPTER TEN. Paris, 1948

1. Lemkin stayed in room 518 at the Hotel Claridge.
2. Ricardo Joaquín Alfaro Jované (1882–1971).
3. Quintin B. Paredes (1884–1973). See letters dated December 17, 1949, from Lemkin to Paredes, and Ingles praising both.
4. In his *Essays in Criticism*, Arnold wrote: "The French Revolution derives from the force, truth, and universality of the ideas which it took for its law, and from the passion with which it could inspire a multitude for these ideas, a unique and still living power; it is—it will probably long remain—the greatest, the most animating event in history. And as no sincere passion for the things of the mind, even though it turn out in many respects an unfortunate passion, is ever quite thrown away and quite barren of good, France has reaped from hers one fruit—the natural and legitimate fruit though not precisely the grand fruit she expected: she is the country in Europe where the people is most alive."
5. Sigrid Undset (1882–1949) won the Nobel Prize for Literature in 1928.
6. Clarence E. Pickett (1884–1965) was an organizational member of the United States Committee for a United Nations Genocide Committee. In March 1949, Lemkin wrote to Pickett, then of the American Friends Service: "Dear Mr. Pickett: Thank you again for the very effective help you gave me in Geneva and Paris, during the discussions by UN of the convention on genocide. Now we have a convention unanimously adopted by the Assembly and we hope that the U.S. Senate will act promptly in ratifying the convention. I am grateful for your prompt arranging for me to meet members of the American friends Service on Friday. I will be in your office around 12:30. I take the liberty of enclosing my recent article on genocide and also the article from *New York Times* which gives a short story of the fight for outlawing genocide. With renewed thanks and best wishes, I am Sincerely yours, Raphael Lemkin."
7. Riad el-Solh (1894–1951).
8. William Ball Sutch (1907–1975).
9. Peter Fraser (1884–1950).
10. New Zealand signed the convention on January 12, 1951, but did not ratify it until December 28, 1978.
11. Begum Shaista Ikramullah (1915–2000). Ikramullah's speech so impressed Lemkin and the United Nations that her words were used to describe the

purpose of the Genocide Convention in an official United Nations book series which began: "What is the Purpose of the Genocide Convention? The full title of the Convention gives the answer: to prevent and punish genocide. 'Genocide has been committed through the ages,' said Begum Ikramullah, of Pakistan, at the Assembly," and ended with Ikramullah's speech quoted by Lemkin.

12. Agha Shahi (1920–2006).

13. William Ewart Gladstone (1809–1898). Gladstone is of course referring to the Hamidian massacres in the late 1800s, not the events of 1915. Lemkin, or one of his research assistants, recorded Gladstone's report in the *London Times*, January 14, 1895 (although the correct date is December 31, 1894). "On his eighty fifth birthday, December 29, 1894, Mr. E. W. E. Gladstone made a long and eloquent speech to a deputation of members of the National Church of Armenia, in which he said: ' . . . Do not let me be told that one nation has no authority over another. Every nation, and if need be every human being, has authority on behalf of humanity and of justice. These are principles common to mankind, and the violation of which may justly, at the proper time, open the mouths of the very humblest among us. . . . The intelligence which has reached me tends to a conclusion which I still hope may not be verified but tends strongly to a conclusion to the general effect that the outrages and scenes and abominations of 1876 in Bulgaria have been repeated in 1894 in Armenia. As I have said, I hope it is not so, and I will hope to the last, but if it is so it is time that one general shout of execration, not of men, but of deeds, one general shout of execration [directed against] deeds of wickedness [sic], should rise from outraged humanity, and should force itself into the ears of the Sultan of Turkey, and make him sensible, if anything can make him sensible, of the madness of such a course. . . . If these tales of murder, violation, and outrage be true, then it will follow that they cannot be overlooked, and they cannot be made light of. . . . If allegations such as these are established, it will stand as if it were written with letters of iron on the records of the world, that such a government as that which can countenance and cover the perpetration of such outrages is a disgrace to civilization at large, and that it is a curse to mankind. Now that is strong language. . . . Strong language ought to be used when facts are strong, and ought not to be used without strength of facts. I have counseled you to retain and to keep your judgment in suspense, but as the evidence grows and the ease darkens, my hopes dwindle and decline; and as long as I have voice I hope that voice, upon occasions, will be uttered on behalf of humanity and truth.' "

14. Angelo Giuseppe Roncalli (1881–1963). He became Pope John XXIII in 1963.
15. Dr. Jean Nussbaum (1888–1967). In 1946, he opened the Association Internationale Pour la Défense de la Liberté Religieuse (International Association for the Defense of Religious Liberty), of which he was the secretary general.
16. John Foster Dulles (1888–1959). Dulles was U.S. secretary of state from 1953 to 1959.
17. Sir Muhammad Zafarullah Khan (1893–1985) was the first foreign minister of Pakistan and was president of the United Nations General Assembly from 1947 to 1954.
18. Erling Wikborg (1884–1992) was a member of the Norwegian Nobel Prize Committee (1967–69) and foreign minister of Norway (1963). Lemkin is most probably referring to Thomas Carlyle (1795–1881).
19. Lemkin is referring to the French art historian Henri Focillon (1881–1943).
20. Possibly Aleksandr Ivanovich Gertsen (1812–1870).
21. Sture Petrén (1908–1976) later became judge of the European Court on Human Rights (1971–76).
22. Abbe Pierre born as Henri Marie Joseph Grouès (1912–2007).
23. Sir James Plimsoll (1917–1987).
24. Genêt writes: "Lemkin is a sad, witty, middle-aged man . . . he became a lawyer, which he now regrets because he feels that lawyers are against progress. In the course of studying genocide, he has, he says, discovered when authorities burn books, they are likely to start burning people next, and he wants a law against both."
25. Jean Louis Barthou (1862–1934) was prime minister of France in 1913.
26. The International Criminal Court did not enter into force until July 1, 2002. Two ad hoc International Criminal Tribunals were established, the first in 1993 (International Criminal Tribunal for the Former Yugoslavia) and in 1994 (International Criminal Tribunal for Rwanda).
27. Article VIII of the Genocide Convention reads: "Any Contracting Party may call upon the competent organs of the United Nations to take such action under the Charter of the United Nations as they consider appropriate for the prevention and suppression of acts of genocide or any of the other acts enumerated in Article 3."
28. John Maktos (1902–1977). On January 18, 1948, Lemkin wrote the following to Maktos: "Dear Mr. Maktos, It is a great pleasure to communicate with you again. I hope you are all right and that you had a pleasant holiday. Let me at this occasion express to you my best wishes for a happy and prosperous New

Year. I am taking the liberty in sending to you a short memorandum as to my views relating to the last resolution of the General Assembly concerning genocide. I am enclosing also my recent article on this subject which appeared in the U.N. Bulletin of January 15, 1948. I might drop in soon for a short while to Washington and I will make a special point to call you. With kindest regards, Sincerely yours, Raphael Lemkin." In an interview, when asked if the subject of genocide was a special interest for him, Maktos replied, "I must admit that it was. I tried to be objective, as objective as I could be, but there is no doubt that the killing of millions of human beings had really moved me. On the other hand, I could not but present the issues to the Department in an objective manner, for instance as to what legal provisions should be incorporated in the treaty that was to be drafted. And I prepared a draft, not with any personal feelings, but with a viewpoint as to what provisions would be effective. For instance, I thought of including a ban against extermination of political ideologists. I felt that that would be inadvisable because some countries might not accede to the treaty to be prepared, because of political difficulties. They may think that they may be accused of being genocidal should they take certain steps in relation to parties not forming part of an existing government. Therefore, I excluded that from enumeration of the kinds of classes—racial, ethnic, religious—that should be treated in the convention. But my appointment to the committee to draft the genocide convention was not because of my personal views, but because of my functions."

29. Article IX reads: "Disputes between the Contracting Parties relating to the interpretation, application or fulfillment of the present Convention, including those relating to the responsibility of a State for genocide or any of the other acts enumerated in Article 3, [conspiracy to commit genocide; direct and public incitement to commit genocide; attempt to commit genocide and complicity in genocide] shall be submitted to the International Court of Justice at the request of any of the parties to the dispute."

30. Article XIV reads: "The present Convention shall remain in effect for a period of ten years as from the date of its coming into force. It shall thereafter remain in force for successive periods of five years for such Contracting Parties as have not denounced it at least six months before the expiration of the current period. Denunciation shall be effected by a written notification addressed to the Secretary-General of the United Nations."

31. Robert Schuman (1886–1963) was also prime minister of France twice.

32. John Hohenberg (1906–2000).

33. Those nation-states were Australia, Bolivia, Brazil, Chile, the Dominican Repub-

lic, Ecuador, Egypt, Ethiopia, France, Haiti, Liberia, Mexico, the Kingdom of Norway, Pakistan, Panama, Paraguay, Peru, the Philippine Republic, the United States of America, Uruguay, and Yugoslavia. According to the United Nations, twenty-one nation-states added their signature to the convention in 1948.

CHAPTER ELEVEN. Climbing a Mountain Again

1. Next to the typed title, Lemkin wrote, "The Years of Trial," perhaps as an alternative title.

2. Joseph Benedict Chifley (1885–1951). Ben, as he was known, was prime minister for the Australian Labor Party from July 1945 until his death. Chifley's ratification bill, read in parliament and sent to Lemkin, reads: "The purpose of this bill is to seek the approval of the Parliament for Australian ratification of the International Convention on the Prevention and Punishment of the Crime of Genocide. Genocide, which means the wholesale or partial destruction of religious, racial or national groups, has long shocked the conscience of mankind. The term itself, however, only came into general use at the time of the Nuremberg trials. It was then used to describe the destruction by the Nazis of groups of human beings on racial or religious grounds. The General Assembly of the United Nations at its first session, in December, 1946, unanimously affirmed that genocide was a crime under international law which the civilized world condemned. It decided that a draft convention to outlaw the crime should be prepared. After much preliminary work by the Economic and Social Council and its organs, a final text was drawn up and unanimously approved by the General Assembly at Paris on the 9th December, 1948. In approving the convention, the Assembly recommended it for signature and acceptance by member States. It has already been signed by more than twenty States. In the convention the term 'genocide' covers various acts committed with intent to destroy, in whole or in part, a national, ethnic, racial or religious group as such. The contracting parties are obliged to give effect to the provisions of the convention and to provide effective penalties for genocide. The convention will come into force on the nineteenth day following the date of deposit of the twentieth instrument of acceptance. The bill also approves that the Secretary-General of the United Nations be notified of the extension of the convention to territories for the conduct of whose foreign relations Australia is responsible. This is in accordance with Article 12 of the convention and a separate resolution of the General Assembly which recommended that States apply the convention to their dependent territories."

3. The minister of foreign affairs in Norway wrote to Lemkin on May 19, 1949: "Dear Mr Lemkin: I very much appreciated your letter of the 5th instant and beg to thank you for your kind words regarding the part played by the Norwegian Delegation in the discussions of the Genocide Convention. As you will probably already have heard from our Permanent Delegation to the United Nations, the agenda of the present session of our Parliament is a very heavy one. It may therefore still take some time before the Government will be able to ratify the Convention, especially so as the Governments [*sic*] proposition was printed only a few days ago owing to the difficult printing situation prevailing in this country. However, I have not failed to inform the Chairman of our Foreign Relations Committee, Mr. Terje Wold, of the contents of your letter, and I trust that he will do his best to speed up the handling of the matter by the Parliament. For your information I enclose a copy of the document presented by the Government to the Parliament. Very sincerely yours, Erik Dons." Terje Wold (1899–1972) was a supreme court judge and a minister in the Labor Party in Norway. Paal Olav Berg (1873–1968) was also a Norwegian jurist and Labor politician. Berg was one of several intellectuals who appealed for a Genocide Convention.

4. The date is an oversight by Lemkin. Nevertheless, the ratifications came in quick succession. After Ethiopia ratified on July 1, 1949, Australia ratified on July 8, Norway on July 22, and Iceland on August 29. All ratifications came into effect on January 12, 1951.

5. It was Yépez who nominated Lemkin for the Nobel Peace Prize in 1950. On June 13, 1949, Lemkin wrote the following letter to Yépez: "My dear Professor and friend, It was a great honor and pleasure to have you with us at Yale on Saturday. Your visit will long remain in the memory of the University, and will serve as an incentive for renewed and strengthened spiritual contacts between our universities and countries. Thank you very much for your deep interest in the genocide convention. Your delegation did a great and constructive work on this subject in the United Nations. I will be grateful to you, therefore, if you will be kind enough to convey to your President my cordial thanks for your country's support of this great humanitarian cause. Your President, who is a man of the people, will, I am sure, appreciate the importance of this treaty which was called recently in an editorial in the *New York Times*, 'a treaty for the people.' If your Parliament will be one of the first to ratify the convention, I am sure the gratitude of the entire world will center on your splendid country. With renewed thanks and warm regards, I am Sincerely yours, Raphael Lemkin."

6. Amalia de Castillo Ledón (1898–1986) was a playwright, jurist, journalist, and

an ambassador. Lemkin wrote to her in January 1950 in her position as chairman of the International Commission of Women and the Pan American Union: "My dear Mrs. Ledone [*sic*], Thank you most cordially for your letter and most efficient help. Now you are becoming the apostle of the genocide convention, I am very happy and grateful for your intervention with Mariblanca Aloma Sabes. It worked so well. How could it be otherwise? I am preparing now my report to Latin America on genocide and since your activities are described there I will send you a copy as soon as the text is ready for distribution. With renewed thanks and best wishes for a Happy New Year, I am, Very sincerely yours, Raphael Lemkin."

7. Dr. Octavio Méndez Pereira (1887–1954). Lemkin also wrote to Pereira on December 17, 1949: "Dear Dr. Pereira: My absence from Yale prevented me from thanking you earlier for your so important letter announcing ratification of the genocide convention. Certainly your personal contributions have been remarkable because you put the great prestige of your personality in the service of this cause. Your help with other countries is also of the greatest importance because, as I am informed by Rector Duram, the presidents of the Latin American Republics have reacted favorably to your resolution of Panama. I gave the Guatemala resolution to the delegate of Guatemala in the United Nations and he made a statement about it. Thanking you again, and wishing you a Merry Christmas and a Happy New Year, I am, Sincerely yours, Raphael Lemkin."

8. Pierre Montel (1896–1967) and Louis Léon Marcel Plaisant (1887–1958). In a letter to Monsieur l'abbe de Lattre, Lemkin wrote that he "discussed ratification with two important French parliamentarians Marcel Plaisant, President of the Senate Foreign Relations Committee and with Pierre Montel, Chairman of the Defence Committee in the National Assembly. Both are ready to help [with France's ratification of the CPPCG]."

9. Édouard Herriot (1872–1957) and Leon Blum (1872–1950).

10. Lemkin is possibly referring to Jean Minjoz (1904–1987).

11. Lester Bowles Pearson (1897–1972) is, to date, Canada's only Nobel Peace Prize recipient.

12. The following letter to Lemkin from the Anti-Defamation League of B'nai B'rith demonstrates the nongovernmental lobbying toward Canada's ratification: "Dear Professor Lemkin: I thought you would be interested in the following information which I have just received from our Canadian contacts. The information is that Hon. Lester B. Pearson, Secretary of State for External Affairs of Canada, in a reply to a request made by Mr. Samuel Bronfman,

National President of the Canadian Jewish Congress, for ratification of the Genocide Convention by Canada, assured that: 'Careful consideration has been given to the question of ratification by Canada of this Convention ever since I had the privilege of signing it on behalf of Canada on November [illegible,] 1940. It is the view of the Canadian Government that everything should be done to promote the humanitarian cause which is given expression to in the Convention, and that the bringing into force of the Convention would be a step in that direction. It will be necessary to secure approval of Parliament for the ratification of the Convention and I am hoping that it may be possible to do so early in the next session. We are somewhat concerned about the reservations made by the Soviet Union, Ukraine, Byelorussia and Czechoslovakia when they signed the Convention last December, and we are examining the position to determine what our attitude should be to these reservations.'"

13. Canada signed the CPPCG on January 1, 1951, and ratified on September 3, 1952.

14. Lemkin is most likely referring to Carlos Peña Romulo (1898–1985). He became president of the United Nations General Assembly between 1949 and 1950.

15. The Philippines signed and ratified the CPPCG on January 12, 1951.

16. Syngman Rhee (1875–1965) was the first president of South Korea, serving from 1948 to 1960.

17. Lemkin capitalized on Nussbaum's deep international influences, as demonstrated in the following letter from Lemkin to Nussbaum, after Nussbaum's visit to Yale. "Dear Dr. Nussbaum: I am writing to you from Washington whereto your letter was forwarded to me. Thank you very much for your efforts on behalf of the Genocide Convention. I am so grateful to you that you have decided to discuss this matter personally with your prime minister of France and with the Mother Queen of Holland. I am sure that these two persons can bring about quick results. A few new developments on genocide will be of interest to you. The British Delegate to the United Nations Assembly, Mrs. Barbara Castle, accused Soviet Russia of practicing genocide on the three Baltic nations. Ecuador has completed the ratification and Brazil is completing it this week. Next week an important international Labor conference will take place in London and I shall try to get a resolution on ratification from this conference. If you have contacts with the French Labor Movement, maybe you could kindly ask the French delegation to support or to propose a resolution on genocide. Enclosed you will find a draft resolution on genocide which

might be used at the Labor conference in London. As you know, Denmark recently signed the Genocide Convention and if something can be done there to speed up ratification it would be of great importance. I was told that the Minister of Justice in Holland is interested. You might mention to him that his advisor, Professor Duynste, who is now in Lake Success, urged ratification. I will be frank with you and maybe you can help. The Legal Advisor of the Dutch Foreign Office, Mr. Francois, is a very skeptical man, who has however, great influence. If you can persuade him personally, Holland will ratify. The points to develop with Francois are as follows: (1) The Nuremberg law left crimes committed in time of peace unpunishable and therefore there is actually no law against genocide. (2) Ratification of the Convention will crystallize world opinion in condemning genocide. (3) The motherland of international law should be the leader in this matter. As far as Yugoslavia is concerned, I think it might be useful for you to ask for ratification. You might see also Professor Bartos in the Ministry of Foreign Affairs, who is attacking Russia now very strongly because of Russia's opposition to international law. As far as Belgium is concerned, I was told that the persons who can help most are Senator Henry Rolin, the Minister Carton de Wiart; also, Mr. Rey, Minister of Reconstruction, the coming man of the Liberal Party. In France you will certainly have the help of the Catholic group such as Monseigneur Beaupin, Aba du Bois, and especially abbe de Lattre, who lives at 5 Lamartine Square, Paris. Please keep in touch with me. Dean Sturges, Professor Benton, and my students were very impressed by your visit in Yale. They all send you warm regards and best wishes in your great work for humanity. Cordially yours." The accusation from Barbara Castle received front-page coverage in the press.
18. Sir Carl August Berendsen (1890–1973).
19. Mario José Echandi Jiménez (1915–2011). Jiménez was president of Costa Rica, 1958–62.
20. Trygve Halvdan Lie (1896–1968) was the first secretary-general of the United Nations.
21. In December 1949, Lemkin wrote the following to Dr. Carlos García Bauer. "My dear Mr. Ambassador: I am sending you warm greetings and expressions of hope that you will bring back to Lake Success the document of ratification of the genocide convention which is so close to your heart. The fact that Guatemala is proceeding with ratification in the midst of rehabilitation work resulting from the recent flood shows the great humanitarian tradition of your country. The ratification day by Guatemala will be celebrated as the symbol of the victory of human spirit and idealism over materialistic preoccupations. If

you see Rector Duran please give him my best regards. He made a great contribution by mobilizing the universities in Latin America for this cause. Wishing you a Merry Christmas and a Happy New Year, I am, Sincerely yours, Raphael Lemkin."

22. Guatemala signed and ratified the CPPCG on January 12, 1951.

23. Panama signed and ratified the CPPCG on January 12, 1951. Cuba signed on January 12, 1951, but did not ratify until March 4, 1953.

24. Selim Sarper (1899–1968).

25. It was 4 A.M. on June 25, 1950.

26. Thomas Terry Connally (1877–1963).

27. Carlos Manuel de Céspedes del Castillo (1819–1874) is known as the father of the nation of Cuba, a plantation farmer who freed his slaves and began the war of independence from Spain.

28. After the end of the Soviet Bloc, on March 8, 1989, the USSR officially withdrew its reservation made on Article IX.

29. Sir Robert Anthony Eden (1897–1977).

30. Lemkin could be referring to Sir Alexander Cadogan, who was the permanent U.K. representative, 1946–50.

31. Dr. Ivan Kerno (born Ivan Krno; 1891–1961).

32. Jean Price-Mars (1876–1969) was a diplomat, writer, doctor, anthropologist, and social scientist who defended voodoo as a legitimate religion.

33. Lemkin has written something illegible over the name "Garrand," suggesting that he corrected his misspelling of the ambassador's name. The French ambassador to the United Nations from 1949 to 1952 was Jean Chauvel.

34. Nasrollah Entezam (1900–1980) was the president of the fifth session of the General Assembly in 1950.

35. In a letter to George J. Spatuzza on January 8, 1950, Lemkin writes: "President Truman in his last message to Congress praised highly the genocide convention. In his previous message to the Senate of June 16, 1949, he urged ratification."

36. Article XIII reads: "On the day when the first twenty instruments of ratification or accession have been deposited, the Secretary-General shall draw up a *procès-verbal* and transmit a copy thereof to each Member of the United Nations and to each of the non-member States contemplated in article XI. The present Convention shall come into force on the ninetieth day following the date of deposit of the twentieth instrument of ratification or accession. Any ratification or accession effected subsequent to the latter date shall become effective on the ninetieth day following the deposit of the instrument of ratification or accession."

37. A large photograph accompanied a small report of the "formal operation." According to the *Times*, the following were photographed in the office of the president of the General Assembly: "Dr. John M. Chang of Korea; Dr. Price Mars of Haiti; Nasrollah Entezam of Iran; Jean Chauvel of France; Ruben Esquivel of Costa Rica; Dr. Ivan Kerno, Assistant Secretary General for Legal Affairs; Trygve Lie, Secretary General; Fernando Fournier of Costa Rica and Professor Raphael Lemkin, chief proponent of the pact."

38. At this conference Lemkin said: "The Communists would like to divert the attention from Russian crimes and to scuttle the genocide convention by confusion."

39. According to Lemkin's friend Nancy Steinson Ehrlich, Lemkin met the lawyer Lazar Lowenstein in Lithuania and both came to the United States as refugees. When Lemkin was teaching at Duke University in 1941, Lemkin helped Lazar's daughter matriculate. The Lowensteins and Lemkin were close to the point where Lemkin often stayed with the family. Unfortunately, Lemkin "did wear out his welcome and that . . . was a great disappointment for everyone. Once Mrs. Lowenstein came home to find her maid hadn't done what she was supposed to have done and she said that she [the maid] had been talking with Dr. Lemkin. Apparently he was as interesting to the house maid as he was to anyone else."

40. No story is included in Lemkin's manuscript, but it is more than likely the following article: "The United Nations genocide treaty would make of international record the fact that people may not be exterminated for racial, religious, national or ethnic reasons; that human groups have a right to life, regardless of origins; and that those responsible for mass murders shall be made punishable for their crimes. The Soviet Union is, of course, bitterly opposed to the treaty, which bears on slave labor forces. In this country the Senate is expected to act on its committee's recommendations and to approve the treaty, with certain reservations, at the next session. But twenty-two ratifications—two more than necessary for making the treaty law—have all been deposited with the U.N., and to all intents and purposes the genocide pact should go in effect next January. Yet the fact is that the treaty is in peril. It is quite justifiably assumed that unless the United States is party to the treaty it will never acquire the necessary moral and political striking force. Last week the Legal Committee of the U.N. decided that the International Law Commission should pass on the effect on reservations on treaties—something that may take months or even years of debate. Further, if a state, such as Russia, disapproved reservations of the United States, we could be excluded from the treaty. All this is suddenly

contrary to the practice followed by Secretary General Lie to permit countries to become parties to a treaty, though they might have some reservations. The treaty should grow and develop with new ratifications. The Law Commission can certainly do its work of interpretation at the same time that the Secretary General follows his traditional practice of accepting ratifications. To create a new procedure, just when success seems assured, would be a clear scuttling of the will of the people. The General Assembly should free the genocide treaty."

CHAPTER TWELVE. Nearing the End

1. Arthur B. Spingarn (1878–1971).
2. The editor of *America*, a weekly national Jesuit magazine, between 1948 and 1955 was the Reverend Robert C. Harnett.
3. Lemkin may be referring to the American Hellenic Educational Progressive Association (AHEPA), a philanthropic association dedicated to Hellenism. It began in 1926 in Atlanta, Georgia.
4. Dean Gooderham Acheson (1893–1971) was secretary of State from 1949 to 1953.
5. Warren Robinson Austin (1877–1962) was the U.S. ambassador to the U.N. (1946–1953).
6. Lemkin may be referring to the Danish politician and judge Inger Helga Pederson (1911–1980).
7. Canada ratified on September 3, 1952, and Sweden on May 25, 1952.
8. U Nu (1907–1995) was the first prime minister of independent Burma and ratified the CPPCG on March 14, 1956.

APPENDIX ONE. Outline for Chapter One

1. Lemkin circled this and drew an upward arrow, indicating the section should be placed between sections 1 and 2.

APPENDIX TWO. Summary of Activities and Chapter Outline

1. The Who's Who entry reads:

    First Name: Raphael

    Last Name: Lemkin

Occupation: lawyer

Born: Bezwodne, Poland, June 24, 1900

Details: Son of Joseph and Bella (Pomeranz) L.; student Gymnasium in Bialystok, Poland; LL.D. (J. D.), U. Lwow, Poland, Sec. Court of Appeals, Warsaw, Poland, 1926–29, pub. prosecutor, 1929–34; prof. law Tachkemoni Coll., 1927–39; gen. practice law, Warsaw, 1934–39; lectr. U. Stockholm, 1940–41, Duke U., 1941–42; chief consultant Bd. Econ. Warfare and Fgn. Econ. Adminstrn., Washington, 1942–44, adviser on fgn. affairs, Dept. of War, 1945–47; mem. prosecution staff, U.S. Army as chief prosecutor Axis Criminality in Neuremberg, 1945–46; prof. law, Yale, 1948– . A founder World Movement to Outlaw Genocide (coined the word genocide and transformed it into internat. treaty); prin. adviser to U.N. on genocide conv. Mem. Am. Soc. Internat. Law. Jewish religion. Address: Yale University Law School, New Haven.

2. Lemkin may have been thinking of the *Chicago Jewish Weekly,* where the following was written: "We are here considering the impact upon one group—the Jews. The physical destruction of more than one-third of all of that group in the world intensified its concern over the problem. One thinker has viewed it in the perspective of all the peoples in the world. Raphael Lemkin in his recent book discusses the problem of attacks by warring powers on civil populations and supplies a specific name for this practice—'genocide.' He proposes an international legal prohibition of it in peacetime as well as in war; it shall be a violation of international law to engage in any action infringing upon the life, liberty, health, economic existence, or the honor of the inhabitants in a land. And the principle shall be enforced through the criminal law of each country. Here is a new law for an old crime."

Bibliography

Abulafia, David, Rosamond McKitterick, and Martin Brett, eds. *New Cambridge Medieval History: c. 1198–c. 1300*, vol. 5. Cambridge, Eng.: Cambridge University Press, 1999.

Alessandri, Arturo, Paal Berg, Luis Podessa Costa, et. al. "The Crime of Genocide: U.N. Is Urged to Act on Proposed Convention Now Before It." *New York Times*, November 11, 1947, p. C26.

Alighieri, Dante. *The Divine Comedy.* Henry F. Cary, trans. Harvard Classics, vol. 20. New York: P. F. Collier and Son, 1909–14.

Alston, Charlotte. *Antonius Piip, Zigfrîds, Meierovics, and Augustinas Voldemaras: The Baltic States.* London: Haus, 2010.

America. "History of *America.*" http://www.americamagazine.org/content/about-us.cfm.

American Bar Association Journal. "Tentative Program, 64th Annual Meeting of the American Bar Association," vol. 27 (August 1941): 517.

American Hellenic Educational Progressive Association. www.ahepa.org/.

Arkadii, Vaksberg. *Stalin's Prosecutor: The Life of Andrei Vyshinsky.* Jan Butler, trans. New York: Grove Weidenfeld, 1991.

Arne, Sigrid. "Nazi Victim Helps Repay Debt." *Portland Press Herald*, March 16, 1947, section D, p. 5.

Arnold, Matthew. *Essays in Criticism.* New York: A. L. Burt, 1865.

Aurell, Jaume. "Autobiography as Unconventional History: Constructing the Author," *Rethinking History* 10:3 (2006): 433–49.

Bartlett, Robert Merrill. "By the Way: Pioneer vs. an Ancient Crime." *Christian Century*, July 16, 1956, "Bio- and Autobiographical Sketches of Lemkin," Raphael Lemkin Papers (RLP), New York Public Library (NYPL).

Berger, Jacob Solomon, trans. *The Volkovysk Memorial Book: A Trilogy.* Mahwah, N.J., 2002.

Boswell, James. *The Life of Samuel Johnson, LL.D*, vol. 1. London: John Sharp, 1930.

Broughton, Jeffrey L. *The Bodhidharma Anthology: The Earliest Records of Zen.* Berkeley: University of California Press, 1999.

Buber, Martin. *I and Thou.* Walter Kaufmann, trans. Edinburgh: Clark, 1970.

Carlos P. Romulo Foundation. "General Carlos P. Romulo." http://carlospromulo.org/.

Castberg, Frede. *The European Convention on Human Rights.* Torkel Opsahl and Thomas Ouchterlony, eds.; Gytte Borch, trans. Leiden: Sijthoff; Dobbs Ferry, N.Y.: Oceana, 1974.

Chifley, Ben. "Genocide Convention Bill 1949—Second Reading—House of Representatives Hansard—19 May 1949," Parliament of Australia, hansard80-ID: hansard80/hansardr80/1949–05–19/0084. http://www.aph.gov.au/Hansard/hansreps.htm.

Confucius. *The Sayings of Confucius.* Leonard A. Lyall, trans. London: Longmans, Green, 2007.

Cooper, Eli Louis. "A Law Against Anti-Semitism." *Sentinel (Chicago Jewish Weekly)* 144:3 (July 18, 1948): 7.

Cooper, John. *Raphael Lemkin and the Struggle for the Genocide Convention.* Hampshire, Eng.: Palgrave Macmillan, 2008.

Cortés, Eladio, and Mirta Barrea-Marlys. *Encyclopedia of Latin American Theater.* Westport, Conn.: Greenwood, 2003.

Crockett, Jameson W. "The Polish Blitz, More than a Mere Footnote to History: Poland and Preventive War with Germany, 1933." *Diplomacy and Statecraft* 20:4 (December 2009): 561–79.

Denton, Sally. *The Pink Lady: The Many Lives of Helen Gahagan Douglas.* New York: Bloomsbury, 2009.

D'Itri, Patricia Ward. *Cross Currents in the International Women's Movement, 1848–1948.* Bowling Green, Ohio: Bowling Green State University Popular Press, 1999.

Diplomatic Documents of Switzerland. "Information about Person Petitpierre, Max (1899–1994)." http://db.dodis.ch.

Dolph Briscoe Center for American History. "Tom Connally Papers, 1924, 1931–1952." http://www.lib.utexas.edu.

Downey, Kirstin. *The Woman Behind the New Deal: The Life of Frances Perkins, FDR's Secretary of Labor and His Moral Conscience.* New York: Nan A. Talese/Doubleday, 2009.

Ehrlich Steinson, Nancy. Personal correspondence with the author, April 30, 2011; October 29, 2011; November 2, 2011; February 16, 2012.

Einhorn, Moses. "Destruction of Wolkowisk." www.jewishgen.org/yizkor/volkovysk.

Einhorn, Moses. "Wolkovisk—My Native Town." http://www.jewishgen.org/yizkor/volkovysk.

Eleanor Roosevelt Papers Project. "Teaching Eleanor Roosevelt Glossary—Adlai Stevenson (1900–1965)." http://www.gwu.edu/~erpapers/teachinger/glossary/stevenson-adlai.cfm.

Evatt, H. V. *The United Nations.* Melbourne: Oxford University Press, 1948.

Federation of Jewish Communities of the Commonwealth of the Independent States. http://www.fjc.ru/communities/default.asp?AID=84435.

Foundation Robert Schuman. http://www.schumanfoundation.eu.

France Catholique. http://www.france-catholique.fr/.

Frieze, Donna-Lee. "The Destruction of Sarajevo's *Vijećnica*: A Case of Genocidal Cultural Destruction?" In Adam Jones, ed., *New Directions in Genocide Research.* Oxon, Eng.: Routledge, 2011.

Genêt. "Letter from Paris." *New Yorker*, October 16, 1948, pp. 111–15.

Georgetown University. "Alfaro Family Papers." Special Collections Division, Lauinger Library. http://www.aladin0.wrlc.org/.

Goethe, Johann Wolfgang von. *Herman and Dorothea: A Poem, from the German of Goethe.* Thomas Holcroft, trans. London: T. N. Longman and O. Rees, 1801.

Greenbaum, Alfred A. "Soviet Jewry During the Lenin-Stalin Period I." *Soviet Studies* 16:4 (April 1965): 406–21.

Greene, Julie. *The Canal Builders: Making America's Empire at the Panama Canal.* New York: Penguin, 2009.

Halecki, Oskar. *A History of Poland.* London: Routledge and Kegan Paul, 1983.

Harry S. Truman Library and Museum. "Oral History Interview with John Maktos." http://www.trumanlibrary.org/oralhist/maktosj.htm#17.

HEART (Holocaust Education & Archive Research Team). "Vilnius Ghetto." http://www.deathcamps.org/occupation/vilnius%20ghetto.html.

Heine, Heinrich. *The Poems of Heine.* Edgar Alfred Bowring, trans. London: George Bell and Sons, 1891.

Hunczak, Taras. *Simon Petliura and the Jews: A Reappraisal.* Toronto: Ukrainian Historical Association, 1985.

ICRC (International Committee of the Red Cross). "Agreement for the Prosecution and Punishment of the Major War Criminals of the European Axis, and Charter of the International Military Tribunal. London, 8 August 1945." http://www.icrc.org/ihl.nsf/WebART/350–530014?OpenDocument.

Institute for Advanced Studies on the United Nations. "Alexandre Parodi Scholarships Program." http://www.ihenu.org/.

International Institute of Social History. "Tomáš Garrigue Masaryk Papers." http://www.iisg.nl/archives/en/files/m/10760607.php.

Irokawa, Daikichi. *The Age of Hirohito: In Search of Modern Japan.* Mikiso Hane and John K. Urda, trans. New York: Free Press, 1995.

Karski, Jan. *Story of a Secret State.* Boston: Houghton Mifflin, 1944.

Kaufmann, J. E., and H. W. Kaufmann. *The Maginot Line: None Shall Pass.* Westport, Conn.: Praeger, 1997.

King, Archibald. "Further Developments Concerning Jurisdiction over Friendly Foreign Armed Forces." *American Journal of International Law* 40:2 (April 1946): 257–79.

Kleine, Richard. "Law Teacher's Crusade Against Genocide Laws Down Home Stretch After 35 Years." *Berkshire Evening Eagle,* August 2, 1949, p. 17.

Konwinski, Norbert. *The Mayor: Saga of Stefan Starzynski.* Posen, Mich.: Diversified Enterprises, 1978.

Krakowski, Stefan. "Siedlce." http://www.jewishvirtuallibrary.org/jsource.

Kubler, George. "Henri Focillon, 1881–1943." *College Art Journal* 4:2 (January 1945): 71–74.

Kurek, Jala. *Grypa szaleje w Naprawie.* Krakow: Wydawnictwo Literackie, 1954.

Landau, Rom. *Ignace Paderewski, Musician and Statesman.* New York: AMS, 1976.

Leikin, Ezekiel, trans. and ed. *The Beilis Transcripts: The Anti-Semitic Trial That Shook the World.* Northvale, N.J.: Aronson, 1993.

Leipzig University. "The Simon Dubnow Institute for Jewish History and Culture at Leipzig University." http://www.dubnow.de/Institute.3.0.html?&L=1.

Lemkin, Raphael. "Acts Constituting a General (Transnational) Danger Considered as Offences Against the Law of Nations." Jim Fussell, trans. *Prevent Genocide International,* http://www.preventgenocide.org/lemkin/madrid1933-english.htm.

Lemkin, R[aphael]. *La Regulation des Paiements Internationaux: Traite de Droit Compare sur les Devises, Les Clearing et les Accords de paiments, Les Conflicts de Lois.* Paris: A. Pedone, 1939.

Lemkin, Raphaël. *Valutareglering och Clearing.* Stockholm: P. A. Norstedt and Söner, 1941.

Lemkin, Raphaël. "The Legal Framework of Totalitarian Control over Foreign Economies." Presented at the section of International and Comparative Law of the American Bar Association, Indianapolis, September 29–October 3, 1941.

Lemkin, Raphaël. *Axis Rule in Occupied Europe: Laws of Occupation, Analysis of Government, Proposals for Redress.* Clark, N.J.: Lawbook Exchange, 1944, 2005.

Lemkin, Raphael. "Genocide." *American Scholar* 15:2 (April 1946): 227–30.

Lemkin, R., and M. McDermott. *The Polish Penal Code of 1932 and the Law of Minor Offenses*. Durham: Duke University Press, 1939.

Lemkin, Saul. Personal conversation with the author, January 29, 2009.

Leon, Garth. *Frank Buchman: A Life*. London: Constable, 1985.

Letter from Bella and Joseph Lemkin to Lemkin, Box 1, Folder 4, Raphael Lemkin Collection (RLC), American Jewish Historical Society (AJHS).

Letter from Charles A. Pearce to Raphael Lemkin, August 19, 1958, "General Correspondence, 1954–1959; n.d.," RLP, NYPL.

Letter from Erik Dons to Lemkin, May 19, 1949, Box 2, Folder 1, RLC, AJHS.

Letter from Lemkin to Amalia de Castillo Ledón, January 9, 1950, Box 2, Folder 3, RLC, AJHS.

Letter from Lemkin to Charles Pierce [*sic*], August 6, 1958, "General Correspondence, 1954–1959; n.d.," RLP, NYPL.

Letter from Lemkin to Clarence Pickett, March 30, 1949, Box 2, Folder 1, RLC, AJHS.

Letter from Lemkin to Count d'Oultremont, January 9, 1950, Box 2, Folder 3, RLC, AJHS.

Letter from Lemkin to Curtis-Brown Ltd., October 22, 1958, "General Correspondence, 1954–1959; n.d.," RLP, NYPL.

Letter from Lemkin to Dr. Perozo, July 24, 1948, Box 1, Folder 19, RLC, AJHS.

Letter from Lemkin to Elia D. Madey, January 9, 1950, Box 2, Folder 3, RLC, AJHS.

Letter from Lemkin to Garcia Bauer, December 17, 1949, Box 2, Folder 2, RLC, AJHS.

Letter from Lemkin to George J. Spatuzza, January 8, 1950, Box 2, Folder 3, RLC, AJHS.

Letter from Lemkin to Hamilton National Bank, October 29, 1948, Box 1, Folder 6, RLC, AJHS.

Letter from Lemkin to Jean Nussbaum, November 17, 1949, Box 2, Folder 2, RLC, AJHS.

Letter from Lemkin to John Maktos, January 18, 1948, Box 1, Folder 19, RLC, AJHS.

Letter from Lemkin to Jorge Villagómez Yépez, June 13, 1949, Box 2, Folder 1, RLC, AJHS.

Letter from Lemkin to Judge Ingles, December 17, 1949, Box 2, Folder 2, RLC, AJHS.

Letter from Lemkin to Karl Schlyter, December 31, 1949, Box 2, Folder 2, RLC, AJHS.

Letter from Lemkin to l'abbe de Lattre, January 9, 1950, Box 2, Folder 3, RLC, AJHS.

Letter from Lemkin to Maynard Gertler, December 7, 1946, Box 1, Folder 18, RLC, AJHS.

Letter from Lemkin to Mr. K.P.S. Menon, February 16, 1950, "India," RLP, NYPL.

Letter from Lemkin to Mrs. Marc Somerhausen, January 9, 1950, Box 2, Folder 3, RLC, AJHS.

Letter from Lemkin to Octavio Mendez Pereira, December 17, 1949, Box 2, Folder 2, RLC, AJHS.

Letter from Lemkin to Quintin Paredes December 17, 1949, Box 2, Folder 2, RLC, AJHS.

Letter from Mrs. Harry W. Davis to all Jewish organizations of Duluth, July 14, 1949, Box 2, Folder 10, RLC, AJHS.

Letter from Naomi Burton to Raphael Lemkin, September 11, 1958, "General Correspondence, 1954–1959; n.d.," RLP, NYPL.

Letter from Naomi Burton to Raphael Lemkin, October 30, 1958, "General Correspondence, 1954–1959; n.d.," RLP, NYPL.

Letter from Pearl S. Buck to Lemkin, undated, Box 1, Folder 17, RLC, AJHS.

Letter from Ricardo Alfaro to Lemkin, January 16, 1950, "Panama," RLP, NYPL.

Letter from Sol Rabkin (Anti-Defamation League of B'nai B'rith) to Lemkin, July 26, 1950, "General Correspondence, 1947–1953," RLP, NYPL.

Library of Congress. "Arthur B. Spingarn papers, 1850–1968." http://lccn.loc.gov/mm79040949.

Library of Congress. "Charles Fahy Papers, 1857–1985." http://findingaids.loc.gov.

Library of Congress. "Vance, John Thomas, 1884–1943." http://catalog.loc.gov.

The Lima News. "Yale Professor Feels Russia Has Dire Mass Plan," June 18, 1951, p. 4.

Loewen, Gertrude. *Crusader for Freedom: The Story of Jean Nussbaum.* Nashville: Southern Publishing, 1969.

Long Beach Independent. "Outlaw of 'Genocide' Recommended by U.N.," December 10, 1948, p. 2.

Maclean, Pam, Michele Langfield, and Dvir Abramovich, eds. *Testifying to the Holocaust.* Sydney: Australian Association of Jewish Studies, 2008.

Malik, Charles Habib. *The Challenge of Human Rights: Charles Malik and the Universal Declaration.* Oxford: Charles Malik Foundation, Centre for Lebanese Studies, 2000.

Manuscript on the Turkish Massacre of Armenians (undated), Box 8, Folder 14, RLC, AJHS.

Marquis Who's Who. http://www.marquiswhoswho.com/.

Martin, Douglas. "John Hohenberg, 94, Former Pulitzer Prize Official, Dies," *New York Times*, August 8, 2000, pp. A23, 25.

McDonough Frank. *Neville Chamberlain, Appeasement, and the British Road to War*. Manchester: Manchester University Press, 1998.

McGinnis, Jon. *Avicenna*. New York: Oxford University Press, 2010.

Mongols, undated, Box 9, Folder 9, RLC, AJHS.

Moors and Moriscos, Box 7, Folder 9, *Raphael Lemkin Papers*, American Jewish Archives.

The Moriscos of Spain: Their Conversion and Expulsion, Box 9, Folder 10, RLC, AJHS.

"Nadson: The Poet of Despairing Hope." *Slavonic and East European Review* 15:45 (April 1937): pp. 680–87.

National Archives. "Passenger Lists of Vessels Arriving at Seattle, Washington, 1949–1954." Micropublication M1398, RG085, Washington, D.C.

National Archives. "Records of the Tennessee Valley Authority [TVA]," Record Group 142. http://www.archives.gov/research/guide-fed-records/groups/142.html#142.14.

National Archives of Australia. "Fact sheet 82—Joseph Benedict Chifley." http://www.naa.gov.au/about-us/publications/fact-sheets/fs82.aspx.

National Archives of Australia. "United Nations—Convention on Genocide—Commonwealth Ratification," 1949–1957, Series no. A463, Control No. 1957/6413. http://recordsearch.naa.gov.au/scripts/Imagine.asp.

National Archives Southeast Region. "Atlanta, GA," RG 147, Box 218.

National Library of Australia. "Papers of Sir James Plimsoll," MS 8048. http://www.nla.gov.au/ms/findaids/8048.html.

New York Times. "Genocide," editorial, August 26, 1946, p. 17.

New York Times. "U.N. Representatives Ratifying Pact Against Genocide," October 17, 1950, p. 18.

New York Times. "The Genocide Treaty," November 1, 1950, p. 34.

New York Times. "The Crime of Genocide," October 20, 1957.

New York Times. "Guillermo Belt, 83, Ex-Cuba Envoy to U.S.," obituaries, July 7, 1989, p. 12.

Nobelprize.org. "Bio—Erling Wikborg." http://www.nobelprize.org/nobel_prizes/peace/articles/committee/unclist/bios/wikborg.html.

Nobelprize.org. "Lester Bowles Pearson—Biography." http://www.nobelprize.org.

Nobelprize.org. "Nomination Database—Peace." http://www.nobelprize.org/nobel_prizes/peace/nomination.

Nobelprize.org. "Sigrid Undset—Autobiography." http://nobelprize.org/nobel_ prizes/literature/laureates/1928/undset.html.

Norwegian Social Science Data Services. "Terje Wold." http://www.nsd.uib.no/ polsys.

Ogden Standard Examiner. "Britain Accuses Russians of Genocidal Terror," October 16, 1949, p. 1.

Ogilvie, Marilyn, and Joy Harvey, eds. *The Biographical Dictionary of Women in Science: Pioneering Lives from Ancient Times to the Mid-20th Century.* New York: Routledge, 2000.

Pearson, Lester B. *Mike: The Memoirs of the Right Honourable Lester B. Pearson.* Toronto: University of Toronto Press, 1972.

Perez, Jizchok Lejbusch. *Ojb Nischt Noch Hecher: A Hasidishe Dertseylung.* Hagen: Katholische Akademie Schwerte, 1996.

Permanent Mission of France to the United Nations, "Previous Ambassadors." http://www.franceonu.org/spip.php?article3629.

Pinson, Koppel S. "Simon Dubnow: Historian and Philosopher." In Koppel S. Pinson, ed., *Nationalism and History: Essays on Old and New Judaism/Simon Dubnow.* Cleveland: World Publishing; Philadelphia: Jewish Publication Society of America, 1961.

Polin, Pinkas Hakehillot. *"Wolkowysk": Encyclopedia of Jewish Communities in Poland,* vol. 8 (Vaukavisk: Belarus), Yad Vashem. http://www.jewishgen.org/ yizkor/pinkas_poland/pol8_00298.html.

Ravel, Marcel, ed. *Rainer Maria Rilke: His Last Friendship.* New York: Philosophical Library, 1952.

Romanowicz, Wiesław. *Poleszuks as an Ethnic Community.* http://rozprawy-spole czne.pswbp.pl/pdf/romanowicz.pdf.

Rosenberg, Alfred. *The Myth of the Twentieth Century: An Evaluation of the Spiritual-Intellectual Confrontations of Our Age.* Newport Beach, Calif.: Noontide, 1982.

Rothwell, Victor. *Anthony Eden: A Political Biography, 1931–57.* Manchester: Manchester University Press, 1992.

Rowley, Hazel. *Christina Stead: A Biography.* Port Melbourne: Minerva, 1993.

Schildgen, Robert. *Toyohiko Kagawa: Apostle of Love and Social Justice.* Berkeley, Calif.: Centenary, 1988.

Severo, Richard. "William Proxmire, Maverick Democratic Senator from Wisconsin, Is Dead at 90." *New York Times,* December 16, 2005, p. 13.

Shannon, Magdaline W. *Jean Price-Mars, the Haitian Elite, and the American Occupation, 1915–1935.* New York: St. Martin's, 1996.

Shawcross, Hartley, and Baron Shawcross. *Life Sentence: The Memoirs of Lord Shawcross.* London: Constable, 1995.

Sienkiewicz, Henryk. *Quo Vadis.* W. S. Kuniczak, trans. New York: Macmillan, 1993.

Simon, Boris. *Ragman's City.* Sidney Cunliffe-Owen, trans. London: Harvill, 1957.

Sōshitsu XV, Sen. *The Japanese Way of Tea: From Its Origins in China to Sen Rikyū.* V. Dixon Morris, trans. Honolulu: University of Hawaii Press, 1998.

Stepanov, Nikolay. *Ivan Krylov.* New York: Twayne, 1973.

Storozynski, Alex. *The Peasant Prince: Thaddeus Kosciuszko and the Age of Revolution.* New York: St. Martin's Griffin/Thomas Dunne, 2009.

Time. "Death of a Hero," 34:16 (October 16, 1939): 48.

The Times. "The Armenian Question," December 31, 1894, p. 6.

Tolischus, Otto D. *They Wanted War.* New York: Reynal and Hitchcock, 1940.

Tolischus, Otto D. *Through Japanese Eyes.* New York: Reynal and Hitchcock, 1945.

Tolischus, Otto D. *Tokyo Record.* New York: Reynal and Hitchcock, 1943.

Tolischus, Otto D. "Twentieth-Century Moloch: The Nazi-Inspired Totalitarian State, Devour of Progress—and of Itself." *New York Times,* book reviews, January 21, 1945, p. 102.

Troubetzkoy, Alexis S. "The Life and Death of Feodor Kuzmich." In *Imperial Legend: The Disappearance of Tsar Alexander I.* New York: Arcade, 2002.

United Kingdom Mission to the United Nations. "Former Permanent Representatives." http://ukun.fco.gov.uk/en/about-us/whos-who/former-permanent-repre sentatives.

United Nations. *Convention of the Prevention and Punishment of the Crime of Genocide,* U.N. Treaty no. 1021. http://treaties.un.org.

United Nations. "General Assembly of the United Nations: Nasrollah Entezam." http://www.un.org/en/ga/president/bios/bio05.shtml.

United Nations. "Participants to the *Convention of the Prevention and Punishment of the Crime of Genocide.*" http://treaties.un.org.

United Nations. *What the UN Is Doing: The Convention on Genocide.* New York: United Nations, 1949.

United States Holocaust Memorial Museum. "Frequently Asked Questions: About the Holocaust." http://www.ushmm.org.

United States Holocaust Memorial Museum. "Śmigły-Rydz Becomes Field Marshal, 1936." http://www.ushmm.org/research/collections/highlights/bryan/video/detail.php?content=prewar_smigly.

University of Iowa Libraries. "Henry A. Wallace Collection." wallace.lib.uiowa .edu.

University of Vermont Library. Warren R. Austin Collection, Special Collections. http://cdi.uvm.edu/findingaids/collection/austin.ead.xml.

Wallace, Henry A. *The Century of the Common Man.* Russell Lord, ed. London: Hutchinson, 1940.

Washington Post. "Genocide," editorial, December 3, 1944, p. B4.

Wilgress, Dana. *Memoirs.* Toronto: Ryerson, 1967.

Wisse, Ruth R. *The I. L. Peretz Reader.* New Haven: Yale University Press, 2002, pp. 178–80.

Woolsey, Lester H. "George A. Finch, September 22, 1884–July 17, 1957." *American Journal of International Law* 52:4 (October 1957): 756.

Yad Vashem. "Lithuania." http://www1.yadvashem.org.

Yale Law School. "Judgement: War Crimes and Crimes Against Humanity." *The Avalon Project*, Lillian Goldman Law Library. http://avalon.law.yale.edu/imt/judwarcr.asp.

Yale Law School. "Memorandum of a Conversation Held on the Night of August 23rd to 24th, Between the Reich Foreign Minister, on the One Hand, and Herr Stalin and the Chairman of the Council of People's Commissars Molotov, on the Other Hand." *The Avalon Project*, Lillian Goldman Law Library. http://avalon.law.yale.edu/20th_century/ns053.asp.

Yeghiayan, Vartkes, ed. *The Case of Soghomon Tehlirian.* Glendale, Calif.: Center for Armenian Remembrance, 2006.

YIVO. "Guide to the Papers of Shalom Schwarzbard (1886–1938)," RG 85.

YIVO. "Simon Dubnow," RG 87.

Young, Robert J. *Power and Pleasure: Louis Barthou and the Third French Republic.* Montreal: McGill–Queen's University Press, 1991.

Index

Acheson, Dean, 220
Ackerly, Nancy. *See* Steinson Ehrlich, Nancy
Admado, Gilberto, 136, 156
Aesop, 17, 21
Africa, 122, 185, 187
Albania, Genocide Convention ratification, 241n2
Alexander I, tsar of Russia, 85–86
Alfaro Jované, Ricardo Joaquín, 122, 150, 151, 172, 175, 200, 210
Amado, Gilberto de, 136, 156, 161
America (Jesuit weekly), 219
American Bar Association, 109, 116
American Hellenic Educational Program Association, 220, 264n3
American Jewish Historical Society, xxvii
American Scholar (journal), 120, 122
Ammoun, Fouad, 158
Angel, Jaime, 187–88
Anti-Defamation League of B'nai B'rith, 259–60n12
anti-Semitism: Nazi Germany and, 31, 77–78, 116-17 (*see also* Holocaust); Poland and, xii, 34, 100; tsarist Russia and, xi, 12–13, 17, 18–19, 21, 48–49, 52, 54, 168
Arab caliphs, 130
Armenian convention (N.Y.), 220
Armenian genocide (1915), xi, 19–20, 51, 103, 141–42, 166, 183–85, 200–201, 220; Hamidian massacre (1894), 254n13; economic consequences of, 183
Arne, Sigrid, xxi
Arnold, Matthew, 154
Association de Liberté Religieuse, 161
Association of Catholic Writers, 160
Assur (biblical), 52
Assyrians, xii, 140
Athens, ancient, 141, 184
Aurell, Jaume, xxi
Auschwitz (death camp), 248n13
Austin, Warren, 124, 220
Australia, 96–97, 274n8; Genocide Convention signing/ratification, 186, 187, 210, 252n13, 256n33, 258n4; U.N. delegation, xvii, 142–43, 144–45, 150, 151, 190
Avicenna, 130
Axis Rule in Occupied Europe (Lem-

Axis Rule in Occupied Europe (cont.)
  in), xiv, 68, 121, 122, 128, 129, 152,
     155, 232
Azkoul, Karim, 157, 158
Azmi, Mahmoud, 137–38
Aztecs, 149, 181

Babi Yar massacre, 127
Baikal Lake, 86–87
Balkans, 168, 169
Baltic states: neutrality of, 29, 44, 60,
     61, 65, 70, 73; Soviet invasion of, 76,
     260–61n17. *See also* Latvia;
     Lithuania
barbarism, international crime of, xii,
     22, 64, 68, *See also* genocide
Barth, Alan, 120
Barthou, Jean Louis, 174
Bartlett, Robert Merrill, xxiv, xxv
Bauer, Carlos García, 199–200
Beiulis, Menahem Mendel, 18
Belgium, 62, 74, 109, 261n17; Gen-
     ocide Convention signing, 245n3
*Belgium Review of Penal Law and Crim-
     inology*, 120
Belt, Guillermo, 123
Berendsen, Sir Carl, 195–96
Berg, Paul Olaf, 186, 258n3
Bey, Nimet Eloui, xviii
Bialik, Chayim Nachman, 17
Bialystok pogrom, 17
Bible, 10, 15, 16–17, 50, 52
Birobidjan (Jewish Autonomous Re-
     public), 87
blood libel, 18
Blum, Leon, 191
Board of Economic Warfare and For-
     eign Economic Administration,
     U.S., xiv, 112

Bodidharma, 90
Boergner, Pastor, 160
Bolgatz, Abe, ix
Bolivia, Genocide Convention signing,
     256n33
Brazil, 136, 161; Genocide Convention
     signing/ratification, 256n33,
     260n17
Bronfman, Samuel, 259–60n12
Bryson, Thaddeus, 105
Buber, Martin, 244n2
Buchman, Frank, 252n17
Buck, Pearl S., 136
Buddha, 89–90
Buddhism, 90–91, 196, 206
Bulgaria, 190; massacre, 254n13
Bureau for the Unification of Criminal
     Law, 22
Burke, Edmund, 184, 185
Burma, Genocide Convention ratifica-
     tion, 222
Burton, Naomi, ix–x

Cambodia, 194
Cambridge Medieval History, 82
Canada, xxiii, 97, 139–42, 191–92;
     Genocide Convention sign-
     ing/ratification, 191–92, 222,
     252n11, 260n13, 264n7
Carlyle, Thomas, 166
Carnegie Endowment Fund, Interna-
     tional Law Division, 116, 129
Carthage, destruction of, 1
Carton de Wiart, Henri, 62, 74, 245n3,
     261n17
case system (law study), 104
Castberg, Frede, 121
Castle, Barbara, 260–61n17

Castro, Héctor David, 202
Catholics, 188; Japanese seventeenth-century destruction of, 1, 91–94, 138; support for Genocide Convention by, 160–61, 170, 261n17
Caux Palace Hotel (Montreux), 252n17
Cecil, Robert, Lord, 135
Center for Jewish History (N.Y.), xxvii
Center of Foreign Affairs (Paris), 156
Céspedes del Castillo, Carlos Manuel de, 202
Ceylon, 190, 196
Chacon, Angela de, 196
Chagall, Marc, 147
Chamberlain, Neville, 28, 73
Chambers of Commerce, 105, 111
Chang, John M., 219, 263n37
Charles XII, king of Sweden, 73
Chaumont, Henri, 128
Chauvel, Jean, 210, 211, 262n33, 263n37
cherry blossom season (Japan), 89–90
Chicago, 69, 99, 219, 220
Chicago Jewish Weekly, 265n2
Chifley, Joseph Benedict, 186, 257n2
children: forcible transfer of, 80, 131, 168–69, 173, 219–20; trade in, 23, 122
Chile, xv, 131, 149; Genocide Convention signing, 256n33
China, 81, 196; Japanese occupation of, 166
Christians: Ottoman destruction of (*see* Armenian genocide); Ottoman taking of children of, 168, 169; Roman destruction of, xi, 1, 17. *See also* Catholics; Protestants

Cleon, 141
Code of Offenses Against the Peace and Security of Mankind, 203, 205, 220
collective destruction. *See* genocide
colonialism, 93–94, 96–97, 193, 194
Combat, Le (French newspaper), 145
Commission on the Rights of Women, U.N., 222
Confucius, 59
Congressional Record, 220
Connally, Tom, 202
Convention on the Prevention and Punishment of the Crime of Genocide. *See* Genocide Convention
Cooper, John, *Raphael Lemkin and the Struggle for the Genocide Convention*, xxvii
Corbett Ashby, Margery, 123, 124
Correa, Jose, 187
Costa Rica, 187, 196–98, 202, 211
covenant with God, 48–49, 52–53, 54
crime: constructing definition of, 151–53. *See also* international crimes; war crimes
crime of barbarism and vandalism, xii, 22, 64, 68. *See also* genocide
crimes against humanity: elements of, 119–20; Genocide Convention and, 209–10; lack of definition of, 205–6
Cuba, xv, 123, 129, 187, 190; Genocide Convention signing/ratification, 200, 262n23; honoring of Lemkin by, 202–3, 233
cultural genocide, xxiv, 22, 125, 127, 131, 138, 166, 168, 172–73, 241n1, 249n6; meaning/implications of, 172, 180–81, 186

Curtis Brown Agency, ix, x
customary law, 207
Czechoslovakia, 25, 34, 125, 126–27,
    260n12

Dante, *Divine Comedy*, 67, 245–46n4
Daumier, Honoré, "They Are Thirsty," 6
death marches, 166, 184
Declaration of Human Rights. *See*
    Universal Declaration of Human
    Rights
democracy, 115–16, 119
Denmark, 74; Genocide Convention
    signing, 261n17
deportations, 166
de Valera, Éamon, 134–35
Dihigo, Ernesto, 129, 249–50nn6, 24
dining customs: American, 106; Swed-
    ish, 73, 75–76
Diodotus, 141
Dominican Republic, 187; Genocide
    Convention signing, 256–57n33
Dons, Erik, 258n3
Douglas, Helen Gahagan, 124
Draft Code of Crimes Against the
    Peace and Security of Mankind,
    203, 205, 220
Dubno massacre, 55
Dubnow, Simon, xiii, xxiv, 71–72; last
    words of, 72, 246n5
Duell, Sloan and Pearce, x
Duino Elegies, The (Rilke), xix
Duke University, 74, 109, 111, 155,
    232, 263n39; Lemkin's first impres-
    sion of, 101–3; Lemkin's law school
    faculty appointment, xiii–xiv, 63,
    79, 99, 103, 104
Duke University Press, 63

Dulles, John Foster, 162, 177, 233
Dunant, Jean Henri, 146, 172
du Parcq, Herbert, 28–29
Duvan, Carlos, 189

Eastern Bloc. *See* Soviet Bloc
eastern Poland (now Belarus), xiii, 29–
    31, 55–56, 260n12; invasions of, x,
    xx, 55, 110; Lemkin's youth in, x,
    3–18. *See also* Wolkowysk
Eberstein, Gosta, 75, 82
Echandi, Mario, 197–98
Economic and Social Council, U.N.,
    133–34, 136, 138, 143, 149, 152,
    257n2
Ecuador, Genocide Convention sign-
    ing/ratification, 187, 198–99,
    257n33, 260n17
Eden, Sir Anthony, 204
Egypt, xv, xviii, 137; Genocide Con-
    vention signing/ratification, 138,
    252n8, 257n33
Eichmann, Adolf, trial of, 247n6
El Salvador, 187, 194–95, 202; Gen-
    ocide Convention ratification, 208
Enchandi, Mario, 196, 197–98
England. *See* United Kingdom
English language, ix, xiv, xxii, xxvi,
    101–2
Ennals, John, 135, 136, 138
Entezam, Nasrollah, 211, 261n37
escapees from Poland, xii–xiv, xxv, 25–
    40, 42–62, 74, 232; descriptions of,
    xxii–xxiii, 27–31; interactions
    among, 42–43. *See also* refugees
Esquivel, Ruben, 263n37
Estonia, 76
Ethiopia, Genocide Convention sign-

ing/ratification, 186, 257n33, 258n4

ethnic groups. *See* racial and ethnic groups

Eurasian movement, 70, 86

Europe: first Genocide Convention ratifications from, 187; Hitler's threat to (*see* Nazi Germany: World War II); Lemkin's comparison of American systems with, xxiii, 101, 103–6; Mongol conquest of, xxiii, 1, 80–82

Evatt, Herbert, 142–43, 148, 150, 162, 171–74, 177, 186, 204, 208, 210, 233; statement on Genocide Convention, 172; tribute to Lemkin, 252n12

extermination, meaning of genocide vs., 131

extradition, 174

fables, 17–18, 21

Fahy, Charles, 129, 131

farm life, xxv, 4–13, 15, 30–31

Federal Republic of Germany, 190

Fifth Conference for the Unification of Penal Law (1933). *See* Madrid conference on penal law

Finch, George A., 116, 129, 248–49n4

Flanner, Janet (Genêt), xvi–xvii, 172

Flowers, Robert Lee, 103

Focillon, Henri, 166

forced labor, 77, 78, 166

forest, 4, 7–8, 27–29, 32–33, 232

Fournier, Fernando, 263n37

France, xii, xv, 109, 128, 148, 173–74, 177, 209–11; Genocide Convention signing/ratification, 174, 190–91, 194, 210–11, 253n18, 257n33, 261n17; sixteenth-century massacre of Huguenots, 1, 17, 160; World War II, 28, 34, 74. *See also* Paris

France Catholique (newspaper), 161

Fraser, Peter, 158

Frederica, queen of Greece, 219

French Revolution, 154, 207

Fussell, Jim, xii

Fyfe, Sir Maxwell, 128

Gabriel, Alexander, xxvi

Gandhi, Mohandas, 123

Garth, Leon, 252n17

geishas, 90, 91

General Assembly, U.N.: first regular session of (1946), xiv, 121–23, 205, 257n2; genocide indictment by, 68 (*see also* Genocide Convention); Lemkin's hopes for, xxiv; meeting of 1948 (Paris), xv, 133, 143, 145, 147, 150–79, 257n2; meeting of 1949 (Lake Success), 186–218; meeting of 1950 (Lake Success), xvi, 186, 201, 203–22; signing of Genocide Convention protocol, 211–12; social life of, 163–64, 175; steering committee resolution, 126–27

Genêt (Janet Flanner), xvi–xvii, 172

Geneva, 133–49

Genghis Khan, 1

genocide: coinage of word, x, xi, xvi, 2, 137, 232; construction of word, 143–44, 181–82; continuing danger of, 171–72; crimes of, 20, 21, 22, 71, 114, 131, 139, 161, 165,

genocide: crimes of (*cont.*)
182–83, 219, 257n2; critics of term, 143–44; of culture (*see* cultural genocide); definition of, xi–xii; as distinct from war, xxiv, 165; economic implications of, 183; enumeration of means of, 166–68; first appearance of word in print, xiv; historical examples of, xi, xii, 1–2, 17, 19, 80–82, 91–94, 102–3, 125, 138, 140–41, 149, 160, 168, 183, 184–85, 193, 196, 254n13; as historically recurring pattern, 138, 168, 222; Hitler's published blueprint for, xii, xiv, xxiv, 22, 52, 76–77, 102, 105, 108–9, 113; human inability to grasp concept of, 113, 114; initiation of treaty against (*see* Genocide Convention); as international crime, xii, 22, 64, 68, 71–72; Lemkin's early interest in/warnings of, xii, xiii, xiv, xxiii–xxvii, 1–2, 22–24, 64, 66, 80, 102–3, 108–9, 113–17, 169–70, 180–81, 232; limitation of group reproduction as, 167–68; national and international levels of, 139; overriding intent and, 166–69; war crime issue of, xxiv, 118–19, 144, 156, 165. *See also* Armenian genocide; Holocaust

"Genocide and Human Experience: Raphael Lemkin's Thought and Vision" (2009 conference), xxvii

Genocide Convention, x, xiv–xv, xvi, 150–79; Article V, 220; Article VIII, 174–75, 204; Article IX, 175, 204, 262n28; Article XIII, 211–12; Article XIV, 176; Article XVI, 176;

birth of, 118–32; dates of formal enactment/expiration of, 176; debated inclusions in definition of "genocide" and, 152–53, 157, 161–62, 165–69, 205, 210, 257n2; draft resolution for, 122; first country to ratify, 186; idealism and, 165; initiation of, 114–15; legal enforcement of, 139, 171, 173–74, 175, 208, 210, 257n2; Lemkin on importance of, 140–41; Lemkin's conception of, xx, xxi, xxii, 20, 21; misconceptions about, 156; moral weight of, xxiv; Nuremberg Judgment's limitations vs., 68, 118, 144, 145, 156; opponents of, 132, 156–57, 159, 162, 170–71, 176, 203–6, 209–11, 212, 214, 216–17, 219, 222; original sponsors of, 202; protection of small nations by, 159; purpose of, 182, 253–54n11; ratification protocol, 211–12; refutations of misconceptions about, 156; reservations to, 175, 204, 214, 215, 260n12, 263–65n40; resolution for, 120–21; resolution vote for, 131, 160, 177, 232; signing as parliamentary intent to ratify, 178; sponsors of, 122; state-sovereignty concerns and, xv, 22; text approval, xv, 176–77, 257n2

Genocide Convention ratification campaign, xi, xiv–xv, xvii, xviii, xx, xxii–xxv, xxvii, 176, 180–218, 219–22, 241n2; first four ratifying nations and, 186, 258n4; imperilment of, 263–64n40; Latin America and, xx, 136, 187–89, 194–95, 200, 221;

Lemkin's strategy, xx, 186; twentieth ratifying nation, 211; U.N. nonmember nations and, 190, 193–94

German language, 146

Germany, 19, 55, 109, 110, 113, 190. *See also* Nazi Germany

Gertsen, Aleksandr Ivanovich, 168

Gladstone, William Ewart, 160

Glion (Switzerland), 147, 148, 156

Goethe, Johann Wolfgang von, *Hermann and Dorothea*, 58

Golden Horde, 81

Goldman, Mrs. Pendleton, 222

Grady, Henry, 220

Graebe, Hermann, 55

Gray, John, 124

Greek children, kidnapping of, 168, 219–20

Greek language, 181

Greek Orthodox Youth Group, 220

Grippe Is Raging in Neprava, The (Kurek), 36

Gromyko, Andrei, 220

Guatemala, 187, 199–200; Genocide Convention signing, 262n23

Gunewardene (Ceylonese diplomat), 196

Hague Conventions, 108–9

Hahnloser, Robert, 252n17

Haiti, xxi, 189, 211, 257n33; Genocide Convention ratification, 195, 208–9

Hamidian massacres (1894), 254n13

Harnett, Robert C., 264n2

Hassidic tradition, 244n2

Hay, John Milton, 250n10

Hayworth, Mike, 178

Hebrew language, x, 13, 14, 15, 17, 48, 50, 51, 247n6

Heian Maru (Japanese ship), 96

Heine, Heinrich, 49

Hereos tribe, genocide of, 185

Herriot, Édouard, 191

Herrissay, Jacques, 160–61

High Point (N.C.), 111

Hinton, Alex, xxvii

Hirohito, emperor of Japan, 95

Hitler, Adolf, 28, 29, 71, 73; mass group destruction blueprint of, xii, xiv, xxiv, 22, 52, 76–78, 102, 105, 108–9, 113; *Mein Kampf*, 52, 76–77; Nuremberg judgment failure and, 118

Hohenberg, John, 177

Holocaust, xiv, 22, 52, 76–78; death of Lemkin's parents in, xvi, 111, 117, 248n13; Jewish religious fatalism and, 49, 52–53, 55; Jewish "resistance" and, 244n3; Lemkin's warnings about, xxiv–xxv, 52, 114–17, 247n6; moral reaction in aftermath of, xv, 121, 122; rumors in United States of, 117; as specific term, 247n6

Honduras, 187

Hossovan, Zahir, 191

Hugo, Victor, 75

Huguenot massacre, 1, 17, 160

Humanitarian, Social, and Cultural Committee, U.N., 171

human rights, xv, xxi, 157, 170, 171, 172

Hungary, 190; Mongol depopulation of, xxiii, 80–81, 82

Ibn Rushd, 130
Iceland: Genocide Convention signing/ratification, 187, 258n4; original culture of, 137–38, 186
Ikramullah, Begum Shaista, 159–60
Imperial Palace (Tokyo), 95
Incas, 149
India, xv, 123, 129, 159, 177
Indonesia, 222
Ingles, Judge, 151–52
Innocent IV, Pope, 82
Inter-American Commission of Women, 188–89
International Association of Criminal Law, 62
International Bureau for Unification of Penal Law, 21
International Council of Women, 192
International Court of Justice (The Hague), 139, 164, 173, 174, 175; Genocide Convention reservations and, 204, 214, 215, 262n28
international crimes: domestic vs., 22, 71, 139; examples of, 23, 122; factors in formulation of, 152; genocide as, xii, 22, 64, 68, 71–72; intent as basis of, 210; Nuremberg failure to set precedent on, 118
International Criminal Court (proposed), 173–74, 209–10, 255n26
International Criminal Tribunals for Rwanda and Former Yugoslavia, 255n26
international law, 23, 64, 154, 159, 205–8, 210; genocide as component of, x, xvi, 2, 22, 118–19, 131, 139, 171, 173, 177, 257n2; small nations' protection under, 187;

state sovereignty vs., xv, 20, 22; statute and judgment principles of, 205
International Law Commission, 214, 263n40; report of, 203
International Military Tribunal (London, 1945): war crimes definition, 118–20, 249n1. *See also* Nuremberg Tribunal
International Red Cross, 146, 172
international treaties. *See* treaties
Iran, 211
Isaiah (prophet), 16
Israeli Declaration of Independence (1948), 257n6
Italy, 190
"I-Thou" relationship, 48–49
Ivan the Terrible, tsar of Russia, 84

Jackson, Robert, xiv
Jacobs, Steven, xxvii
Jadwiga, queen of Poland, 64
Jagiello, king of Lithuania, 64
Janissaries, 168
Japan, xxiii, 96–97, 166, 193; destruction of seventeenth-century Catholics in, 1, 91–94, 138; Lemkin's impressions of, 88–96
Jehoiakim, 17
Jewish Federation and Community Council, 247n6
Jewish Holocaust Centre (Melbourne), 226
Jews, xxiv, 3, 23, 192, 259–60n12; autonomous Soviet republic for, 87; fatalist attitude of, 49, 52; Hebrew education of, 13, 14, 16–17, 50; persecutions of (*see* anti-Semitism;

Holocaust); *shtetl* and religious daily life of, xxiv, 48–54

Jim Crow, 100

Johnson, Colonel (Australian delegate), 143, 144–45

Jordan, 190; Genocide Convention ratification, 201

Joye, Judge (Filipino official), 193

justice, 17–18, 20, 21

Kagawa, Toyohiko, 96

Kantouraty, 168

Karens (Burmese people), 222

Karsavin, Lev Platonovich, 70, 86

Karsavina, Tamara, 70

Karski, Jan, 249n5

Kaunas, xxiv, 65, 66–70

Kerno, Ivan, 206–7, 263n37

King, Archibald, 108, 109

King, Charles D. B., 208

Kirishitans (Japanese Christians), 92

Kirsten (U.S. congressman), 220

Korea. *See* South Korea

Korean War, 201–2, 219

Kosciuszko, Thaddeus, 105

Kowel, 45

Krakow, 80

Kremlin (Moscow), 83, 84, 95

Krylov, Ivan Andreevich, 17

Kublai Khan, 196

Kural, Adnan, 200, 201

Kurek, Jalu, 244n6

Kuzmicz, Fedor (legendary), 86

Kyoto, 89–94, 95

La Fontaine, Jean de, 17

Lake Leman, 134, 141, 145

Lake Success (N.Y.), xvi, 186–222

languages, 69–70, 138; cultural genocide and, 172; hybrid roots in, 143–44, 181

Laos, 190, 194

Lash, Joseph, 222

Latin America, 152, 160, 161, 177, 210; Genocide Convention ratification and, xx, 136, 187–89, 194–95, 200, 221; number of small nations in, 187; solidarity among U.N. delegates from, 122–23

Lattre, Abbe de, 259n8, 261n17

Latvia, xiii, 70–72, 76, 82, 246n5

law: Lemkin's study of comparative systems of, xxiii, 21, 104, 105; motivations and, 165. *See also* international law; penal law; rule of law

lawyers, Lemkin's view of, 66–67

League of Nations, xii, 22, 23–24, 34, 62, 68, 134–35, 154, 173–74

Lebanon, 157–58

Ledón, Amalia de Castillo, 188–89, 194, 258–59n6

Legal Committee for the Genocide Convention, U.N., 128, 129, 131, 150–54, 159, 161–75, 249n6; cultural genocide article and, 172–73; drafts before, 169, 174, 205; hurdles in, 156–57, 161–63, 209–10, 214–15, 263n40; Lemkin's lobbying of, 153–54

Leger (Haitian diplomat), 195

Lemkin, Bella (née Pomerantz) (mother), x, xi, xiii, 9, 11, 12, 14, 18, 72, 82, 110–11; last letters from, xx, 65, 79, 109–10; last meeting with, xxiv, 29–30, 56–59; moral in-

Lemkin, Bella (*cont.*)
fluence of, 15–16, 17–18; Nazi gassing of, xvi, 111, 117, 248n13
Lemkin, Elias (Eliyahu) (brother), xv, xx, 56, 248n13
Lemkin, Joseph (father), x, xiii, 18; farm of, 4–13; last letters from, xx, 65, 79, 109–10; last meeting with, xxiv, 29–30, 56–59; Nazi gassing of, xvi, 111, 117, 248n13
Lemkin, Raphael: birthplace of, 3; campaign against genocide of (*see* genocide; Genocide Convention); characterizations of, xvi–xvii, xxi; childhood of, x–xi, xxv–xxvi, 1, 2, 3–18, 31; coinage of word "genocide" by, x, xi, xvi, 2, 137, 232; death of, ix, xix; digitalized archives of, xxvii; early adult years of, 19–24; education of, x, xi, 14–19, 20; financial problems of, 220–21, 222; flight from Warsaw of, xii–xiv, xxii–xxiii, 25–40, 41–59, 155; honors and tributes to, xiv, 202–3, 233, 252n12, 258n5; ill health of, ix, xv, xx, xxvi, 117, 178–79, 181, 214, 215–18; inner life of, xviii–xix, xxiv, 15–18; intellect and political skill of, xvi, xxiii, 48; Jewish identity of, xxiv; law studies/career of, xi–xii, 20, 21–22, 48, 66–67, 152–53; linguistic skills of, ix, x, xiv, xxii, xxiii, xxvi, 45, 69–70, 72–73, 75, 101–2; loneliness of, xv–xvi, xvii, xviii, 10, 58, 163; loss of family of, xi, xv–xvi, xix, 110–11, 117, 248n13; moral conscience of, x, xi, 10, 15–18; on personal happiness, 66; refugee status of, xii–xiv,

xxii, xxiii, xxv, 67–68, 82–97; resurgence of scholarship on, xxvii; U.S. haven for, xiii–xv, 97, 98 111; Who's Who entry for, 264–65; works by: articles on genocide, 120, 156, 168; autobiography, ix–x, xix–xxii, xxv, xxvi; *Axis Rule in Occupied Europe*, xiv, 68, 121, 122, 128, 129, 152, 155, 232; *The Birch* (poem), 242n5; *Exchange Control and Clearing*, 74–75; "Totalitarian Control over Foreign Economies," 116
Lemkin, Samuel (brother), xix
Lesbos, 141
Leszek the Black, 80
Liberia, 198, 208; Genocide Convention signing, 257n33
Library of Congress, 106, 107–8, 109, 116
Lidice massacre, 127
Lie, Trygve, 199, 211, 263n37, 264n40
Lincoln Memorial, 107
Lithuania, xiii, xxiv, 34, 44; culture and language of, 69; ethnic groups in, 3, 4; Lemkin's escape to, 29, 57, 60–70, 155; Soviet invasion of, 76. *See also* Vilnius
Lithuanian language, 69–70, 73
Lithuanians, 192, 219, 220
Litvinov, Maxim, 135
Lodz, 32
London Conference of Prosecutors (1945), 68
Lowenstein, Lazar, 263n39
Lublin, 80
Lumbre, El (Colombian magazine), 196
Lwow (now Lviv), xi, 20, 34
Lynchburg (Va.), 100

Madrid conference on penal law (1933), xii, 22, 23–24, 68, 232
Maginot Line, 34
Maktos, John, 175, 255–56n28
Malik, Charles, 149
marriage restrictions, 167–68
Martin, Morris H., 158, 252n17
Masaryk, Jan, 126–28, 233
Masaryk, Tomás Garrigue, 127
McDermott, Malcolm, xiii–xiv, 63, 74, 99, 101–2, 106, 111, 155
Mein Kampf (Hitler), 52, 76–77
Méndez Pereira, Octavio, 189
Merkis (Lithuanian premier), 69
Mexico, 188; Genocide Convention signing, 257n33
Meyer, Eugene, 120
Michael, Archbishop, 219
military tribunals, 118–19
Minjoz, Jean, 191
Mitylene, 141
Monaco, 190, 194
Monde, Le (French newspaper), 156, 168
Mongols, xxiii, 1, 4, 80–82, 141, 196
Montel, Pierre, 190–91
Montreux, 147, 148; casino dancer, xvii, xx, 148–49
Moors, 1, 133, 183
Moral Rearmament Movement, 147–48
moral standards, xxiv, 21, 63–64, 165; conscience of humanity and, 37, 216; genocide as outside of, 184–85; Jewish covenant with God and, 48; Lemkin's conscience and, x, xi, 10, 15–18; women and, 125
Morganthau, Henry, Sr., 184–85

Morocco, 137; Genocide Convention ratification, 252n7
Moscow, xxiii, 82–84, 86
Mother, The (sculpture), 72
Mottu, Philippe, 252n17
Munich crisis (1938), 25, 28, 73
Muslims, 1, 130, 133, 163–64, 168, 183; genocide in Pakistan of, 159

Nadson, Semyon, 16, 17–18, 23
Nagasaki, 92
Napoleon, 4, 71, 84, 86
Nazi Germany, 79, 86; Allied silence on mass murders by, 117; broken nonaggression pacts by, 22, 34, 61; mass European resettlement aim of, xii, xiv, xxiv, 22, 52, 76–77, 80, 81, 102–3, 105, 108–9, 113–15; war crime indictments of, 118–20, 232. *See also* Holocaust; World War II
Nero, emperor of Rome, x, 1
Netherlands, 74, 169, 260–61n17
neutrality, xiii, 29, 44, 60, 61, 70, 78, 109, 134, 136, 146, 155; Sweden's choice of, 73, 74
New European Order, 76
Newland, Mrs. (New Zealand U.N. delegate), 158–59
New Yorker (magazine), 172
New York Herald Tribune, 120–21, 212–13, 220
New York Post, 177, 222
New York Public Library, donation of Lemkin papers to, xxvi
New York Times, Genocide Convention support, xxv, 120, 124, 199, 211, 215, 220, 221, 222, 258n5
New Zealand, 164–65, 195–96; Gen-

New Zealand (*cont.*)
ocide Convention signing/ratification, 253n10
Nijo, castle of (Kyoto), 91
Nobel Peace Prize, xiv, 233, 258n5, 259n11, 233
North Carolina, xiii, 105, 106–7, 111
North Korea, 201–2
Norway, 74, 121, 165–66; Genocide Convention signing/ratification, 186, 187, 257n33, 258n4
Novosibirsk, 85, 86–87
Nu, U, 222
Nuremberg Judgment, 205, 206–7, 209–10, 214; limitations of, 68, 118, 144, 145, 156, 157, 261n17
Nuremberg Tribunal, xiv, xx, 55, 68, 118–20, 122, 126, 128, 145, 232
Nussbaum, Jean, 161, 194, 260–61n17

Opprecht, Hans, 145–46
Orthodox Church, 82, 168, 220
Ottoman Empire: genocides by, xi, 19–20, 168, 169, 184–85, 200, 254n13. *See also* Turkey
Oultremont, Count d', 169
Ozerisko (farm), 3, 4–18

Paderewski, Ignacy Jan, 34
Pakistan, xviii, 159–60, 163–64; Genocide Convention signing, 257n33
Palais de Chaillot, 150, 157, 170, 178
Palantova, Madame (Czech U.N. delegate), 125
Pale of Settlement, xxiv, 48–49
Panama, 122, 126, 150, 151, 187; Genocide Convention signing/ratification, 189, 200, 249–50n6, 257n33, 262n23

Pan American Union, 194
Pandit, Vijaya Lakshmi, 123
Paraguay, 257n33
Paredes, Quintin B., 151, 193
Paris, xv, 6, 21, 74, 133, 143, 145, 147, 150–79, 257n2; atmosphere of, 150, 153, 154, 175; Lemkin's talk on genocide in (1948), 169–70
Parodi, Alexander, 128
Paul-Boncour, Joseph, 134–35
Pearson, Lester B., 191–92, 222, 233
peasants, 11–12, 39–40, 44, 46, 47
Pederson, Inger Helga, 222
Pédone (publisher), 23, 62, 154–55
Pédones (mother and daughter), 62–63, 68, 155–56, 159
penal law, 21–22, 152–53
Perez, Leib, "Higher Than the Sky," 50
Pérez Perozo, Victor Manuel, 133, 135, 161, 165
Perkins, Frances, 124
Perry, Matthew C., 94
Peru, Genocide Convention signing, 257n33
Petitpierre, Max, 146
Petliura, Symon, xi, 21
Petrén, Sture, 169
Peyer, Erich, 252n17
Philippines, 151, 190; domestic law against genocide, 193; Genocide Convention signing/ratification, 193, 257n33, 260n15
Pickett, Clarence E., 157
Pierre, Abbe, 170
Pilsudski, Józef Klemens, 34–35
Pinson, Koppel, 246n5
piracy, 122
Plaisant, Marcel, 190, 191

Plato, 141, 144

Plimsoll, Sir James, 171

pogroms, xi, 17, 19, 21, 52; Jewish self-defense and, 54–55

Poland: anti-Semitism in, xii, 34, 100; critics of political/social policies of, 34–37, 71; escapees from, xii–xiv, xxv, 25–40, 42–62, 74, 232; government-in-exile of, 79; Mongol depopulation of, xxiii, 80, 81, 82; Nazi blitz/conquest of, xii, xxii, 25, 31, 35, 37–38, 41, 71, 74; Nazi genocidal aims in, 76–77, 117, 152, 166, 167–68; Nazi nonaggression pact with, 22, 34; Soviet invasion of, 34, 44–45; U.N. delegation, 166, 167–68. *See also* eastern Poland; Warsaw

Poles, 3, 4, 77, 116, 192

Polesie province, 44

Polish Committee on Codification of Laws, 21, 152–53

Polish Group for the Association of Penal Law, 21–22

Polish-Lithuanian kingdom, 64

political groups, debated inclusion in Genocide Convention of, 157, 161–62

Politis, Nicolas, 135

Portugal, 109

positive law, 207–8

PreventGenocide.org (website), xxvii

Price-Mars, Jean, 208–9, 263n37

Protestants, 1, 17, 160, 161

Proxmire, William, 241n2

Quakers, 157

Quenco, Jesus, 193

racial and ethnic groups, intended destruction of, 22, 23, 77–78, 108–9, 116–17, 161, 165

Ravel, Maurice, xviii–xix

Red Square (Moscow), 83

refugees, xii–xiv, xxii, xxv, 82–97; consulates as meeting places of, 70, 74; entry into United States by, xiii–xiv, xxiii, 97, 98–99; mental state of, xiii, 67–68; travel through Soviet Union by, 79, 82–88

religious groups, intended destruction of, xi, 1, 17, 22, 23, 124, 141, 161, 165, 168

reproduction of group, 167–68

Rhee, Syngman, 193

Riad, Judge (Egypt), xviii, 129–30, 131

Riga, xiii, 70–72, 82, 246n5

Rilke, Rainer Maria, xviii–xix; *The Duino Elegies*, xix

Roberto (Panamanian diplomat), 126

Rodriguez, Consuelo, 188

Rolin, Henry, 261n17

Romania, 124, 190

Roman persecutions, xi, 1, 17

Romulo, Carlos Peña, 193

Roncalli, Angelo Giuseppe (later Pope John XXII), 160

Roosevelt, Franklin D., xiv, 15, 114, 115, 149n5

Rosenberg, Alfred, *Myth of the Twentieth Century*, 108

Roth, Arthur, x

Rowley, Hazel, xxi

rule of law, 114–15, 123, 207–8; Genocide Convention implementation and, 173–74

Russia, tsarist, x, 84–86, 110, 124; Jew-

Russia (*cont.*)
ish repression in, xi, 12–13, 17, 18–19, 21, 48–49, 52, 54, 168; Mongol rule in, xiii, 80, 81. *See also* Soviet Union
Rydh, Hanna, 124–25

Sabbath, 49, 53–54, 244n5
St. Basil's Church (Moscow), 83–84
Samitisen (Norwegian magazine), 120
Sandomierz (Poland), 80
Sanskrit, 69
Sarper, Selim, 201
Saudi Arabia, 129, 201
Schlyter, Karl, 29, 62, 74–75, 155
School of Military Government (Charlottesville, Va.), 116
Schuman, Robert, 177, 211, 233
Schwarzbard, Shalom, xi, xii, 21
Scotta-Lavina (French journalist), 148, 156
Seattle, 97, 98–99
Second International Congress of Comparative Law (1937, The Hague), 106
Security Council, U.N., 175
Senate, U.S., 219
Serbs, 77
Shahi, Agha, 160, 163
Shawcross, Sir Hartley, 128, 129, 157, 160, 162, 250n6
sho'ah (Hebrew term), 247n6
Shōwa, emperor of Japan, 246n6
shtetl life, xxiv, 48-54
Siberia, 70, 83–87, 126
Siedlce, 29; massacre of Jews, 31
Siegel, Judith, xxvii
Sienkiewicz, Henryk, *Quo Vadis*, xi, 1

Silesia, Mongol depopulation of, xxiii, 80, 81
Simon, John Lord, 28
Simon and Schuster (publishers), x
slave labor, 251n40, 263n40
slavery, 23, 122, 195
Śmigly-Rydz, Edward, 34–35
Socrates, 184
Solh, Riad el-, 157
sonnet-songs, 15–16
South Africa, 177, 210
South Korea, 186, 211; Genocide Convention ratification, 190, 193–94, 202, 219; North Korean invasion of, 201–2
Soviet Bloc, 151, 152, 168, 220; Genocide Convention and, 204, 260n12, 262n28, 263n38
Soviet Union: genocidal practices and, 260–61n17, 263n40; Genocide Convention and, xv, 126, 127–28, 165, 204, 260n12, 263n40; invasion of Baltic States by, 76; invasion of Poland by, 34, 44–45, 56; Lemkin's travel as refugee across, xxiii, 79, 82–88, 232; Nazi invasion of, 248n12; Nazi nonaggression pact (1939), 34, 61; police detention of Lemkin, xii, xxiii, 44–48; troops in Vilnius, 60–61, 62
Spain, 133, 183, 193
Spanish language, 152
Spartans, 141
Special Committee on Genocide, U.N., 158, 166–67, 169
Spencer, Stuart, 186
Spingarn, Arthur, 219
Starzyński, Stefan, 42

State Department, U.S., 220
state sovereignty, xv, 20
Statute of the International Military
    Tribunal, 118–19
Steinson Ehrlich, Nancy, ix, xi, xvi,
    xviii, xxvii, 263n39
sterilization, 167
Stevenson, Adlai, 124, 126
Stockholm, 72, 75, 79, 82
students: American vs. European, xxiii,
    101, 103–5; Lemkin's relationship
    with, 183–85, 191
Sutch, William Ball, 158–59
Sweden, 4, 62, 157, 169; Genocide
    Convention signing/ratification,
    222, 243n1, 245n3, 264n7; Lem-
    kin's refuge in, xiii, xxiii, 29, 58, 63,
    66, 70, 72–78, 79, 82, 155, 232;
    neutrality of, 73, 74, 109. *See also*
    Stockholm
Swedish language, 72–73, 75
Swiss dialect, 146
Switzerland, 109, 134, 115–16. *See
    also* Geneva

Taft, William Howard, 124
Talaat Pasha, xi, 19–20, 184–85
tea ceremony (Japan), 90–91
Tehlirian, Soghomon, xi, 20, 21
Tennessee Valley Authority, 113–14
terrorism, 173–74
Thomas, Dylan, 87
Thomas, Lowell, 178–79
Titulescu, Nicolae, 135
Tokyo, 95, 96
Tolischus, Otto, 120, 124
Tolstoy, Lev, 18, 84
Tomkiewicz, Benjamin, 65–66

torture, 1–2, 17, 92–93, 125, 147, 166,
    191
Trans-Siberian railroad, 84–85
treaties, 23, 114, 171; sanctity of, 207–
    8, 210
Treblinka (death camp), xvi, 148n13
Truman, Harry, 202, 211, 219
Tsurga (Japan), 88, 89
Turkey, 200–201. *See also* Ottoman
    Empire
TVA project (U.S.), 113–14

Udrie (Latvian official), 70–71
Ukraine, xi, 21, 260n12; Genocide
    Convention ratification, 241n2
Ukrainians, 4, 34, 192
Undset, Sigrid, 157
United Kingdom, 19, 128–29, 169,
    260–61n17; Genocide Convention
    ratification, 252n14; opposition to
    Genocide Convention, 143–44,
    157, 159, 160, 162, 203–4, 205,
    210, 212, 214; World War II, 28–
    29, 61, 73
United Nations, x, xv, 68; Genocide
    Convention and, xiv–xv, xvii, 120–
    21, 174–75; golden age of, xxi; hu-
    man rights program, xv, 157, 170,
    171, 172; limited member nations
    in 1949 of, 190; women's rights pro-
    gram, 222. *See also* Economic and
    Social Council; General Assembly
United States, 103, 107; Genocide
    Convention late ratification date
    (1988), xxv; Genocide Convention
    ratification struggle, 202, 219–22,
    241n2; Genocide Convention sign-
    ing, 257n33; Lemkin's impressions

United States (*cont.*)
of, xiii–xiv, xxiii, 97–111; Lemkin's planned escape to, 58, 62, 63, 79; Lemkin's warning about Nazis' genocide plans and, 113–15, 117; neutrality of, 78; U.N. delegation from, xv, 123–24, 126, 129, 131, 162, 175, 210
United States Holocaust Memorial Museum, 247n6
Universal Declaration of Human Rights, U.N., xv, 157, 170, 171, 172
University of Guatemala, 189
University of Heidelberg, xi
University of Kaunas, 70
University of Lwow, xi, 20
University of Panama, 189
University of Stockholm, 75
University of Vilnius, 63
Urijah (prophet), 17
Urquia, Rafael, 194
Uruguay, Genocide Convention signing, 187, 257n33

Vance, John, 106, 107–8
Vancouver (Canada), 97
vandalism, international crime of, xii, 22, 64, 68
Vatatzes, king of Nicaea, 82
Venezuela, 133, 161
Venizelos, Eleftherios, 135
Versailles peace conference, 19
Vietnam, 194
Villa Rigot (Geneva), 136–37
Vilnius, xi, xiii, 44, 60–66, 155
Vishinsky, Andrey, 127, 128
Vladivostok, 87–88
Voice of Birobidjan (newspaper), 87

Walfora, Madame (Czech U.N. delegate), 125
Wallace, Henry A., 113–14
war crimes: crime of genocide vs., xxiv, 118–19, 144, 156, 165; crimes against humanity and, 119–20, 205–6, 209–10; International Military Tribunal (1945) list of, 119, 249n1; Nuremberg Judgment's limitation to, 118, 156; trial of Turkish, 19–20
War Department, U.S., xiv, 108, 109, 232
Warsaw, 100; ghetto decree (1940), 77–78; ghetto uprising, 49; Lemkin's flight from (*see* escapees from Poland); Lemkin's legal career in, xii, 21–22; Nazi bombing of, 74, 110; Polish defense of, 42
Washington, D.C., xxiii, 106, 107–9, 194–95, 232; wartime atmosphere of, 112–13, 115
Washington Post, 120
White House, 107
White Russians, 3, 34
White-Ruthenian language, 44, 45
White-Ruthenian zone, 62
Wikborg, Erling, 165–66
Wilgress, Dana, 139–42
Willis, Lord, 212
Wilno. *See* Vilnius
Wold, Terje, 186
Woldemaras (Lithuanian premier), 69
Wolkowysk (eastern Poland), x, xi, 3–4, 18, 29–30, 46; Lemkin's final visit to, 56–59; Nazi bombing/invasion of, xx, 111; Nazi transport of Jews from, 248n13; Sabbath description,

244n5; territorial sovereignty changes in, 19, 55–56, 110

Wolynia province (Poland), xxiv, 48

women: escapees from Poland, 42–43; Genocide Convention support by, 124, 188–89, 192, 222; moral feelings of, 125; rights campaign, 196, 222; trade in, 23, 122

Woolsey, Lester, 249n4

World Court. *See* International Court of Justice

World Federation of the United Nations Associations, 135, 136, 138

World War I, xi, 55, 109, 110, 113. *See also* Armenian genocide

World War II, xx–xxi, xxii–xxiii, 193; alliances and, xii, 28–29, 34; Britain and, 28–29, 61, 73; Japan and, 96–97, 166, 274n8; Nazi invasions and occupations, xx, 25, 31, 71, 74, 76–77, 108–9, 116–17, 166–68; neutral nations and (*see* neutrality); quick defeat of Polish army, xxii, 31, 35, 37–38, 74; as transitional period, 63–64; war crimes indictments, 118–20

World Women's Alliance, 124–25

Wroblewski, Bronislaw, 63–64

Yad Vashem, 247n6

Yale Law School, 131, 168, 180–85, 187, 191, 211

Yépez, Jorge Villagómez, 187

Yeshiva University Museum, Lemkin exhibition (2009), xxvii

Yiddish language, 50–51, 87, 247n6

Yokohama, 88, 94–96

Yugoslavia, 257n33, 261n17

Yustschinsky, Andrey, 243n10

Zafarullah Khan, Sir Muhammad, xviii, 163, 177, 178, 201

Zalkauskas, Mr (Kaunas jurist), 68–69

Zen Buddhism, 90–91